TODAY'S CHANGING JOB MARKET DEMANDS A BETTER RESUME

In the past five years, the job market has changed radically. The drastic ways jobs have been restructured or combined, increasing competition for those jobs being offered, and frequent requests for "faxed" resumes are warning signals that the old way of writing and sending an all-purpose resume will *not* get you hired in the '90s. Now you can overcome all these obstacles and make yourself the top candidate for the job by creating a "mini sales" presentation that has proven 90 percent effective in the tough New York job market. This extraordinary, advice-packed guide tells you everything you need to know, including:

- The 250 "CAN-DO'S" to offer employers
- How to target different jobs by varying your resumes
- Winning strategies to pique the interest of picky employers
- When a two-page resume is essential
- Blueprints for resumes, letters, salary history, fax sheets
- And much more!

WINNING RESUMES

MATTHEW GREENE is the president and founder of a New York City firm that specializes in resume writing and has written or edited nearly 10,000 resumes. He was the personnel manager in a Fortune 500 company and conducts workshops to help laid-off workers find employment.

MATTHEW GREENE

WINNING RESUMES

A PLUME BOOK

PLUME

Published by the Penguin Group
Penguin Books USA Inc., 375 Hudson Street, New York,
New York 10014, U.S.A.
Penguin Books Ltd, 27 Wrights Lane, London W8 5TZ,
England
Penguin Books Australia Ltd, Ringwood, Victoria, Australia
Penguin Books Canada Ltd, 10 Alcorn Avenue, Toronto,
Ontario, Canada M4V 3B2
Penguin Books (N.Z.) Ltd, 182–190 Wairau Road,
Auckland 10, New Zealand

Penguin Books Ltd, Registered Offices:
Harmondsworth, Middlesex, England

First published by Plume/Meridian,
an imprint of Dutton Signet,
a division of Penguin Books USA Inc.

First Printing, August, 1994
10   9   8   7   6   5   4   3   2   1

Ⓟ REGISTERED TRADEMARK—MARCA REGISTRADA

LIBRARY OF CONGRESS CATALOGING-IN-PUBLICATION DATA:
Greene, Matthew.
    Winning resumes / Matthew Greene.
        p.   cm.
    Includes bibliographical references and index.
    ISBN 0-452-27136-3
    1. Résumés (Employment)   I. Title.
HF5383.G723   1994
808'.06665—dc20   93-21291
                                                   CIP

Printed in the United States of America
Set in Gill Sans and Janson

Designed by Steven N. Stathakis

BOOKS ARE AVAILABLE AT QUANTITY DISCOUNTS WHEN USED TO
PROMOTE PRODUCTS OR SERVICES. FOR INFORMATION PLEASE
WRITE TO PREMIUM MARKETING DIVISION, PENGUIN BOOKS USA
INC., 375 HUDSON STREET, NEW YORK, NEW YORK 10014.

In memory of my father, Rev. Gershon Gad,
mother, Hilda Sarah,
and elder brother, Max.

And in remembrance of my maternal grand-
father and grandmother, uncles, aunts, nephews
and nieces who did not survive the Holocaust
(1939–1945).

May they all know eternal peace.

Acknowledgments

This book is about selling yourself on paper and in person—the art of marketing one's value to employers. As such, it owes a great deal to the contributions of Robert Half, Richard Lathrop, Douglas B. Richardson, and Tom Washington.

The original manuscript weighed an awesome 6 lbs 4 oz, but thanks to Deborah Brody, my senior editor at Plume, it is now "reader friendly." Her suggestions have been invaluable. Thanks also to Deb's able assistant, Jennifer Moore and the talented production team at Dutton Signet.

I owe a special debt of gratitude to Rachelle Daina, Dr. Samuel Fishbain, Neville Grusd, Abraham Hecht, Helen Grunfeld-Privitera, Catherine Meehan, Theodore Smith, and Beverly Zimmerman who assisted in various ways; also to Louis, Antonio, Joe, Johnny, Corazon, and Spiro.

The timely cooperation of Ronelle du Plessis (Johannesburg), David Gad, Raphael Joseph, David Richardson, and James Sheehan of Brother International, is gratefully acknowledged.

Edward Knappman of New England Publishing Associates was very patient and helpful at all times.

To those of my clients whose resumes and success stories have been featured in this work, I say thank you. May you continue to be successful.

Last, but not least, I wish to express my appreciation to Ailauna, Anne (Newcastle), Ashley, Berta D., Carolyn, Harvey, Henie P., Justin, Kathleen C., Martin, Maurice L., Miles, Millicent, Paul P. (London), Ray G. (Cape Town), Raymond B., Robert, and Temma.

Prof. Randall S. Schuler of New York University advised me on current research in the area of the employment interview.

Above all, thanks be to God.

Contents

ix

CONTENTS

PART THREE: WINNING RESUMES FOR THE '90s

PART FOUR: HOW TO OPEN DOORS TO DIFFERENT JOBS

Preface

HOW TO GET HIRED IN THE NASTY '90s

Winning Resumes gives you all the answers you need to get hired in today's job market because times have changed and finding a job has become more challenging. The book is easy to read and just as easy to use. It will help you succeed—from entry level to management.

But first, are there any jobs out there? Of course there are, and people *are* getting hired. Hiring has continued during every economic downturn, recession, or depression—even throughout the 1930s. But tough employers expect much more from you and your job resume today. What you need to know is what to offer them and how to market yourself *on paper*, because landing a job interview is much more difficult today.

It is important to understand that the content of many jobs has changed and will continue to change. Job titles don't tell you much these days. Because companies are redefining and combining positions, one person now has to do the work of two or three. To apply for these "restructured" positions, you would need to offer a wider range or combination of your skills. For example, today's "office secretary" is also expected to do the work of an administrative assistant. (S)he now has to be able to make certain decisions the manager or owner used to be responsible for. And some "blue collar"

workers need to perform office tasks with computers. These are today's "new collar" workers.

How to look for a job has also changed because most employers are no longer reading your cover letters. Nowadays, selling yourself depends largely on your job resume. But the "basic" type of resume presented in many resume books can't help you do that today. More focused ones are required—to address the specific needs of various audiences.

Because the new job market is a buyer's market, *Winning Resumes* is a different type of resume book. For this reason, all of the sample resumes (one-pagers as well as two-pagers) will show you how to present your best selling points to picky employers. You are also given hundreds of writing samples to copy or adapt—entire sentences and phrases for every level and most types of work. (Unlike the academic descriptions you'll find in most career and resume books, these are written in the language of hiring and cover some of the 8,431 skills you may have!) All job seekers love those winning words, and employers enjoy reading them—even the pickiest ones! In addition, there are many well-written job objectives, targeted skills summaries, and forty special samples of how to describe your work experience and achievements. There are also lists of new and more dynamic action words to use in the '90s. In short, this book offers you more writing samples than any other resume or career book in the library. (See the **Resume Finder**, on pp.116–118.)

Chapters 8 and 10 contain all of the tools you'll require for the job search using either a one-page or two-page approach—as well as a wide selection of resume categories. (More experienced job seekers will usually need a longer resume.)

Instead of giving you vague and general advice, *Winning Resumes* addresses common resume-writing problems such as having too little formal education, having very little or the wrong type of work experience, or being overqualified. That is why there are chapters that address the special needs of recent college graduates (Chapter 11), the needs of more experienced job seekers (Chapter 10), and how to target various jobs (Chapter 12). In Chapter 13 you'll be shown how to "fix" awkward dates and what to do if you've had too many jobs, have been too long in the same job, or have a work history that looks like a fruit salad!

Finally, there are discussions of how to avoid making fifty fatal resume mistakes and how to evaluate professional resume services and others whose advice and/or assistance you might seek (Chapter 14).

All of the sample resumes presented are *combination* resumes (one-pagers and two-pagers) that have already worked for others. These are much stronger than the old basic or general resume. Each has an appealing "top" and "bottom." That "top" contains the "sell" of a cover letter. In other words, a combination resume is a resume and covering letter rolled into one! This is the best resume format to use in the nasty '90s because it is the only type of resume that is an effective sales or marketing tool. It has already worked for thousands of job seekers, and for every level and most types of work.

The actual time taken by nearly 10,000 job seekers to get hired was greatly reduced. Most job searches required far less effort (and involved much less frustration) than these people dreamed possible—despite the keen competition for jobs. Success was achieved in:

DAYS INSTEAD OF WEEKS,
WEEKS INSTEAD OF MONTHS, and
MONTHS INSTEAD OF YEARS.

This was mainly because they had presented their "CAN DO'S" effectively on paper. That, in turn, helped employers to hire them.

A combination resume is not only powerful but also flexible. You can create as many different and unusual ones as you like—to offer varying combinations of your skills and experience. You'll need such *tailored* resumes to compete successfully in the new job market.

You also need to figure out who may be hiring. Visit your local "goldmine"—the microfiche section of your library—and ask to see help-wanted ads in Sunday newspapers that are six to thirty-six months old. One in twelve of those positions might now be vacant but is not being readvertised. Send them your impressive combination resume. You might be considered *without* any competition from 200 others who also replied to last week's ads! In my view, it's the most effective job search technique there is because it is in the unadvertised ("hidden") job market that most of today's hiring is being done. And this is where your friends and acquaintances could act as your eyes and ears—to help open those doors for you.

It's not how qualified you are for a position that is crucial. It's how well you *present* yourself to an employer—on paper and in person. A winning resume presentation can often swing it for you—even if your credentials are quite ordinary. The reality is that it's not necessarily the best qualified candidate that gets hired. (For example, a microbiologist was recently hired as a bookkeeper in Manhattan's garment district. She'll be using her computer skills to figure out a new software package and then train staff! A friend had introduced her.)

So, good luck in all your job searches and be thankful for every "no" you get. It brings you one interview closer to the last and joyous one when you'll be hired. You see, there *is* a "yes" at the end of most job search tunnels, but if some of these seem longer and darker these days it's because so many companies and jobs have been "re-engineered."

—MATTHEW GREENE
New York City
February 1994

Part One

DISCOVERING YOUR "CAN DO'S"

WINNING RESUMES FOR TODAY'S JOB MARKET

New age job seekers know that they inherently are problem solvers. They think like entrepreneurs. They ask: "What is wanted and needed out there that I have to offer?" They are the ones who know their value and how to communicate it.
—Tom Jackson, "A Fresh Approach to Getting Yourself Hired" [34]*

WHAT TODAY'S EMPLOYERS EXPECT TO SEE IN A GOOD JOB RESUME

In the highly competitive job market of the '90s, your resume is your most important job search tool. If well written, it can market your value to ten picky employers in a single day. But recruiters expect a better resume from you—a focused one that tells them what you're able to do for their companies. They want to hear about your CAN DO'S.

In the '70s and '80s, job seekers were taught to write a "basic" or generic resume that presented only their facts—their education and work experience. It concentrated almost entirely on their past I-DID-I-DID'S and, as a rule, the same version was sent to every prospective employer. That type of resume omitted to say that you were efficient, that you knew how to cut costs, that you had good organizational and teamwork skills, and so on. (Selling yourself was done in a separate cover letter.)

Today, busy employers prefer to read everything

about you in a *single* document—your facts and your sell. This requires a different type of resume format—one that allows you to include your school/work experience as well as details of your skills, abilities, and achievements. In other words, a *combination* resume. It is a stronger type of resume and is more effective than any of the resume formats used in the '80s.

You see, basic resumes were usually "headless." They omitted to say what you were looking for because job seekers were advised to stay loose and flexible—to keep *their* options open. Instead, they relied on a cover letter to state what position they were interested in and what they were offering. In this way, they expected employers to find a suitable slot for them. But such resumes are being screened out today. Why?

Because the job market has changed and is now a buyer's market in which 50 to 300 job seekers might be applying for each vacancy. As a result, overworked personnel clerks and secretaries have stopped reading those cover letters. (Nowadays, they ask you to fax only your resume, seldom a cover letter!) In short, most hiring authorities will

*Bracketed figures refer to the numbered lists in the Bibliography.

be looking only at your resume. They expect to see what position(s) you are seeking and what your CAN DO's are. Only a combination resume can help you give them all they need to know because it's a resume and cover letter rolled into one.

Except when mailed to the head of a department by name, a formal covering letter is no longer an important part of your total sales package. Today it is only a cover "note"—a *routing* device to direct it to the right party—not a sales tool. It should *not* contain anything important.

Today's employers expect your resume to address their specific needs. Instead of the all-purpose resume of the '80s, you'll have to focus yours and even tailor it to match their needs. This book shows you how to do it, on a word processor or PC. You'll learn how easy it is to create two or more combination resumes that offer a different "mix" of your skills and work experience. This is how you explore your job options today.

WHAT ARE YOUR CAN DO'S?

Even in the '80s, many employers complained that basic resumes told them little or nothing about the job seeker's skills (other than a few technical ones such as typing, WordPerfect 5.1, Lotus 1–2–3, and so on). To find out what you were *able* to do, ordinary managers or departmental heads had to scrutinize your resume from A to Z and try to figure out your CAN DO's. All too often they either couldn't, or didn't bother. (You can't expect an employer to be a qualified skills analyst as well.)

Picky employers won't play this guessing game any longer. They want your resume to tell them that you're a problem solver, that you have strong analytical skills, that you are able to meet deadlines, and so on. In particular, they'll be looking for answers to two hiring questions: "What are your skills?" and "What can you do for us?" In short, they expect *you* to help them to hire you. Thus, a basic resume—a laundry list of facts—won't satisfy recruiters today. They want far more than your dates, job titles, and work descriptions.

To illustrate the difference between the old and the new type of resume, let's review the two resumes of Mary Parker (not her real name). The first is the basic (I-DID-I-DID) resume of the '80s. The second offers Mary's CAN DO's plus her I-DID-I-DID's. It is the type of resume most employers prefer today—a combination resume.

4

THE OLD TYPE OF BASIC RESUME

MARY PARKER

95 Gramercy Park East #4 • New York, NY 10003 • (212) 677-0000

EXPERIENCE   <u>Secretary</u>   5/93–Present
FASTBUCKS CORPORATION, New York, NY

Assist analysts and traders with securities research. Provide administrative support. Pinch hit for the Operations Manager. Research and resolve trade problems. Produce daily statistical reports. Perform general secretarial duties, including word processing, record keeping, and general office duties.

<u>Assistant to Credit Manager</u>   8/90–4/93
APEX HOME RENOVATIONS, Jersey City, NJ

Assisted Credit Manager in collecting outstandings. Researched credit applications and inquiries. Maintained records of accounts. Posted and balanced payments. Prepared and recorded legal documents.

EDUCATION   **Rutgers University,** New Brunswick, NJ

Degree: B.S. in Business Administration   (6/90)
Minor: Accounting

SKILLS   Typing (55 wpm), WordPerfect, Lotus 1–2–3, dBase III.

REFERENCES   Available upon request.

THE NEW RESUME FORMAT FOR THE '90s

MARY PARKER

95 Gramercy Park East #4 • New York, NY 10003 • (212) 677-0000

OBJECTIVE: A position as **Administrative Assistant/Secretary.** Seek an opportunity to assist one or more busy executives to get the job done. Am efficient and effective. Have strong research and problem-solving skills.

SUMMARY:
- B.S. degree in Business Administration and Accounting.
- Experience in fast-paced trading and credit/collections environments.
- Routine bookkeeping.
- Thorough knowledge of office operations and administration; preparation of statistical reports.
- Research, record-keeping and file maintenance.
- General secretarial skills and experience.
- Strong organizational, liaison and follow-up skills.
- IBM PC . Lotus 1–2–3 . WordPerfect 5.1 . dBase III . Typing (55 wpm).
- Work well under pressure; able to meet deadlines.

EXPERIENCE: **Administrative Assistant/Secretary**
1993–Present   FASTBUCKS CORPORATION, New York, NY

—Pinch hit for Operations Manager during his absences.
—Assist analysts and traders with securities research.
—Provide administrative support; maintain records.
—Research and resolve trade problems.
—Produce daily statistical reports.
—Perform general secretarial duties, word processing (IBM PC) and general office duties.

1990–1992   **Assistant to Credit Manager/Secretary**
APEX HOME RENOVATIONS, Jersey City, NJ

—Assisted Credit Manager in researching credit applications.
—Collected outstandings; maintained records.
—Posted and balanced payments.
—Prepared routine legal documents.

Details of additional employment and references will be provided at an interview.

EDUCATION: **B.S. in Business Administration/Accounting**   (6/90)
RUTGERS UNIVERSITY, New Brunswick, NJ

BASIC VERSUS COMBINATION RESUMES

Which of Mary's two resumes will sell a prospective employer? Mary's old (or basic) resume concentrates on work experience, on what: she-DID-she-DID-she-DID-she-DID for two previous employers. But what is there to pique the interest of a busy reader who might be receiving hundreds like this one?

By contrast, her combination resume has an eye-catching "top" and attention-getting bullets. Each is a *selling point* that tells the reader what she is offering. These are her CAN DO's. It makes an excellent first impression and it sells—in the first five to fifteen lines (or 10 to 20 seconds). Also notice her new and improved job titles. What a difference they make! (Much more on this later.)

The rest of Mary's combination resume—the "bottom"—is virtually identical to what she wrote in her basic one, except that it now looks more readable and has "eye appeal." (Instead of two gray, run-on paragraphs that look like mashed potatoes, her new resume has the definition and appeal of golden French fries. Every statement now commences with a dash to guide the reader's eyes.)

To summarize, Mary's basic resume has no "sell," but her combination resume offers her CAN DO's as well as her I-DID-I-DID's. It will help her to compete successfully. With her new resume, Mary can sell herself *without* the use of the outdated cover letter. Now let's look more closely at how to transfer the sell of a cover letter to a combination resume.

TRANSFERRING YOUR "SELL" FROM COVER LETTER TO JOB RESUME

Let me repeat. In the '80s, job seekers used a basic job resume to present their facts (what I've done for others) and a separate cover letter to sell themselves (what I can do for you). But nowadays, this strategy is outdated because most employers are ignoring those letters. So how can we rescue the important selling message of that letter?

You can easily do this by transferring your "selling points" to the top portion of your resume. In Mary's new resume, the top portion is her sell. It now tells employers what she wants *and* what she is offering. Both her facts and her sell are recorded in a single document—her combination resume.

On the next two pages you'll find the "old" cover letter and "new" combination resume of a young executive whom we'll call Phillip Smith. Phillip felt that his letters were not being read. He therefore transferred those selling points to his resume. All twenty of them! (The letter itself was repetitious, anyway, as most cover letters tend to be.)

A TRADITIONAL COVER LETTER

(Will It Be Read If 100–300 Others Like It Are Also Received Per Job Opening?)

January 10th, 1994

The Personnel Manager
New York Times
T7470
New York, NY 10108

Dear Advertiser:

I am applying for the FINANCIAL ANALYST position as advertised in the New York Times of January 8th and enclose a copy of my resume for your consideration and review.

I graduated in 1993 with a Bachelor of Science degree in Finance and a minor in Accounting [1] from the University of Massachusetts. [2] Due to my strong analytical skills [3], I obtained an A grade in Financial Statement Analysis [4]. In addition, I was awarded A and B+ grades for special papers in related business courses. These involved researching investment publications over a five-year period.[5]

For nearly three years, I have worked in two commercial banks [6]—in Money Market trading [7] and Customer Service. [8] I performed well in each position and exceeded corporate objectives. [9] During this period, I made an intensive study of monthly indicators of the state of the economy [10] using Lotus 1–2–3 spreadsheets. [11] I have also acquired a wide knowledge of banking products and services. [12]

My writing skills are excellent. [13] In high school I was awarded a scholarship in Journalism [14] and, on campus, it was my communication and presentation skills [15] that helped me get elected President of the Students Union. [16] I was also Vice-President of the Finance Society. [17]

At work, my performance evaluations have been "outstanding." [18] In particular, my superiors feel that I have a good head for business [19] and perform very well under stress. [20]

All in all, I feel confident that I would be an asset to your brokerage house as an Analyst and look forward to meeting with you.

Thank you for your time and consideration.

Sincerely,

Encl. Resume

"SELL" AND "FACTS" IN ONE COMBINATION RESUME
(Contains All 20 Selling Points of Cover Letter on Left.)

OBJECTIVE: Position as FINANCIAL ANALYST where a Finance degree, experience **(1)** in trading/banking, and strong research, analytical, and writing skills **(6) (7)** would be of value. **(5) (3) (13)**

SUMMARY:
- B.S. degree with A grades in Finance/Accounting. **(1) (4)**
- Experience as Money Market Trader; understanding of the economy and **(7)** its monthly indicators; extensive knowledge of banking products. **(10) (12)**
- Analysis of financial statements of companies to determine areas of weakness and risk (A grade). **(4)**
- Outstanding performance evaluations. **(18)**
- Research skills, including securities research. **(5)**
- Strong communications skills, orally and in writing. **(15) (13)**
- Leadership positions (President, Students Union). **(16) (17)**
- Computer skills (Lotus 1–2–3, Reuters, and Telerate). **(11)**
- Able to work well under stress; business acumen. **(20) (19)**

EXPERIENCE: CENTURY BANK TRUST COMPANY, Chicago, IL **(6)**
1993–Present **Trader** (Money Market) **(7)**

—Research and solicit new corporate accounts. **(5)**
—Analyze economic indicators for market movements. **(10)**
—Trade Eurodollars and Federal Reserve Funds—overnight to three months.
—Also trade in Hong Kong market.
- Exceeded quota for new corporate deposits. **(9)**

1991–1992 AMERICA BANK NA, Boston, MA **(6)**
(Part-time) **Customer Service Representative** **(8)**

—Researched and resolved customer inquiries. **(5)**
—Authorized adjustments to customers' accounts.
—Acquired a knowledge of banking products/services. **(12)**
- Received excellent performance evaluation. **(18)**

1991 (5 months) MANAGEMENT STRATEGIES, INC., Boston, MA
Assistant to Controller

—Worked for a group conducting financial seminars.

EDUCATION: UNIVERSITY OF MASSACHUSETTS, Amherst, MA **(2)**
B.S. degree in Finance (Minor: Accounting, 1993) **(1)**
<u>Activities</u>: President of Students Union **(16)**
Vice-President of Finance Society **(17)**
Scholarship for Journalism (high school) **(14)**

9

ARE COMBINATION RESUMES ONLY ONE PAGE LONG?

Combination resumes are *not* only one page long (as most resumes were supposed to be in the '80s). More experienced job seekers (such as secretaries who seek advancement to Administrative Assistant), supervisors and others may sometimes need a longer resume. (The detailed reasons for this are discussed at length in Chapter 10.)

Patricia Kelly (not her real name) was "disemployed." She had worked as a Broker on Wall Street for eight years but had been laid off and now had to explore other options. She had developed many skills "on the Street" and had made valuable contacts with the investor community. (She had strong "people" skills, could interact well with high-net-worth individuals, and had a broad knowledge of financial products.)

At first, Pat used a basic one-page resume that presented only her education and work experience—her previous job titles, dates, and responsibilities. (Like many job seekers, she wanted everything down on one page.) But this one-pager didn't work—mainly because it said too little about her skills and had no "sell." That's why she needed a longer presentation. (A two-pager can sometimes work better for you, as long as your selling message—the marketing "top"—appears on page 1.) Her winning combination resume can be found on pages 11 and 12. It's a marketing gem.

The longer resume helped Pat get many interviews. Within one month she obtained the type of position she was looking for—dealing with high-net-worth business and professional persons. But she first needed a bigger and better marketing "top" (and a longer presentation) to get her to those interviews!

TWO-PAGE COMBINATION RESUME

PATRICIA KELLY

JOB OBJECTIVE

Seeking a SALES-oriented position where my successful experience on Wall Street and proven ability to build ongoing relationships within the investor community would be of value. Am very competitive.

Able to transfer my skills and experience to related areas such as:

Institutional Sales . OTC . Municipals . Corporates . Stocks

SUMMARY OF SKILLS AND EXPERIENCE

- Nearly nine years' experience as liaison between buyers and sellers—as Broker and Broker's Assistant in fiercely competitive Wall Street environments.
- Able to identify potential customers and anticipate their needs by monitoring the market and what they are involved in.
- Excellent communications and interpersonal skills with decision makers and high-net-worth individuals.
- Entertainment of clients to build relationships; able to compile quality information.
- Success in satisfying the daily requirements of major brokerage houses such as [deleted] for Government Securities.
- Communication of data concerning bids and offerings to primary dealers on a second-to-second basis via trading/sales desks.
- Broad-based knowledge of brokerage operations—from back office to the "trenches."

RELATED SELLING EXPERIENCE

1992–Present   **Broker**
FLETCHER & CARTWRIGHT, G.S.I., New York, NY
One of the five broker shops on Wall Street

—On being hired, brought the government bond business of two major clients to the firm—"Mega-Mega-Bucks" and "Big-Bucks."
—Satisfy the day-to-day requirements of these two clients for zero to two-year Treasury Bonds.
—Handle Buys . . . Sells . . . Swaps.
—Receive bids and offerings.
—Find sellers for specific issues by interacting with other traders and bond shops; compete for Swaps at auctions.
- Increased the level of interest in my firm by entertaining clients and becoming known in the 2,000-strong trading community.

(continued)

PATRICIA KELLY

RELATED SELLING EXPERIENCE (continued)

1989–1991   **Rotation Broker**
EAST-WEST BROKERAGE, INC., 60 John Street, New York, NY
Dealer-owned Brokerage House

—Responsible for backing up other brokers.
—Transacted customer business per telephone.
—Handled government bonds (zero to five-year).
—Kept long and short positions for traders on desk.
—Previously in charge of clerical staff on the floor.
—Assisted in the computerization of bids, offers, and trades.

1985–1988   **Broker's Assistant**
PRESIDENT BROKERS, INC., 40 Chambers Street, New York, NY
Division of Water Street Brokers

—Obtained Series 7 license.
—Verified trades with the primary dealer community.
—Ran a manual board that orchestrated all brokers in the room.

Previously worked as New York <u>Sales Representative</u> for GEO. BROWNING (USA)
INC. Promoted the sale of sporting goods and equipment to stores. Details provided at
a personal interview.
Sales Manager once wrote: **"Trish, you could sell broken baseball bats!"**

EDUCATION AND TRAINING

REGISTERED REPRESENTATIVE, Series 7 (1988)

LONG ISLAND UNIVERSITY, Brooklyn Campus, NY
Bachelor of Science degree (1984)

REFERENCES

Furnished upon request.

WHY COMBINATION FORMATS ARE BETTER THAN CHRONOLOGICAL OR FUNCTIONAL ONES

Throughout the '70s and '80s, the most widely used resume formats were the chronological (work history) and the functional ("skills") resume. The former stresses your previous employment (i.e. the bottom portion of the resume); the functional format has a top that describes things you're *able* to do, usually under three to four different categories. (See p. 14) But each of these two resumes told employers barely *half* of what they needed to know about you. That is why an additional cover letter was always required—to complete your sales pitch. Unlike today's combination resume, neither of these formats allowed you to emphasize both your *sell* (CAN DO'S) and your *facts* (HAVE DONE'S) in the same document.

But the work history and functional formats also have other shortcomings or disadvantages. For example, the chronological resume highlights your dates, job duties, and education—from the time you left grade school to the present. (At best, it may also include an achievement or two.) But this format does *not* allow you to present your most important skills and abilities such as your communication skills, "people" skills, and your ability to solve problems. Where would you record them? (That is why the words "*able to*" or "*ability*" do not appear in work history resumes.)

The need to state your last job first is another serious problem because that may not be the most enjoyable or responsible job you've had or wish to emphasize. To have to bury your best work experience under more recent but less interesting positions would really be bad marketing! This is why the chronological resume tends to be so weak as a sales device.

Even worse, is that a chronological format will only present "perfect" careers in a favorable light. It can be downright detrimental to use it if you've moved around a lot; if there are gaps in your employment history; if you have not been given increasing responsibility at regular intervals; or if you are changing careers (Taunee Besson). For many job seekers—those with less-than-perfect credentials, it can be a "killer" resume.

Because a simple work history format can have such a downside, a functional resume is often suggested as the solution for many of your resume-writing problems. It is supposed to help you highlight your skills while covering up or concealing your blemishes. But most job seekers tend to shy away from it because it seems so strange and difficult to compose. Why else do only 5 in 100 ever go "functional"? To write this type of resume requires a high level of analytical and verbal skills that only an experienced resume professional may have. (It is seldom easy to dissect your life/work experiences and translate them into functions you can perform.) And the resulting resume may even look odd! Why? Because it will usually be top-heavy—all functions but hardly any work history.

Not only that. This format is actually *disliked* by most employers because they're used to seeing a "normal" work history—one with dates. They realize only too well that a functional presentation endeavors to hide or camouflage your true facts and they're generally suspicious of it. In particular, they can never match up what you say you're able to do with *when*, *where* and *for whom* you actually did it. That's why many won't even read it (Douglas B. Richardson). They resent a resume that tries to control what they should know about you—that presents the tasks you say you can perform but obviously tries to disguise your dates of employment, actual job duties, and previous employers.

To summarize, neither the functional nor the chronological resume will impress employers today. And each requires an additional covering letter which may be ignored. (To write a "blinding" cover letter is seldom easy, as any English major can confirm. It requires the combined talents of an advertising copywriter, a writer of sales literature, and a self-marketing expert!) But even such talents won't resolve the problem of "Fax me your resume." Only the combination format enables you to record both your *strengths* and your *accomplishments* in the same document. It gives employers what they want—with or without a formal cover letter.

RESUME FORMATS USED IN THE '80s
(Suitable for a Seller's Market.)

OUTLINE OF CHRONOLOGICAL RESUME
(Used by 90 to 95 Percent of All Job Seekers.)

Objective: Omitted (usually); stated in a separate cover letter.

Education: Stated (with dates).

Experience: Heavy emphasis on dates, names of employers, and detailed descriptions of present and past duties and responsibilities. Sometimes results or achievements are mentioned.

Skills: Typing (45 wpm), Lotus 1–2–3, WordPerfect 5.1. Omitted are all crucial nontechnical skills. These are mentioned in the cover letter.

References: Available upon request.

OUTLINE OF FUNCTIONAL RESUME
(Used by 5 Percent of All Job Seekers.)

Objective: Specified only as a job title.

Functions: Administrative: (Description of functions performed.)

Public Relations: (Description of functions performed.)

Supervisory: (Description of functions performed.)

Work History: One-line statements of job titles and names of employers; *no* job descriptions are given. Dates are usually omitted because these might be "awkward."

Education: Stated. (Dates are often omitted.)

The combination resume is valuable because it includes the best features of other resume styles. On the one hand, its marketing top reflects the *breadth* of the functional format (in order to present a wide range of your skills and strengths). But, instead of offering employers a list of vague and mysterious functions, they will now read a series of impressive *selling points*. And its bottom presents the *depth* of the chronological resume, showing what work experiences you've had.

Above all, the way a combination resume can target jobs, is vastly superior to the old "targeted" resume format which was divided into "Capabilities" and "Work Experience." (In that impractical format, many of the so-called capabilities actually looked more like job duties!)

In short, today's combination resume is a successful blending of the best features of the chronological, functional, and targeted resume formats. Combining focus, depth, and breadth in a single document creates impact. Most employers are impressed by such resume power, even today!

A FLEXIBLE RESUME FOR TARGETING JOBS

The combination resume is not only stronger than either the chronological or functional formats, but has the advantage of being more flexible. Thus, its content can easily be tailored to address the needs of many different audiences. Because its marketing "top" can quickly be varied to offer various combinations of your skills and experience, you can now write two to four different resumes to target different jobs. (Don't worry, with today's PCs and word processors this is easier than you think. See Chapter 12, "Targeting Jobs with Different Resumes.")

More than 10,000 job seekers have already used a combination format successfully over the past decade. Personnel managers have been impressed, as well as executives in hundreds of major banks, corporations, businesses, and factories throughout the United States and England. They hired. That amount of positive feedback is the best type of validation for this old/new style of job resume!

The combination format is definitely the most effective one for marketing your selling points in a tough job market. It is a powerful and proven self-marketing tool. Indeed, the successes achieved with it have sometimes been dramatic.

In the Oxford American Dictionary, the word *strategic* is defined as "To gain an advantage." That is what you'll achieve by using a combination resume to market your CAN DO'S—in one, two, or three different versions. All you need to construct it (or them) is presented in the pages of this book.

Why shouldn't you pay attention to those who tell you that a good job resume is *only* a "key" with which to unlock doors?

Why would it be unwise today to rely exclusively on selling yourself in person at interviews? The answers follow.

WHY IT IS UNREALISTIC TO SAVE UP YOUR SELL FOR INTERVIEWS

Nowadays it has become very difficult to meet with employers. Landing a job interview isn't easy. In fact, the competition for most jobs is so keen that you need to presell yourself—on paper—just to get to see the hiring authority. Everything is being done to screen you out, fax you out, and keep you out.

But a good job resume does much more than open doors for you. It *markets* you. Sadly, many (if not most) job seekers continue to underestimate the impact that a well-written resume can make. Instead, they choose to save up many of their best selling points for the interview itself. In other words, they elect to rely on the skill of the interviewer to extract their "sell" from them. That is like playing roulette! The vast majority of managers and departmental heads are *not* trained to interview you; they don't know how to get at your skills and often can't "match up" what you've done before with what they need you to do now. Most employers actually hate the process of interviewing and want to get it over with. (See Chapter 3.)

That is why a focused presentation of your CAN DO'S on paper will do much to clinch it for you. It enhances your perceived worth and will continue to reassure the party who has to make the hiring decision. Once he or she has your impressive document in writing, much of the resistance to you will fade. The printed word will usually impress more than hastily scribbled notes.

There is considerable evidence that a combination resume both presells your value to the reader and is the best type of resume to leave behind you after an interview. (By then, up to 85 percent of what you have told them in person has probably been forgotten.) That is why thousands of job seekers have felt that their combination resumes did much more than "unlock" doors for them; the resume (and selling points) helped employers hire them!

All of these job hunters presented their best CAN DO's up front. They decided *not* to rely on employers to figure out what these might be and wisely chose not to depend too much on their own interviewing skills. The simple truth about many job interviews is that if your job resume gives a recruiter the impression that you are (a) organized, (b) focused, and (c) able to address 50 percent or more of his or her needs, the following happens:

- The "halo effect" (I'm-so-impressed-with-your-resume-*and*-with-you) will start to work in your favor, the atmosphere will be positive, the "chemistry" between you will feel good, and tough questions might never be asked.
- A combination resume that offers your skills will score many points in your favor—before, during, and after that meeting.

SUMMARY: WHY COMBINATION RESUMES ARE THE BEST JOB SEARCH TOOLS FOR THE '90s

COMBINATION resumes are stronger than those of the '80s

COMBINATION resumes are easy to write

COMBINATION resumes make a winning first impression

COMBINATION resumes address the buyer's needs

COMBINATION resumes are marketing devices ("sell" plus "facts")

COMBINATION resumes sell you in the first 5 to 15 lines

COMBINATION resumes are focused, not general

COMBINATION resumes address the interviewer's main questions

COMBINATION resumes focus on "What can you do for us?"

COMBINATION resumes present your CAN DO'S (skills and achievements)

COMBINATION resumes help employers hire you

COMBINATION resumes can be mailed without a cover letter

COMBINATION resumes can be faxed as is

COMBINATION resumes are flexible (they can easily be varied)

COMBINATION resumes help you to explore more options

COMBINATION resumes can be used to target various jobs

COMBINATION resumes lead to low-stress job interviews

COMBINATION resumes market your value before the interview, sell you during that meeting, and represent you before selection committees

COMBINATION resumes are proven (many employers have hired)

2

WHICH OF THE 8,431 SKILLS CAN YOU OFFER?

There are probably 8,431 truly different skills that human beings possess....The average job-hunter can only do 700 of those.
—RICHARD BOLLES, *What Color Is Your Parachute?*
[2]

Most people are not in touch with all of their valuable skills—with those that might be job related. But to succeed in any job search, you need to know what you're good at and what you'll enjoy doing.

Selling yourself to employers means selling your skills. Skills are your value—the CAN DO's that employers want to hear about. That is why the most important questions asked in job interviews will be those that refer to your skills (or lack of them):

"WHAT CAN YOU DO FOR US?"
"WHAT ARE YOUR STRENGTHS?"
"WHAT IS YOUR BIGGEST WEAKNESS?"

And that is why you need to discover what your job-related skills might be. Thus, well before meeting with any employer, you need to know what to write about your skills, mainly in your job resume.

Those who have recently graduated (and many returning-to-work homemakers) tend to have a similar problem—too little or no work experience.

And nearly all career changers have credentials that are less than perfect. Why? Because their previous work experience and/or education might not be relevant to the needs of future employers in new fields.

For such job seekers, their *transferable* skills will be crucial—those that are also marketable. But the same applies to those aged 50 or older.

DEFINING YOUR SKILLS

For purposes of the job search, the most practical definition of *skill* is that given in the Oxford American Dictionary. It is the "ability to do something well."

Notice that the word *skill* does not necessarily mean the ability to do something *extremely* well or better than anyone else—only that you're able to do it "well." Never be afraid to state that you do have this or that skill. You won't be claiming any special expertise and you've probably got enough of it to satisfy the employer's needs. A "strong" skill would be any specialized knowledge, talent, or gift you might have. If you do possess an exceptional amount of any particular skill or ability, you're justified in claiming *expertise* in that area.

To most employers, skills equal abilities. They use the terms interchangeably. That is why, in their help-wanted ads, recruiters often ask for the following types of skills and abilities:

- "Must be detail oriented."
- "Should be able to work well under pressure."
- "Must have strong organizational skills."
- "Able to supervise staff."
- "Must have good communications skills—orally and in writing."
- "Knowledge of Lotus 1–2–3 a plus."
- "Proven ability to lead and direct a team."
- "Must have good teamwork skills."

This is the practical language of skills—the language of hiring. It has very little in common with the examples of "skills" found in most career books. [Not even the job seeker's "bible"—the *Dictionary of Occupational Titles**—shows you how to communicate your skills to employers in *their* language.]

WHY *SKILLS* IS THE "S" WORD FOR MOST JOB SEEKERS

Whenever I ask job seekers to tell me about their best skills, they usually freeze, look at me sheepishly, or start to apologize. The following are typical of the responses I get:

- "I have typing (W/P) skills." (Clerks/typists/secretaries/administrators)
- "I know Lotus 1–2–3 and dBase III+." (College graduates)
- "I don't have any job skills." (Returning-to-work homemakers)
- "I have never had time to acquire any skills." (College professors)

*U.S. Department of Labor, Fourth Edition. Washington, D.C., 1977.

Each seems to be limiting "skill" to something one learns in a classroom situation—technical skills. Because of this misconception about the nature of skills, such job seekers are marketing only twenty to thirty percent of their total value. (That is, the "technical" content of the average job.) The remaining 70 percent or so of the tasks that people perform in most jobs (at every level) involve basic or nontechnical skills such as people skills, communication skills, and, above all, problem-solving skills. Tom Jackson, a well-known job skills expert, confirms this.

Even in fairly technical jobs, we see after task analysis that about 70% of the job is nothing more than basic skills . . . [3]

The truth is that many valuable skills or abilities—often the most important ones—are neither acquired nor developed in formal learning situations and are *not* the technical ones you need to upgrade. This is an especially important point for returning-to-work homemakers or recent college graduates who might have very little (if any) work experience. It is equally crucial for all career changers who, by definition, might only have the "wrong" work experience or education to offer.

The reality is that if you're able to perform *any* activity better than many of your peers (and they've told you so), the skill involved might be one of your strongest ones. (Relatives, friends, and work colleagues will often comment about something you do particularly well.)

As a college student you might have displayed excellent organizational, leadership, or people skills in campus activities. You might have been Social Chairperson of a fraternity/sorority or vice-president or treasurer of an economics club. You might have been captain of a sports team or a senator or ambassador who had to use good "communications" skills. And so on. You might have contributed your writing skills to a college newspaper and your public relations and fund-raising skills to raise money for the "War Against Poverty" or some other worthy cause.

The average, efficient homemaker has developed far too many skills to mention here. Just review a typical day in the life of your family and what you must do in order to cope. Are you well organized? Can you coordinate and schedule family activities? Do you manage your time well? Do you prepare meals on time (and within budget)? Are you good at budgeting the family's finances? Do you have to mediate in disputes? Do you manage to solve a wide range of problems?

All of these activities involve the same basic skills used in the workplace. And the fact that you might not have had a single day of paid employment will not diminish the value of those skills. They are all transferable and highly *marketable*.

However, to try to identify your best skills on your own is seldom easy because it's so difficult to be objective about oneself. We cannot see ourselves as others see us (Robert Burns). In fact, we need outside parties—our relatives, friends, teachers, and employers—to help us by answering the crucial question: "In your view, as you know me, what do you think I'm good at?"

Another reason why we aren't always aware of how good we are at something is because we are told to be modest when talking about ourselves—not to toot our own horns. (In our Judaeo-Christian culture, humility is a most desirable virtue.) Thus, we seldom talk about our skills. That might be construed as boasting or bragging. The result? Many job seekers omit some of their best skills from their job resumes. In short, they fail to make good "hiring music."

More serious are the putdowns—repeated (negative) criticism of our efforts to learn by well-meaning parents, teachers, and friends and the fact that our daily achievements and accomplishments are seldom recognized. Is it any wonder that many of us feel we have very little of value to offer an employer?

But to get a job in the tough, competitive '90s, the need to know your strongest and most marketable skills is crucial to your success. You should never rely on any employer to figure this out for you. Most employers are *not* qualified to analyze either you or your resume in order to identify your skills. They're bound to overlook some important ones and then conclude that you don't have them.

Now let's look at 250 skills statements and phrases, each of which describes one or more job-related skills or abilities. These will help you get hired in any job market.

250 CAN DO'S YOU CAN OFFER: YOUR VALUE

Test Question: "Name five of your best skills."

See? It isn't easy. Let's help you do it. In the next few pages you'll find 250 carefully worded sentences and phrases that express the skills (and combinations of skills) that all employers require. They frequently advertise for these. They always need them. They are yours to copy or adapt. Every item has previously been used in 500 (or more) winning resumes. They are therefore employer tested and approved.

These are the words you'll need to use in offering your value (or CAN DO's) to employers—sentences that add sell to your resume. Such writing samples provide you with the specialized vocabulary you need to market your skills. (You won't learn these in English 101.)

The six checklists on pages 24 to 26 cover many of your basic skills. These are the building blocks—the elements involved in performing many tasks—in every type of work and at all levels, from entry to management. They will certainly qualify you to perform 70 percent of the work in most offices. (The only exceptions are "technical" tasks such as computer programming.) The checklists are classified as follows:

BASIC (GENERAL) SKILLS

DISCOVERING YOUR CAN DO'S

Your job search campaign starts here, with an easy exercise

a. to help you discover ten or more of your job-related skills and abilities, and

b. to identify your strengths.

In addition to the 250 skills sentences and phrases that follow, a further 750 or more writing samples appear in the pages of this book. Each is a valuable CAN DO that will help you get hired. If properly used, they will be music to an employer's ears. They are your best selling points.

Begin by scanning pages 24 to 28. Check (✓) any items that describe you well. Then transfer about ten of these *basic* skills to the worksheet, marked "A," found on this page. (If necessary, make a choice between similar items or modify the wording to make an item fit you better.) Next, *underline* your best or strongest skills and number them in order of importance from 1 to 10.

(These words, phrases, and sentences will be used in writing Job Objectives, Skills Summaries, and cover letters, and during any face-to-face meeting with employers. More on this later.)

A. MY STRONGEST BASIC (GENERAL) SKILLS

1. _Enthusiastic_
2. _Team Player_
3. _Can Do Attitude_
4. _Hands on Supvisery_
5. _Able to Train_
6. _Able to organise_
7. _Able to Com w/ Man, Tec, clerical_
8. _Research Data._
9. _Able to complet Jobs._
10. _Tactful._

Now turn to the Resume Finder on pages 116 to 118. Locate the type of work you wish to perform (or something similar). In column 2 (Resumes) and column 5 (Skills Summaries) you'll see where to find groups of more *job-specific* skills sentences that apply to your field. (If by any chance yours does not seem to be covered, don't worry. There are ninety or so Skills Summaries in this book, each offering approximately ten skills and abilities.) Transfer a few of these to worksheet B (page 22). Next, underline your best or strongest job-specific skills and number them in order of importance.

B. MY JOB-SPECIFIC SKILLS AND ABILITIES

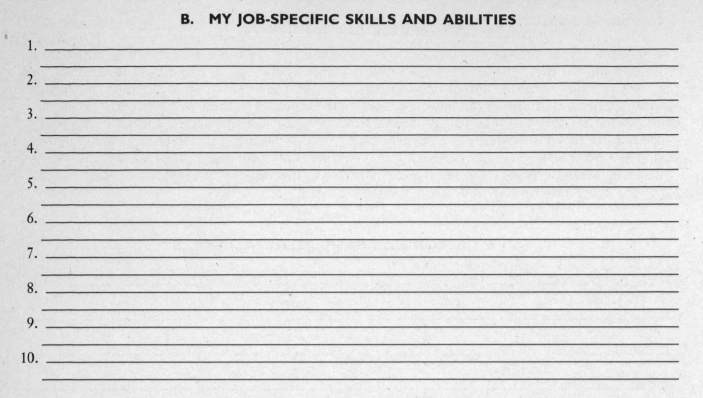

1. _____
_____
2. _____
_____
3. _____
_____
4. _____
_____
5. _____
_____
6. _____
_____
7. _____
_____
8. _____
_____
9. _____
_____
10. _____

Next, think about jobs you've held (full-time and part-time), hobbies, school, home, and other activities, such as volunteer work. You have probably picked up quite a few valuable skills along the way, especially if you've had to "pinch hit" or "cover" for someone. Which of these CAN DO'S seem transferable to work situations? In the present job market, which seem to be the most marketable? What type(s) of work could they "fit"? Record this data below under "C." (We'll return to this subject in Chapter 3 when we'll see what employers are willing to buy.)

C. MY TRANSFERABLE AND MOST MARKETABLE SKILLS

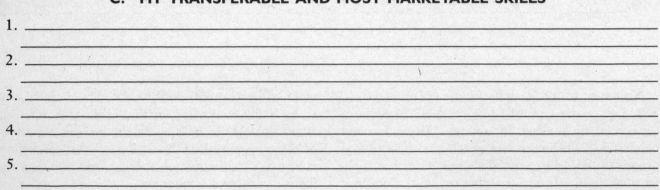

1. _____
_____
2. _____
_____
3. _____
_____
4. _____
_____
5. _____
_____

PREPARING FOR JOB INTERVIEWS

Your preparation for a job interview starts here with a very important worksheet—one that covers any achievement or accomplishment of yours, something you're proud of. (Everyone has done well at something somewhere—in school, at work, or anywhere else.)

Employers want to know not only what you've done but *how well* you have performed. If you can demonstrate past achievements, your attractiveness as a possible hire will increase geometrically! And the more job-related these are, the better.

The point is that any achievement will demonstrate a few of your skills. (These are probably your *strengths*.) For example, your success as a fund-raiser might have been due to your excellent telephone skills, your ability to communicate well with high-net-worth individuals, your strong organizing or teamwork skills, or your persistence and hard work.

Why do you consider your achievement to be so special? What problems or difficulties did you need to overcome? Was it the only, the first, or the best of anything? (Imagine that the employer is not easily impressed.)

Briefly describe three of your achievements. How did you make a difference? Which of your skills were involved? Were any measurable results achieved? Employers love objective numbers and percentages that make you seem like a valuable hire!

D. ACHIEVEMENTS AND ACCOMPLISHMENTS

1. _____
_____
_____
2. _____
_____
_____
3. _____
_____
_____

SKILLS AND ABILITIES EMPLOYERS NEED

PERSONAL SKILLS AND QUALITIES

- Enthusiastic
- Friendly manner; agreeable; good sense of humor
- Energetic; have high energy level; am a "go-getter"; dynamic
- Hardworking; conscientious; willing to work overtime
- Cooperative; willing to pitch in to get the job done
- Able to write neatly and legibly
- Interpersonal skills; teamwork skills; willing to lead the pack
- Scheduling skills
- Able to organize people (paperwork, events); organizational skills
- Coordinating skills
- Liaison skills
- Able to work well with little or no supervision
- "Can do" attitude; "stick-to-itiveness"; persistence; perseverance
- Efficient and effective in getting work done; able to prioritize
- Able to work well under pressure; able to meet deadlines
- Able to cope with a heavy workload
- Have problem-solving skills; am a creative problem solver
- Willing to learn; fast learner; able to adapt very quickly
- High personal standards; thorough; meticulous
- Able to set and achieve high personal goals; ambitious; achiever
- Creative; innovative; resourceful
- Leadership skills (captain of ____; leader of ____ group)
- Well-groomed; professional appearance and manner
- Positive and professional image

GENERAL SKILLS AND APTITUDES

- Detail-oriented; attention to detail; eye for detail
- Aptitude for figures
- Mathematical aptitude
- Clerical skills and experience; clerical aptitude
- Able to use a wide range of business machines
- Research and data collection skills; able to interpret data
- Analytical skills
- Follow-up skills; follow-through skills
- Able to handle a heavy workload and meet deadlines
- Able to work well under both time and accuracy pressures
- Able to complete projects on time and within budget
- Able to exercise sound independent judgment; able to make decisions
- Able to identify potential problem areas
- Strong troubleshooting skills
- Able to find alternative or low-cost solutions to problems
- Tact and diplomacy in handling sensitive (delicate) situations (documents)
- "People" skills; able to deal with "difficult" clients; able to mediate
- Able to train others; able to supervise people/activities/events
- Business sense; business acumen; entrepreneurial skills; money-driven

COMMUNICATION SKILLS

- Excellent telephone/switchboard skills; pleasant voice/manner
- Able to screen and direct callers—in person and per telephone
- Excellent listening skills; able to identify a buyer's needs
- Able to compose own correspondence and memorandums
- Able to draft legal documents and memorandums
- Writing skills; report-writing skills
- Strong communications skills—both orally and in writing
- Interviewing skills; screening and assessment skills

- Individual and group counseling skills
- Excellent one-on-one communications skills
- Strong advocacy and mediation skills; representation skills
- Able to make excellent oral presentations
- Able to make effective (winning) presentations to decision makers
- Platform (public speaking) skills
- Public relations skills; excellent promotions skills
- Liaison skills with other departments or agencies
- Able to communicate well with members of a multidisciplinary team
- Able to communicate effectively with managerial/technical/clerical personnel
- Able to communicate effectively with professionals/paraprofessionals
- Effective communication with programmers and end-users
- Able to write clear and concise reports for senior management
- Able to write effective telemarketing scripts (or detailed call reports)
- Able to write sales literature, promotional brochures, and newsletters
- Demonstrated ability to write effective sales letters (speeches)
- Bilingual (English and Spanish); excellent command of spoken English
- Foreign language skills (fluent in French; working knowledge of Afrikaans)

"PEOPLE" SKILLS

- Sensitivity to the needs/feelings/perceptions of clients/co-workers
- Excellent interpersonal skills with fellow employees
- Team person (team player); strong teamwork skills
- Able to deal tactfully with the needs of celebrities and VIPs
- Able to interact well with a wide range of people and personalities
- Able to relate well to upscale business and professional clients
- Able to interact effectively with clients

- Relationship-building skills
- Able to interact well with both individual and corporate clients
- Able to establish excellent rapport with clients
- Success in dealing with high-net-worth individuals
- Excellent customer service skills
- Strong liaison and follow-up skills
- Able to satisfy the needs of discriminating customers
- Skill in dealing effectively with demanding clients
- Sensitivity to the budgetary constraints of clients
- Able to work effectively with all levels of management and staff
- Able to supervise professional, technical, and clerical staff
- Able to oversee the work of other professionals
- Able to train, supervise, and motivate staff; get the best out of staff
- Strong "people" skills
- People management skills

SUPERVISORY SKILLS

- Hands-on supervisory style; willing to pitch in
- Able to substitute (pinch hit) for any member of office support staff
- Able to hire, supervise, and terminate junior clerks and typists
- Able to oversee an office/store/factory floor
- Able to supervise both technical and non-technical personnel
- Able to supervise both professional and clerical staff
- Able to train, cross-train, and retrain clerical personnel
- Strong organizational and scheduling skills and experience
- Able to prioritize, coordinate, and oversee work assignments
- Demonstrated ability to take charge during a manager's (boss's) absence(s)
- Able to oversee a variety of ongoing (simultaneous) projects

25

- Proven ability to get the job done; able to delegate effectively
- Able to ensure the proper execution of time-sensitive projects
- Track record of setting and meeting departmental goals and objectives
- Able to monitor budgetary expenditures and control expenses
- Excellent time management skills; efficient and effective
- Able to communicate clearly and avoid misunderstandings
- Decision-making skills; able to exercise sound independent judgment

- Proven ability to troubleshoot actual and potential problem areas
- Able to mediate (negotiate) and resolve staff disputes
- Able to administer discipline, as and when required
- Proven ability to motivate staff to increase their productivity
- Able to raise the productivity of staff and reduce/eliminate waste
- Able to win the respect of staff; lead by example
- Strong supervisory skills

MANAGERIAL SKILLS

Planning: Able to see the "big picture"; able to set goals and objectives; able to attain/realize corporate objectives; able to anticipate/forecast manpower requirements in order to schedule sufficient staff and eliminate wastage/costly overtime; proven ability to develop and implement more efficient procedures that have shortened response times to internal/external inquiries and/or that expedited the shipping of orders and/or that have reduced daily proof time (in a bank); able to forecast financial requirements and monitor budgetary expenditures in order to reduce or eliminate nonessential expenses; excellent time management skills; able to cover a territory in a minimum amount of time.

Organizing: Proven ability to organize manpower and equipment in order to achieve maximum operational effectiveness; able to streamline the workflow; able to delegate and assign appropriate workloads to individuals in order to attain optimum performance; excellent people management skills; effectiveness in cross-training individuals in order to avoid costly disruptions and/or downtime; success in promoting staff; excellent organizational, coordinating, and follow-through skills and experience.

Directing: Able to lead and direct a team; able to make sound independent judgments; strong decision-making skills; able to conduct productive staff meetings that result in effective action being taken; highly developed problem-solving skills; creative problem-solving skills; able to analyze and troubleshoot actual and potential problems (or problem areas); able to recommend appropriate (cost-effective) solutions; precision in written communications in order to minimize errors of interpretation; effective oral communication skills; tactful and to the point in dealings with customers and staff; able to write clear and concise reports.

Controlling: Able to develop performance standards and/or formulate reasonable expectancies in order to evaluate staff; able to increase the effectiveness of individual members of a team; proven ability to raise the morale of a group; demonstrated ability to increase the productivity of staff by _____ percent; proven ability to reduce/eliminate waste and/or unnecessary duplication of work; strong analytical skills; able to detect and correct faults through coaching and/or taking corrective action; skill and good judgment in administering discipline, including arranging transfers; decisive in terminating staff when necessary.

Negotiating: Able to negotiate well; strong negotiating skills; able to drive a hard bargain with vendors; able to negotiate favorable prices, terms and conditions; proven ability to renegotiate the terms and conditions of vendor contracts and/or maintenance agreements and/or health/pension/insurance plans; able to mediate in and resolve staff disputes; able to negotiate effectively with labor unions.

"People" skills: Demonstrated ability to select, train, motivate, and develop subordinates; achievements include reducing labor turnover by ____ percent and lowering absenteeism ____ percent; able to provide/create incentives to motivate staff; proven ability to win the respect of staff; counseling skills; able to create definite career paths for employees in own area; able to provide one-on-one training where required.

Track record: Steady promotions to positions that included management-level (supervisory) responsibilities; successful experience as a manager in ____ and ____; effective in getting the job done within acceptable cost-timeframes; proven ability to complete projects on time and within budget; success in turning around a project that was behind schedule and running over budget; demonstrated ability to turn around an ailing department, division, or company; success in consistently meeting/exceeding sales/profit objectives.

3

WHAT TODAY'S EMPLOYERS WANT TO BUY

All businesses are looking for people who can produce more sales or profits by correcting and improving operations. Recession does not affect that kind of hiring.
—ARTHUR P. GOULD, President, Merchant Bank [31]

Forget about the '80s. Today's employers would like you to

a. address *their* needs and self-interest, and

b. write (and speak) what they want to hear. Show employers that you understand what they need to have done and offer to help them do it. To succeed, your approach should be:

Not: I-WANT-AND-EXPECT-FROM-YOU

But: I-CAN-DO-FOR-YOU.

Instead of focusing on what you might have done in the past and how the next job will fulfill your own needs, reverse your job search telescope and try to see through the eyes of the present buyer. What are his or her most urgent needs? What is his or her company looking for? Your experience in D.E.F. Company and with BOZO Inc.—your I-DID-I-DID's—might *not* be a good "fit." So, which of your CAN DO's could be valuable? This is what you need to offer or sell.

In short, what is troubling your future boss and how can you make life easier for him or her? If you succeed in finding that out (or guess at the most likely answer), you will be well on your way to getting hired.

WHAT DOES THE MARKET— THE BUYER—NEED?

In the brutally competitive '90s, most companies are doing everything to become more efficient, more competitive, and more profitable. All one reads these days are the words *productivity, streamlining, restructuring, re-engineering,* and *downsizing.* Even companies that are prospering are engaged in exercises which they describe as "rightsizing" their organizations. This has led the American Management Association to comment that corporate downsizing has become "an addiction." Today's employers are hiring people who can help them achieve these goals.

For example, as a secretary, can you help your boss become more organized? Can you reduce inefficiency in any area? Can you minimize waste and reduce expenses? Could you help doctors or dentists become more productive by shielding them from patients they don't need to see? Do you know how to get more mileage out of software?

Could you streamline operations or shorten response or delivery times? Can you suggest where their product or service could be marketed and how this should be done? Are you able to show an employer how to avoid or reduce the risk of costly lawsuits?

Practical suggestions or answers to such problems will always be music to an employer's ears. And because each will help them save or make more money, you will be a valuable person to have on board.

TAILORING THE JOB SEARCH (TOOLS) TO THE JOB

Recently, Arthur P. Gould, the president of a New York merchant bank and investment company, wrote a letter to the *New York Times* [31] that contains valuable advice for every job seeker—from entry level to senior executive.

All businesses are looking for people who can produce more sales or profits by correcting and improving operations. Recession does not affect that kind of hiring. If I had applicants who would "ring the cash register" after they came on, I would do a lot more hiring. So would others. . . .

Target a company you want to be associated with and study it. Determine what its problems are in the area of your competence. Figure out how you would solve them. . . .

Search out the executive at the company who has responsibility over the area that interests you. Write to that person. Outline the problem you have researched and the solution you would propose. Present yourself as an applicant to handle that assignment and others like it. . . .

When you research the company, study its customers and their relationships with the company. Customers are one of the best sources of information about a company. If you explain what you are doing, they are often willing to provide the information you are looking for. . . .

People who hire respect this approach. In fact, we are ready to hire such applicants.

A more effective strategy might be to show a prospective employer that you have already solved problems similar to those facing him or her now, and that you obtained immediate results. However, you want to appear capable of solving the problem (or rather, the "challenge") without coming across as a smart aleck. No employer likes to be told how to run his or her business.

It is for such reasons that many of the sample Job Objectives, Skills Summaries, and Achievements in *Winning Resumes* will demonstrate how to show employers what you have already achieved for others and would also be able to do for them.

THOSE WHO HIRE VERSUS THOSE WHO SCREEN

The writer of the letter in the previous column has the authority to hire you—unlike a personnel officer or secretary who only screens you out. He wants to know if you can help improve any area of his business.

In other words, those who do the actual hiring—the "upstairs" people—are interested mainly in whether you'll be able to help them meet their goals. But to meet with them, you first have to get past the "downstairs" people—those who hold the "key" to the boss's door.

Unfortunately, such people have a very different mindset and look for formal "requirements." Do you have the right education? Do you have experience? And so on. That's why you need to impress them with a winning resume, or learn to bypass them by developing a few telephone skills. Only then will you get a chance to persuade the "real" boss that you can do the job—even without the right experience. And that's the time when "must have" requirements are often downgraded. (Philip R. Lund's *Compelling Selling: A Framework for Persuasion* [6] teaches you what to say to telephonists and secretaries. This is probably the most valuable job-hunting skill of all. It really opens doors!)

SEVENTY PERCENT OF JOB FUNCTIONS ARE SIMILAR

How often have you said to yourself, "I could do that." Or, "I could do better than that." You were probably right much of the time! In fact, many jobs are more similar than different even though they might have widely differing job titles. This is so because job titles don't mean much and because 70 percent or more of the tasks or functions performed in those jobs involve combinations of the same basic or general skills you read about in Chapter 2. Those five pages cover many of the skills required in thousands of jobs.

There are therefore more types of work that you can handle than you could ever imagine. And it won't take you long to acquire the required amount of experience or additional knowledge.

The proof of this is all around you. Tens of thousands of people are doing well at jobs they were not "qualified" for when they started. Many were once asked to pinch hit for a qualified person during a crisis and did so well at it that they were later given the job on a permanent basis. (One psychology graduate assisted a corporate accountant during a summer vacation and impressed everyone so much that when the accountant's health failed, the graduate was asked to take on the job. (Only then did he enroll for a bookkeeping course—by correspondence!)

Similarly, Andrea, a successful Controller who supervises a computer room, has a B.A. in Education and English, no formal education in accounting, and has never taken a training course in computers! She is entirely self-taught!

TOO LITTLE EDUCATION?

What if you have too little education or the "wrong" major? Judy, a Seven Sisters history major, consistently outperforms eighteen Ivy League M.B.A.s in a major Wall Street brokerage house. When she started, she knew nothing about computers or finance, but the job involved selling to institutions and interacting with high-networth individuals. Judy quickly learned to use a PC and the right "numbers" to present to clients. She already knew how to talk to those that buy.

Similarly, many ex-teachers with Master's degrees in Early Childhood have succeeded in administrative, liaison, and sales positions. Martina, an administrative assistant, showed factory engi-

neers how to modify the production line and reduce waste in expensive fabric. And in the home movie business, Louis, an unqualified bookkeeper, developed a new way to reduce his employer's liability for taxation by millions of dollars!

Such people used skills they don't teach you in school. Judy used her "people," presentation, and numbers skills. These were the *real* requirements of the job, not a formal M.B.A. Martina had a lot of common sense and was obsessed with saving money. Louis had strong analytical skills and was creative—even in accounting. (He was a dual major in Latin and Psychology.)

So don't be put off by your own lack of formal experience or education. Your transferable skills may be more than adequate.

GET YOURSELF HIRED BY SMALLER COMPANIES—AVOID PERSONNEL DEPARTMENTS

To help you feel better about your own job prospects, you'll be relieved to hear that in only 15 percent of all companies will you need to deal with rigid and conservative personnel clerks. It's only the bigger companies that have formal personnel departments. Fully 85 percent of all employers have only 10 to 50 (or fewer) employees and tend to be more flexible about their "requirements." (It's a mystery to me why career books go to such great lengths to show you how to impress Fortune 500 personnel clerks—those who are *least* likely to hire you. And in the '90s, big companies are actually doing most of the firing!)

Once and for all, let's take a critical look at personnel departments. Do such people (or a boss's secretary) *really* know what skills or experience or education any position might require? The answer is no! Why? Because to determine this, properly executed selection research would be necessary. But what is the reality? Fewer than one-tenth of one percent of all employers ever do this, or else do it crudely! Thus, most of their formal "job requirements" are actually guesses—neither accurate nor relevant. They are rough checklists for screening out applicants. It is therefore tragic that many highly capable job seekers will also be eliminated because such requirements tend to be vague, loosely worded, and inflated—much more than a position actually requires. You could probably handle certain jobs with *half* the qualifications, if you could persuade the decision maker to let you try. (In a large company, your chances of this would be near zero.)

For example, can an employer claim that in order to succeed as, say, an "accountant" in Swank Bank, NA you would need to offer all of the following?

(a) an M.B.A. degree with an accounting major and a GPA (Grade Point Average) of at least 3.5 (and nothing less)
(b) "Big 6" experience in a public accounting firm (and nothing else)
(c) six years' experience (and not three or four)
(d) near-identical work experience in another bank rather than in a corporate accounting department

The answer is "No, not necessarily" in the case of each and every one of these "requirements" because there is hardly any objective evidence that any or all of them are really needed to be successful as an accountant in Swank Bank. More often than not, these "must have's" are based on a particular recruiter's hunches and personal preferences—almost always on the corporate culture but rarely on what it has taken others to do well in that position. What many tend to look for is the right "image." (Exaggerated requirements are like the higher prices for co-op apartments quoted to outside parties; as you know, much lower "inside" prices are reserved for those already living there.)

A characteristic of nearly all "job requirements" is their *elasticity*. This is so because they're determined (to a large extent) by the ups and downs of the job market, that is, supply and demand. Thus, if too many job hunters are expected to apply, the advertised "requirements" will usually be raised (to discourage some); if too few, then even the most rigid minimum "qualifications" will be lowered. (An obvious example is how the height requirements of police officers, firemen, and flight attendants has yo-yoed in the past. The same idea applies to the way the degree of difficulty of some of New

York City's qualifying tests is sometimes lowered to ensure that ethnic, minority, or other EEO or Affirmative Action quotas will be met. Even colleges and universities have to vary some of their admission criteria from year to year depending on the number of applications received.) And you've already heard how some "requirements" can fall like ninepins if the employer likes you and wants to have you on board. (An added reason is that he or she may feel more secure with you and your shortcomings because you won't be perceived as a threat!)

MOST "JOB SPECIFICATIONS" ARE ONLY GUESSTIMATES

How are job requirements usually agreed upon and then distilled into a formal "job specification"? The process tends to be subjective, arbitrary, and even hilarious! An already overburdened personnel clerk might perform a cursory "task analysis" to describe the main functions that will need to be performed by the appointee. From these, they'll proceed to make guesstimates as to what the minimum qualifications for the position *ought* to be: the required education, experience, intelligence, personality, and so on. As a rule, the process has a lot in common with an African witchdoctor emptying his little bag of bones on the ground and then trying to "read" them. It's not a science or mathematics!

The specific items they agree on for the "spec" will then serve as convenient cut-off points to help them decide whom to *reject* but not necessarily whom to *select*. Why? Because the "upstairs" boss does the actual hiring. For example, one Manhattan employer recently ignored a carefully prepared checklist, preferring instead a semi-qualified candidate who had once worked in the same five-star hotel as him. Who knows what your own chances might be with such bosses? The bad news is that personnel's rigid "spec" will result in many career changers being eliminated, even though they may well be *able* to do the job. That is why you need to present yourself as a good "fit" in your job resume.

Apart from highly specialized work such as an air force or navy test pilot, a physician, nurse, lawyer, or engineer there is little evidence as to what all the "right" qualifications for any particular position really are. For example, shouldn't a hospital physician also be required to have no previous record of his/her license having being suspended or revoked in other states? Meeting this requirement would help reduce the number of costly lawsuits and might be as relevant as being board certified!

Unfortunately, the dearth of objective information about job requirements gives personnel officers free rein to compile rigid (read "phony") "must have's" that are often excessive and irrelevant. And, of course, they'll never disclose items such as "must be willing to work for a boss who always breaks his/her promises" or "must be willing and able to join a company planning major layoffs and/or about to go into Chapter 11." In short, there isn't much truth in the way some job requirements are advertised, and more than a few job descriptions have turned out to be job distortions! (Joan Iaconetti [33]) For hard-to-fill positions, those ads may even contain misleading statements (or promises) to entice you to apply. That's how one trusting bookkeeper got herself hired by five employers who, within months, had to file for bankruptcy!

WHY 80 PERCENT OF HELP-WANTED ADS ARE NOT ACCURATE OR RELIABLE

The people in the personnel department are not solely to blame for the job requirements they advertise in their ads; their "upstairs" bosses can also be faulted. After all, what type of message do they often communicate to personnel? Is it always a clear-cut job specification—like asking for the correct-sized three-pronged plug to connect a word processor? No. Often it is so vague that personnel clerks are obliged to use their own imagination! And later, in rephrasing the ad, the newspaper's ad-taker will probably distort the position's "requirements" even further. In short, up to 80 percent of help wanted ads cannot and do not mean what they say or say what they mean. [1]

Again, I urge you to do everything possible to try to see the real decision maker, to get him or her to talk about their needs (problems) and see how you could help. For example, if the present

supervisor is struggling to get the work out, is it because he or she can't prioritize or schedule or can't or won't delegate or assign tasks, or because poorly trained staff need to be retrained or replaced? What would you suggest? How would you present yourself as the answer to his or her most vexing problem? (Every salesperson needs to identify the buyer's needs or "hot buttons" and also offer practical solutions.)

BE FLEXIBLE!

If you can't go out to fish, try mending nets—ANON.

In the preceding sections you saw how job hunters were hired *without* some of the formal "qualifications" for many positions. Here's another example: Barbara M., a homemaker returning to work, learned some of the things architects and construction people have to do by listening in on her husband's discussions with site foremen—at her kitchen table while she baked the cookies. Without upgrading any other skills, Barbara was later hired as office manager in a Manhattan architectural firm. In short, only if you *really* are short of any knowledge or skills that are considered a "must," do you need to add to your *technical* know-how—the remaining 20 to 30 percent of your CAN DO's—by enrolling for one or two short courses of specialized training.

As we noted in Chapter 2, job-related skills can be picked up anywhere and at any time: during unpaid or volunteer activities; while helping out in a school, PTA, church, club, or any recreational activity; in scheduling the transportation of children; in planning and organizing a successful outing or membership drive or fund-raiser. And if you've ever had to cover for someone (who hasn't?) then you've probably been "cross-trained" to perform at least one or two more work-related tasks or functions. That is how we continually add to our inventory of valuable skills or CAN DO'S.

Your first priority is therefore to discover and market what you already know—your most transferable knowledge or skills. And if all this doesn't qualify you "perfectly" for any position, don't worry.

You'll be joining the silent majority of job applicants who lack "perfect" credentials for most of the jobs they try to get most of the time. The awful truth is that this is the universal condition! (Warren Alverson) Nevertheless, most people (12 out of 14) *are* working at present. They do get themselves hired, on the average, in one to 23 weeks. (Richard Bolles) These are the determined ones who treat job-hunting as a full-time job. And where are the jobs? Mainly in the "hidden" or unadvertised job market. That's where 75 percent of the openings usually are. As we'll see, employers do have thousands of unfilled jobs that, for various reasons, they don't advertise. (Susan Dentzer, *U.S. News & World Report*, June 28, 1993) If only a friend or relative could tip you off about one of these openings!

Flexibility, resourcefulness, and the determination to keep looking are the keys to getting hired in the changing '90s, so as to find new areas where your skills might be valued. To succeed, you'll behave like an entrepreneur trying to market a product or service, only this time the commodity being offered is you! So what do buyers need that you might be able to help them with? And how flexible are you about your asking price? Are you willing to discount it? For example, if you already have some teaching experience and good organizational, "people," and problem-solving skills, you might qualify as a Daycare Administrator. (They earn $25,000 to $45,000 a year.) You can then take child-development courses at a local university. Similarly, out-of-work mechanics who were retrained in the technical school of a labor union in Long Island City, New York, have been hired as computer operators. More than anything, nearly everyone needs to know something about computers today—even "blue collar" factory workers or UPS drivers. Nowadays, many employees are in such "new collar" jobs!

CORPORATE CLASSROOMS ARE CLOSING

In the new job market, some recombined positions will definitely require you to have a wider range of technical skills. But employers are no longer willing to spend money training you on-the-job. Why? Because in hard times the training department is always among the first to be cut or even axed. After all, with so many applicants to choose from, why should companies bear the cost of in-house skills training? (According to Neil Eurich, author of *Corporate Classrooms*, more than ten million employees were trained at company expense in 1988. The total cost? Nearly $60 billion! Nowadays, such activities have been drastically curtailed.)

In the '80s, most college graduates focused only on Plan A—to offer recruiters their major or concentration. Today, however, there's an equal need to implement Plan B and market their minor plus a different mix of skills. (See Cathy Windell, p.158 to 161) Some colleges are even restructuring their degree coursework so that, say, management education is now being combined with manufacturing skills to show graduates how to create value for employers who are competing in today's global economy. Similarly, joint efforts by employers, labor unions, and educational authorities will ensure that the skills offered by applicants will be more job-related. Thus, in the Cincinnati area cooperative education programs supported by local industry have resulted in the nation's highest placement rate—far higher than many other federal or state "retraining" programs. (*Wall Street Journal* [36]) And for those who will not be attending college, Boston's Pro Tech apprenticeship programs are leading the way. (Tom Brokaw, "The Lost Generation," NBC, July 28, 1993).

But let us not exaggerate the amount of additional education or training you'll require. In today's world of smart machines or computers with ready-to-use, state-of-the-art software, only a two-year degree is the new requirement for many industrial and laboratory jobs (such as chemical analysis)—not a four-year degree as before. Why should employers pay for additional knowledge they don't need?

THE EMPLOYMENT INTERVIEW—A BLESSING OR A CURSE?

Before you rush off to buy the latest how-to on how to beat any interviewer at his or her own game, I must shout "Whoa!" You first need to be warned about the inept performance of many employers during job interviews. You see, most hiring authorities don't know how to look for the skills they require and therefore *won't* be asking you suitable questions (except, maybe, for the 15 percent in the largest companies). That's why *Winning Resumes* places such heavy emphasis on selling yourself on paper.

Not surprisingly, more than 100 separate, follow-up studies have already demonstrated that the ever-popular (unstructured) employment interview is a terrible way to judge candidates. It has a lousy track record as the means of predicting the success of new hires on the job. (You can read about its 50-plus years of failure as a selection tool in: R. D. Arvey and J. E. Campion, "The Employment Interview: A Summary and Review of Recent Research," in Randall S. Schuler and Stuart A. Youngblood [eds.], *Readings in Personnel and Human Resource Management*, 2nd Ed. [St. Paul: West Publishing Co., 1984, pp. 129–59].

Why are employers such poor interviewers? "Tell me about yourself" continues to be America's number one interview question although it is notorious for being counterproductive. (It has already "thrown" many, many highly qualified candidates.) In fact, it tells you more about the interviewer than him/her about you—that he or she is unprepared, unfocused, or untrained to question you! Be prepared; it could cost you a job because there is *no* right or wrong answer you can give. (Your best bet is to give a brief summary of your most qualifying experience or achievement for 30 to 60 seconds and then turn the question around: "Please, could you tell me more about the job and what you are looking for. Then I'll gladly try to show you how I 'fit.'") That is why a well-written presentation of your best skills in your job resume is so important—to reassure nervous, fumbling departmental heads that they won't go wrong in hiring you.

Why do so many "wrong" people get hired? This is due mainly to the extreme subjectivity of interviewers in this face-to-face meeting. As Dr. Jeffrey Allen admits after eighteen years of interviewing (in *How To Turn an Interview into a Job*), it is very, very difficult for any employer to resist the "halo effect": the winning first impression that starts in the first few seconds or minutes of the meeting when you and the interviewer "click"

about something, whether relevant to the job or not. The fact is that employers do tend to hire people like themselves. That's why most books on the subject focus on showing you how to identify with the interviewer. (My own preference is for Richard A. Payne's best-selling *How to Get a Better Job Quicker*, 3rd Ed. [Signet], which shows you how to uncover the needs of your prospective employer at the very start of your interview and how to convince him or her that you're the most likely person to get done what he or she needs to get done—whether or not you're the most "qualified" candidate.)

As for matching up what you did before with what they need you to do now, this is more difficult than you might imagine, and you have to help them. Because job applicants don't fit like standard plugs, mechanical dovetailing is seldom possible. As a result, the entire matching process tends to be more sorcery than science! (Richard Lathrop)

WHY THOUSANDS OF POSITIONS ARE UNFILLED

Not too long ago, it was estimated that in a typical year there are 700,000 to 800,000 vacancies for management-level positions of which only 250,000 or so got filled by the end of the year. Any personnel manager or recruiter can confirm how many of these are still on his/her books six months later. (A similar picture applies to positions at most other levels.) Although the total number of job openings is down today (many jobs have indeed been lost), it is still fair to ask why so many existing vacancies are neither filled nor readvertised. Here are some of the reasons why many job openings really do exist and why the employers concerned might be waiting for you to apply at the strategically correct time when they might need to appoint someone in a hurry. This happens more often than you might realize. Things do get out of hand and employers also run out of time. "How soon can you start?" gives you a clue. Let's see what happened in one company.

The Chief Executive Officer of the Gourmet Baloney Company (a small to medium-sized manufacturer) is in serious trouble. (People in top jobs like his don't seem to last more than two years.)

He is in the "hot seat," and his biggest problem is that the company has been losing market share for its products. He needs reports and figures urgently, but the company's computer always seems to be on the blink. He simply doesn't have the time right now to figure out what the problem might be; he must hire a Marketing Manager—real soon. In the interim, these duties are presently being performed (or not performed) by the National Sales Manager.

An ad is duly placed in *The Wall Street Journal*, 200 resumes are received, ten applicants are interviewed, and the CEO is about to make his key appointment. But too late! The Chairman and Board of Directors aren't convinced, act quickly, and fire him. All his hiring plans are put on hold so that the next CEO can recruit his own team. It will be a matter of weeks before CEO number two gives his full attention to appointing a marketing manager, if at all. First, he needs facts and the facts are still slow in coming. Why is G.B.C. losing its share of the market? Are the prices of its products too high? Does he need to spruce up their packaging? More advertising, perhaps? Will the company really need to find new user markets? Perhaps the sales department isn't doing its job. And what about the head of M.I.S.?

Decisions require facts and this takes time. By then our original candidates have either found other positions or have written off this company. Anyhow, you can't call them in for an interview three or four months later. That would seem terribly unprofessional! The position therefore goes unfilled.

But let's say that the new CEO does stick his neck out and appoints a new Marketing Manager from among the outstanding applicants. When the appointee gets to hear of the shakeup in G.B.C. (as he or she must), (s)he gets cold feet and withdraws. The other two short-listed candidates also back off. (Superior applicants don't have to rush in and accept. They are probably in good jobs at present and can afford to continue looking.) Again the position remains unfilled.

"We can't advertise again," argues Bill Jones, the Personnel Manager. "It's too embarrassing to receive applications from the same people we've already written 'thank you, but no thank you' letters to. They'll easily recognize the ad. Instead, let's contact an executive recruiter. They have lots of A1 candidates on their books."

And so they do. After another four to eight weeks of interviewing, the position of Marketing Manager is finally offered to candidate X who accepts. Unfortunately, his existing contract requires him to give two-months' notice. More delay. Finally, his starting date draws near. But wait! His present employer makes him an offer he can't refuse: a shrewd counteroffer which he decides to accept. He'll stay with the devil he already knows and he makes this decision at the eleventh hour, leaving G.B.C. high and dry. Again, the position remains unfilled. (There is also the possibility that a new vacancy may be opening to replace the "disloyal" manager who accepted the counteroffer!)

Another version of this scenario is that X does join Gourmet Baloney for 12 to 18 months but can't get on with the new CEO, an accountant who doesn't understand marketing. During this time, he continues to look around. The fact that he has an excellent track record in the industry is well known to other executive search firms. One or two have persisted in trying to lure him away from G.B.C. (That's how many "headhunters" earn their living; some are called "body snatchers.") Finally, X agrees to start interviewing again, accepts an offer and resigns. The position that had been filled at Gourmet is now vacant again! But none of the original applicants knows this.

Back at the ranch, the CEO recalls what the headhunter's fee had been. They had agreed on $35,000. "We're not wasting that kind of commission again," he bawls. "Or on costly ads. What do we have a personnel department for?" That puts pressure on the Personnel Manager to deliver a replacement Marketing Manager quickly and inexpensively.

Other variations are that the company decides on a six-month hiring freeze, or that the National Sales Manager asks to be allowed to continue being Marketing Manager as well or simply doesn't wish to relinquish power. He waits until matters get out of hand before conceding that someone else needs to be appointed. After all, this could so easily be viewed as an admission of failure on his part.

MANUFACTURING YOUR OWN LUCK

Similar scenarios play themselves out daily for many positions and at many levels. Someone is reluctant to reveal that he or she can't cope with the workload and needs to spend company money getting additional help. His or her superiors might think that (s)he is either inefficient or ineffective. (They've already commented on the high rate of turnover in the department.) Unfortunately, D day is about to arrive when an appointment has to be made. This, dear reader, is the day when you have to be the one who happens to be in the right place at the right time. But what can you possibly do to "manufacture" such luck? A little research—it works! (I know this from my own experience.)

Every boss has his or her problems, and you might easily be the answer to those problems. After all, you do know all about increasing a company's market share. (Didn't you already do that in A and B companies?) But any applicant that'll cost Gourmet too much to hire—in advertising, commissions, and costly interviewing time—won't seem too attractive as a candidate. That's where the less expensive out-of-work applicant might have the edge and even seem like a bargain.

To get there, your first step is to research old Sunday newspapers by using the microfiche section of any major public library. Check all previous ads in your field for the past 6 to 36 months. See who was hiring. One in 12 (or better) may still be unfilled, and your resume might just be the answer to some personnel manager's prayer. (As John Lucht says, your *timing* is crucial.) That manager has probably been accused of doing too little, and your warm body is his or her best answer to that charge. You might also be the only candidate and *won't* have a headhunter's price on your head. Best of all, you're available to start on Monday. What does the company have to lose? They can always fire you if you fail to deliver!

(*Note:* Even though many employers might choose to hide behind P.O. or other box numbers, it is possible for you to obtain the name of any corporation that places an anonymous ad. Read the article by Perri Capell in the Bibliography section. [29]. And just as sellers in the real estate business do sometimes accept "no money down" offers from buyers—if they've waited too long and have run out of time—so, too, can any boss run out of time to make an appointment. That's when formal "job requirements" are at their lowest!)

ESSENTIAL VERSUS DESIRABLE REQUIREMENTS

Now that you understand the rough-and-ready nature of the most rigid-looking "job requirements" and that it is often possible to persuade an employer to settle for less, let us look at a few of the really important or "critical requirements" of every job. There are very few of these. But how do you set about finding out what these are in any job you intend to apply for?

In every help-wanted ad you read, there are usually one or two (or three) items deemed essential to good performance. These are the employer's "must have's." (But even here some flexibility is possible. For example, "equivalent" education or other experience might also be acceptable.) Then follows a list of nonessential requirements—skills or knowledge that is merely desirable ("a plus," "will be preferred," and so on).

Your task is to examine that ad carefully and decide which requirements are "musts" and which you need not have or offer. Unfortunately, this is not always clear from the ad itself.

HOW YOU CAN FIND OUT WHAT THE HIRING AUTHORITY REALLY NEEDS

Quite obviously, you'll need to study the target market. What skills are "buyers" looking to hire? Your experience and common sense might give you the best clues! But there are other steps you should take.

- Study help-wanted ads in major Sunday newspapers, *National Business Employment Weekly*, and trade or professional journals. Write down what they usually specify for jobs in your field.
- Check postings for in-house positions (in

hospitals, local and federal government offices, and so on).

- Network: contact people in the industry who should know, or even a personnel department or employment agency.
- Conduct informational interviews with executives. In preparing for such meetings, first visit a public library or trade association and review a few current editions of a trade or professional journal that discuss current issues or problems in your field or area of expertise. You'll find out what might be troubling the employers you'll be seeing. You'll also discover practical solutions that might work for them—as suggested by the experts. (This know-how could also be used as "bait" to get more interviews.) Armed with this knowledge at any meeting with decision makers, you would sound like a very valuable person to have on board. (This is an easy way to become "well informed" in more than one area; it will help you compete in today's job market.)
- Look up the type of work in a trade reference book such as *Career Opportunities in Television, Cable, and Radio* (Maxine K. and Robert M. Reed), the *Redbook of Advertising*, and similar reference works and CD-ROMs in your local library. [38]
- Consult the *Dictionary of Occupational Titles* (1977) for job descriptions and for some of the skills that might be involved.
- In job interviews, turn around the "Tell me about yourself" question and ask what skills and abilities the employer seeks.

The good news is that a little research will help you determine the needs of many employers and jobs because the similarities between employers and jobs are often greater than the differences.

THE NEED TO PRESENT YOURSELF AS A PERFECT "FIT"

Your aim will be to present yourself as a good or perfect "fit." If you have too little of something (such as work experience), using the word *nearly* (as in "Offer nearly ____ years' experience") will often bail you out—unless they're asking for ten years and you offer two.

If you have too much of something (such as work experience), you should either write "more than" (the number of years they require) or even omit a higher degree such as a Ph.D. (But *never* offer ten years' experience when only two years are required. You will be screened out. Writing "more than two years" might give you a fighting chance.) See pages 57, 110, and 208.

In adjusting your credentials to please the perceiver, you will be doing what many Miss America beauty contestants have done in the past. These ladies know exactly when they have either "too little" of (and have to play up) or "too much" of (and have to tone down) some bodily feature. But, instead of writing "nearly" or "more than" in their resumes, these lovely contestants have been known to use Scotch tape!

In short, your resume has to *look* good to give you a chance to meet face-to-face with your future boss. Now let's do an exercise.

JOB REQUIREMENTS

What does an employer need? In other words, what combination of skills, abilities, knowledge, experience, education, and training is "required" of you for any particular position?

By collecting and studying a few help-wanted ads (recent *and* older ones), you'll see what the "buyers" usually ask for. Some items will be essential or "must have's"; others only desirable ("a plus" or "preferred"). Your own knowledge of what the work involves and what is probably important will help you judge a few likely requirements.

Once you know what to offer (in order to be a good "fit"), you'll also know what selling points to include in your Job Objective(s) and Skills Summaries. (See Chapters 4 and 5.) Don't be surprised to find that the formal requirements for two jobs may be more similar than different!

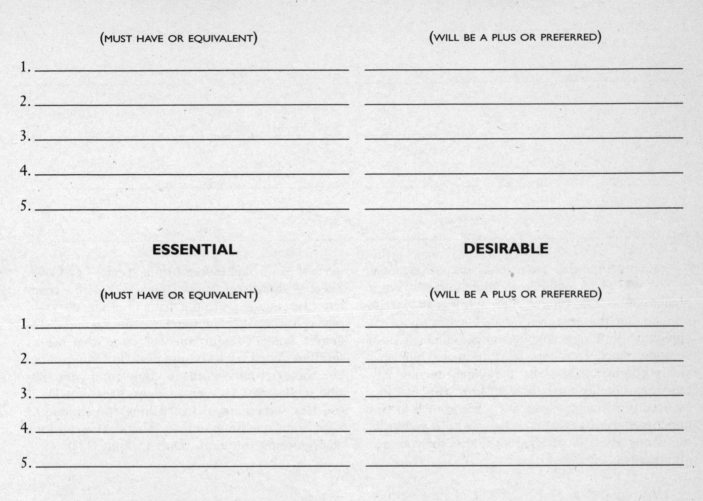

ESSENTIAL

(MUST HAVE OR EQUIVALENT)

1. _____

2. _____

3. _____

4. _____

5. _____

DESIRABLE

(WILL BE A PLUS OR PREFERRED)

_____

_____

_____

_____

_____

ESSENTIAL

(MUST HAVE OR EQUIVALENT)

1. _____

2. _____

3. _____

4. _____

5. _____

DESIRABLE

(WILL BE A PLUS OR PREFERRED)

_____

_____

_____

_____

_____

ANSWERING HELP-WANTED ADS

In their help-wanted ads, employers will be specifying items like:

- Must have a B.S. degree in Chemistry
- Three years' experience as Analytical Chemist in manufacturing
- Knowledge of wet analytical chemistry methods, UV and IR
- Understanding of Quality Control procedures desirable
- Familiarity with Stability Test Procedures a plus

How should you let the recruiter of this pharmaceutical laboratory know that you can offer all or most of these requirements or, at least, acceptable equivalents? that you have more than a B.S. (an M.S.) but without overqualifying yourself? that you have nearly three years' experience (but in a hospital lab) and have only been *exposed* to Stability Test Procedures (i.e., you observed but did not perform them)? Failing to do so clearly and effectively might result in your being zapped by a junior clerk or secretary who usually does the initial screening—before your resume ever gets to an experienced chemist. (How to draft your selling points is discussed in detail on pages 57–62. How to record them in a resume summary is demonstrated in the 38 samples in Chapter 6.) Your exact wording is crucial. Step One is to prepare a comparison table.

YOUR REQUIREMENTS   **I OFFER**

1. _____   _____

2. _____   _____

3. _____   _____

4. _____   _____

5. _____   _____

Completing this table looks deceptively easy, doesn't it? Their requirement(s) followed by your qualification(s)? Be careful. Although it is an exercise in targeting the employer's stated needs, most job applicants do it very sloppily and get eliminated—in seconds. Since recruiters need to match up what you're offering against what they might require, it is *your* responsibility to show them how you "fit," line by line. If in doubt, please ask a friend to help you understand exactly what is being sought. If you make the wrong guess or guesses, it's File C for your application: the circular file.

How to do this exercise on a special Fax Cover Sheet is shown on pages 109–110. But if a cover letter is requested, use the YOUR REQUIREMENTS—I OFFER format in your letter (in the second paragraph). Under "Requirements," copy what the ad specifies. Then try to be the best "fit" you can be. Use the exact *same* words in completing your specific replies next to each of those lines. Finally, if you lack something, write "willing to continue to learn" or something similar. That's more positive than ignoring the item. (Don Erikson [13])

Part Two

MARKETING YOUR VALUE

4

THE FOUNDATION OF YOUR RESUME: THE JOB OBJECTIVE

Job seekers who write "A" resumes know that a well-stated job goal or objective is the foundation upon which the rest of the resume is built ... their goals are specific enough to hook into employer needs ... [and] tell the employer exactly what the job seeker wants to do for the company.
—LINDA J. SEGALL, Employee Relations Manager of a Fortune 500 company [21]

BAITING THE HOOK

In Chapter 2, you identified many of your job-related skills and abilities. Now you are ready to start marketing the best ones—your strengths. The best place to start offering those CAN DO'S to employers is in the Job Objective or Job Goal section of your resume.

Why? To be effective, a sales or marketing device needs to have "hooks"—items that will immediately appeal to the reader's self-interest or needs. These *must* appear in the first line or two of your job resume—in a Job Objective. This is where selling yourself really starts, not in a separate cover letter that might or might not be read or faxed.

A well-written job objective is of *crucial* importance in the '90s. With so many resumes (and letters) to process, employers need to know immediately (a) what you want and (b) what you can do to help them.

Your resume is a "paper with a purpose." That purpose (or goal) must be clear to the reader. Employers shouldn't have to guess what you might want or qualify for. It's *your* responsibility to tell the reader. But more than that, you have to offer them your value—the benefits of hiring you.

As in fishing, your Objective acts as a lure to attract the attention of the reader. Therefore, your choice of which skills or achievements to offer as bait is important. If they are what the buyer wants, you'll get a nibble (of interest) or more—a job interview.

Just as every July 4th Grucci rocket must have a "head," a job resume needs an objective. If yours is "headless," busy readers will probably ignore it. Never omit an objective in order to keep your resume "flexible" in regard to your own options. In the '90s, any resume that tries to be all things to all readers won't work. It will only annoy! (Rather, learn to e-x-p-a-n-d your objectives and widen your options. More on this later.)

WHAT EMPLOYERS EXPECT TO SEE IN YOUR JOB OBJECTIVE

- At what *level* of work are you able to perform? Is it entry level, supervisory, or managerial—or somewhere in between?

- What *type* of position are you seeking? In which field, area, or department?

- What *qualifies* you for such a position? What knowledge, skills, abilities, experience, or achievements do you offer that could be of interest and value to them? Do you have any expertise to contribute? A successful track record?

A good Job Objective says to a busy reader: "Grab me and read me." That helps to get your resume into his or her "A" pile.

THE LEVEL OF THE POSITION(S) YOU SEEK

Employers need to know immediately what level of position you are interested in. Why? The answer is payroll—a critical factor in the new job market when most hiring authorities are engaged in cost reduction programs.

Ideally, you should be aiming for a position slightly above the highest level of work you have managed to perform so far—unless you haven't worked at that level for a long time or are changing careers.

However, before writing down the level of work you are seeking, ask yourself a few pertinent questions. Will the rest of your resume back you up? Do your previous job titles indicate that you would be ready or qualified to handle such responsibility? Are you at least 50 percent qualified for the position you seek? Should you aim at a lower starting level? There are three important things to remember when deciding on what level of position you should seek.

1. You could be screened out if you aim either too high or too low. Some job hunters might have to rachet down their expectations. (Returning-to-work homemakers are an exception. They should generally try to aim higher.)
2. If you have not worked at the desired level for some time (a few years), aim to return to the same type of work but at a slightly lower level. You will be offering superior value, and it will give you a chance to catch up on your skills and earn a promotion to your previous level.
3. Career changers will always have less-than-perfect credentials and should generally ask for (and expect to get) less initially.

MAIN OPTIONS IN STATING THE LEVEL OF POSITION YOU SEEK

Here is a guide to some of your main options in specifying the level of the position you're seeking:

- A position as intern (or management trainee) in . . .
- An entry-level position in . . . where my . . . , . . . and . . .
- A junior-level position in . . . where my . . . , . . . and . . .
- A position in . . . where my supervisory skills and . . .
- A supervisory-level position in . . .
- A position as Assistant Supervisor in . . .
- A supervisory position in . . . that includes management-level responsibilities.
- A management-level position in . . .
- A management position in . . .
- A senior executive position in . . .
- A top executive position in . . .

Note: These statements are phrased very carefully. For example, look at the four that refer to duties or positions that are "supervisory" in nature. The first of these seeks an opportunity to use some of the job seeker's supervisory skills. (S(he) obviously needs more experience.) The next one is stronger. It seeks a "supervisory-level" position (i.e., one with definite supervisory responsibilities). "Assistant Supervisor" is even more specific—it is the title of the person next in line to the supervisor. And "supervisory" position with "management-level responsibilities" speaks for itself. It is clearly a senior position.

As a general rule, it is always safer to request a "_____-level" position rather than shoot for a higher job title by name. All who seek advancement should note this.

THE TYPE OF POSITION(S) YOU SEEK

Next, you will need to state the type of work you are seeking. What is it that you want to do for the employer? Starting with the *level* (or job titles) you have selected, add to it the area and/or field and/or industry you wish to work in.

Entry-level FINANCE position within the International Department of a multinational corporation (or bank) where my ...

Junior position within an ACCOUNTING DEPARTMENT in the banking/brokerage industry where my ...

Management-level position in a HOTEL/ RESTAURANT where my ...

MAIN TYPES/AREAS/FIELDS OF WORK

The following will help you in recording the *type* of work you seek:

Field: Marketing • Accounting • Public Relations • Graphics/Illustration • A&R Administration
Industry: Hospitality • Electronics • Health Care • Banking • Brokerage • Beauty • Radio/TV
Department (Area): Data Processing • Customer Relations • Laboratory • Institutional Sales • Credit & Collections • A/P • A/R
Company: Major • Large • Medium-Sized • Small • International • Multinational • Network

In most cases, you'll need to state only the field or department or area in which you wish to work.

WHAT QUALIFIES YOU? WHAT ARE YOU ABLE TO OFFER?

Now comes the most important part of your Objective—your sales "hooks." You have to tell the reader why you would be valuable in the position you are seeking and/or what you can do for his/her company.

You do this by stating your three strongest skills (or abilities or any achievement) that could be of *value* in the position. For example, your aptitude for figures, strong research skills, problem-solving skills, reconciliation skills, strong negotiating or closing skills, and so on.

Or by stating any special knowledge or expertise you offer (such as niche-marketing expertise) or knowledge of state-of-the-art equipment. Or by mentioning your outstanding track record in a similar position. For example, in streamlining operations, increasing sales in a "soft" market, raising staff productivity, lowering food and beverage costs, lowering absenteeism rates, reducing labor turnover, or whatever. In short, anything that would be music to an employer's ears.

These will be the come-ons that say to the employer, "Please read further and decide to meet with me; I can be a valuable employee to have on board." This is how you make a winning first impression in the '90s.

EXAMPLES OF JOB OBJECTIVES THAT SELL YOUR VALUE

Now let's analyze two sample objectives and see how they were composed to offer employers the value they are looking for. This will be followed by two examples of bad objectives that thousands of job seekers are still writing and that will turn off most employers in seconds. First, two good objectives.

Entry-Level Job Objective:

An entry-level position within the <u>International Department</u> of a bank or multinational corporation where a Finance degree, research skills, analytical ability, and foreign language skills would be assets.

Supervisory-Level Job Objective:

Supervisory-level position in the <u>Operations</u> area of a bank, brokerage house, or insurance company where my proven ability to increase staff productivity, cut response turnaround times, and reduce overtime would be of value. Able to train/cross-train staff.

Notice how these objectives indicate the level and type of position being sought. More importantly, they offer valuable skills and/or achievements that "would be of value" or "would be assets."

This is the language you should use in addressing those reluctant-to-hire employers in the '90s. Focus on *their* self-interest or needs. *Never* ask (or expect) them to "utilize" all of your . . . (even if acquiring your sheepskin did set you back $30,000!).

To summarize:

DON'T WRITE: "A _____ position that will *utilize* all my . . ."

WRITE: "A _____ position where my _____ and _____ would be **of value** [or **assets**]."

Finally, what about the fact that you are ambitious, seeking growth, and looking for future advancement? In such cases, you might add the following phrase:

"A _____ position in a _____ where my _____ would be of value and where my continued professional growth would be encouraged."

(See page 74.)

BAD JOB OBJECTIVES THAT TURN OFF EMPLOYERS

Permit me to digress for a moment. In every batch of 100 or so laser-printed resumes I look at, I still come across about 85 or more with "me-centered" objectives—those that would turn off any prospective employer today. Here are two examples of bad objectives.

"A challenging _____ position within a progressive company or firm where <u>my</u> education, experience, and skills will be utilized to the fullest extent (to enable <u>me</u> to realize <u>my</u> full potential) and where <u>I</u> could contribute to corporate goals and objectives."

"To secure a position that will utilize <u>my</u> business/economics skills while providing <u>me</u> with challenging work and opportunities for <u>my</u> advancement to managerial positions."

Never, never write such job objectives. They are all I-want-I-want—what *you* expect, not what you are able to offer or do *for* the employer. (Unfortunately, some resume-writing services—the paper mills—continue to churn out such verbiage. Today's employers would scoff at them. And enough about wanting to realize your "full potential." Only God knows what that might really be!

JOB OBJECTIVES FOR SEEKING ADVANCEMENT

If you are a secretary seeking advancement to Administrative Assistant but have had very little experience of such work, write:

A position as **Secretary/Administrative Assistant** which will <u>include</u> administrative duties and/or opportunities to be involved in special projects. Offer my strong _____, _____, and _____ skills.

If you are seeking your first management-level position but have never had supervisory responsibilities, phrase your Objective as follows:

A responsible position in [**Industry/ Department-Area**] that will <u>include</u> responsibilities of a supervisory nature. Offer my strong _____, _____, and _____ skills.

By *not* stating your higher-level Objective (a management-level position) and using the word "include," you won't need to have suitable work experience in either management or supervision to support it.

THE FOUNDATION OF YOUR ENTIRE RESUME

Not only is a well-written job objective crucial to luring prospective employers into reading further, it also helps you to select and organize your data for the body of your resume. In fact, stating a clear objective will make it easier for you to decide

- What to include
- What to emphasize
- What to downplay
- What to omit

Each time you start to write a resume, you need to make all four of these decisions. (This will help you to *focus* it. Thus, what to leave out might be just as important as what to include.) If you don't, your marketing tool might end up looking like a strange mix of fruits and vegetables!

For example, any items (be they skills, experience, or education) that don't support or back up your objective should be downplayed or even omitted. If not, they will only cloud or confuse the "theme" of your resume—what you're trying to sell. It is essential that you do this because many employers complain that most resumes are unfocused and carelessly organized. [24]

HOW TO E-X-P-A-N-D YOUR JOB OPTIONS: SOLUTIONS TO A MAJOR DILEMMA

Let's face it, whereas most employers do expect to read a focused job objective, you, the job seeker, have a fear of being screened out. Happily, this dilemma can easily be resolved. Write your objective in a way that will actually e-x-p-a-n-d your options! Here are *three* practical solutions.

1. Print two or three nearly identical resumes, each with a *different* job objective.

For example, in one version of your resume write:

"An entry-level **Auditing** position within a public accounting firm."

In another version write:

"An entry-level position as **Internal Auditor** within a bank or similar financial institution where my ____ would be of value."

"An entry-level R & D position as **Chemist/ Chemical Engineer**
a. in a pharmaceutical laboratory,
b. in the area of industrial polymers,
c. in environmental science and control."

With each objective, highlight your most qualifying course work.

2. Expand your options in the *same* resume by using a slash(/).

Entry-level computer programmers should either write **Computer Programming/Operations** or prepare separate versions for Programming and Computer Operations (a good way of breaking into programming). Similarly, an objective that reads "Position as **Bookkeeper/Assistant Bookkeeper** in a company or firm" will cover you for a position as Bookkeeper in a small firm and for a position in the Accounting department of a large company (as Assistant Bookkeeper/Accounting Clerk).

Note: The two to three job titles must be related.

3. Suggest suitable positions or areas.

"Position as ADMINISTRATOR/COORDI-NATOR/ORGANIZER where my experience in corporate public relations and development offices would be of value.

Able to contribute in the areas of **Public Relations . Publicity . Promotions . Special Events . Fund-raisers."**

"Position in the SECURITY/INSURANCE or related industries where my strong administrative and investigative skills would be of value—either in house or in the field.

Suitable positions: **Insurance Investigations .. Corporate Security .. Security Investigations .. Field Claims Adjustment"**

"A supervisory-level ADMINISTRATIVE position where my administrative, coordinating, and research experience within the Social/Human Services field would be of value.

The ideal position would be as **Project Administrator/Supervisor/Coordinator/ Researcher."**

Note: If you are seeking vastly different positions, you need to prepare entirely different resumes, each with its own objective. (See Chapter 12, "Targeting Jobs with Different Resumes").

Such e-x-p-a-n-d-e-d objectives can be written for nearly every level and type of position, and offer a practical solution to one of your biggest dilemmas as a job seeker—the fear of instant elimination. And relax! Hundreds of employers and personnel agencies have been accepting such double- and triple-barreled objectives for years—because it makes it much easier to see where your CAN DO's could best be plugged in.

OBJECTIVES TO E-X-P-A-N-D YOUR OPTIONS

Here are more examples to show you how and when two related job options can be specified in the same objective. The emphasis is on the word *related*. (Grapes and raisins are "related"; so are

peaches and nectarines. But apples and bananas are very different fruits.) The same idea applies to job titles. Only related positions may be requested in the same job objective. The following example shows you what to do:

• **A professional *** CLOWN/MIME ARTISTE *** with very fine credits offers to increase your sales by attracting and motivating shoppers outside your department store.**

In the foregoing example, this well-known lady clown seeks either of two *related* positions because clowns are also trained in the art of mime. In return, she offers employers value—her ability to get the attention of shoppers and cajole them into entering the store. She doesn't ask them to "utilize" all of her . . . whatever! Instead, she addresses their needs.

All of the objectives that follow have appeared in winning resumes:

• An entry-level **Clerical/Accounting** position where aptitude for figures, attention to detail, and follow-up skills would be of value. Willing to work overtime.
• An entry-level **Clerical/Customer Service** position in which my clerical, communications, problem-solving, and customer service skills would be assets. Am very hardworking.
• A responsible **Secretarial/Word Processing** position where my familiarity with litigation documents, rapid dictation–transcription skills, and the ability to handle a heavy workload would be of value. Willing to work **night** shift.
• A position as **Bookkeeper/Office Manager** in a small firm where my proven ability to reduce expenses and hire, train and supervise low-cost (but reliable) staff would be of value.
• A position as ADMINISTRATOR/COORDINATOR in: the **Arts . Public Relations . Music . Entertainment.** Offer strong research skills and ability to manage special projects.
• An **Administrative/Accounting** position

where my diversified Private/Public sector experience and strong internal auditing skills would be of value. Able to tighten controls and reduce operational costs. Will relocate.

- A senior ADMINISTRATIVE/FINAN-CIAL position where my track record of achieving cost reductions, strong negotiating skills, and ability to increase the productivity of staff would be valued. Willing to travel and/or relocate.

- Senior-level position as **Buyer/Purchasing Agent.** Offer my successful experience in Contract Buying. Able to reduce the number of vendors and obtain volume discounts through greater purchasing "clout"; can also achieve cost-savings by substituting generics.

- A position as **Engineer/Technician** (Voice/ Data/Network communications) where my knowledge of state-of-the-art AT&T equipment and local access networks would be valued.

- A position as **Engineer/Electronics Technician** where my experience in maintenance and repair of high-powered, invisible Laser Cutting, and Barco C.A.D. systems would be of value. Able to train technicians in four languages.

- Position as **Graphic Designer/Mechanical Artist/Technical Illustrator.** Portfolios available upon request.

- Senior-level position in **Production/ Industrial Engineering** where my track record of increasing efficiency and productivity in manufacturing environments would be of value.
Proven ability to improve quality, reduce waste and decrease downtime through O & M/Time & Motion studies, and by reorganizing production and/or assembly-line technology.

- A position in **Merchandising/Product Development** within a Retail, Mail Order, or Manufacturing organization where my proven track record in Buying/Merchandising for major stores would be of value. Willing to travel or relocate.

- A management-level position in the **Hotel/ Travel/Leisure** industry or in Institutional Feeding (Executive Dining Rooms . Hospitals . Universities) . Offer my proven ability in positions requiring strong operations and "people" skills.

- Position as **Project Manager/Coordinator** in the Social/Human Services. Success in designing, modifying and implementing cost-effective and comprehensive programs. Track record of meeting stated goals.

- SALES/MARKETING position in **Corporate Fundraising .. Conference Planning .. Convention Sales.** Offer my valuable contacts in major corporations.

Additional samples of expanded job objectives can be found in 38 Skills Summaries (see Chapter 6) and in sample resumes throughout this book. Refer to the Resume Finder on pages 116–18.

HOW BEING "FLEXIBLE" IN THE '90s DIFFERS FROM THE '70s AND '80s

In the preceding pages you saw why writing a good Job Objective is of major importance in today's competitive job market. In order to be successful in your job search, your resume has to be focused, so as to target an employer's specific needs as closely as possible. You do this by writing an objective that addresses those needs and then adding a selection of supporting skills and experience to back it up—to "argue" your case. (You'll learn how to do this in the next chapter.) [11, 19]

Nowadays, stating a good objective is a way to *avoid* being screened out! It means learning to vary your objectives and your resumes nearly as often as you apply for jobs. To do this well, you need to use a very flexible type of resume format, the combination resume. (At this stage, I ask you please not to worry about the precise "how to" that might be involved. You'll see how easy it is to do it on a PC or memory typewriter in Chapter 12, "Targeting Jobs with Different Resumes.")

To be "flexible" in today's job market means to discover more of your skills and to be able to vary your objectives (and resumes) to make them fit more than one type of position; it doesn't mean to "stay loose" or be vague. It will require a little practice, but is *not* as difficult as it sounds.

This job search strategy is very different from what you might have been taught in school. You see, the old idea was to try to remain "flexible" by *not* writing any Job Objective in your resume. The only place you were supposed to do this was in a separate cover letter. Thus, your resume stayed the same, whatever position you applied for. (It was a basic, all-purpose or generic resume.) This meant writing a cover letter to target each employer's specific needs. (That outdated strategy was developed by those with lingering memories of the Great Depression. They argued that stating what you wanted ahead of time could result in a lost job opportunity.) But today's job market and employers are very different. They are efficiency-, productivity-, and profit-oriented as never before, and they want to see, ahead of time, what *value* you are offering. More value for their money is what today's employers are after, and they want to know how you can help them do that even better. They expect to read this in the Job Objective in your resume. Not surprisingly, they've largely stopped reading cover letters (which can be very time-consuming), and fax is being used as the first screening device. In fact, getting to see an employer today is becoming more and more difficult.

To summarize, the old way of doing things that you might find in many traditional resume books simply won't cut it today. And because this book stresses the writing of a Job Objective when many others (and some teachers) either don't or limit the objective to saying something about wanting to "utilize your education and experience," let us address a few questions that are raised about the entire subject of job objectives *before* you go job hunting in this tough job market.

QUESTIONS AND ANSWERS

Q. Should I state my Job Objective or Goal in my resume?

A. Yes. Your job resume is a marketing tool to sell your skills and experience to employers. It is like any piece of direct mail which needs an opening statement to pique the reader's inter-est, to make him or her want to read further and find out what you have to offer. A well-written Job Objective can achieve this for you. This is where you start to sell yourself and your CAN DO'S in the '90s because the deck is heavily stacked in the employer's favor. It is a buyer's market.

Q. Do most employers expect to see an objective in my resume?

A. Yes. Today's employers need to know immediately what you want and what you can do for them and their companies. With hundreds of resumes to scan and very little enthusiasm or patience for the task, or time to do it in, they search for your objective or goal. Those applicants who state it will definitely be preferred.

Q. But won't stating an objective limit my job options?

A. That cautious approach belongs to the '70s and '80s. But don't worry, stating an objective does not mean that you'll have to foreclose on your options. Simply write two or three near-identical versions of your resume, each with a *different* objective. Or you can easily e-x-p-a-n-d your objective to widen your options (as shown on pages 47 to 49). If you omit a Job Objective in a highly competitive job market, impatient employers might exercise their own option: not to read further.

Q. But I've been told that my resume should be "flexible"?

A. Not in today's job market. Without a Job Objective, you may come across as someone who does not know what (s)he wants. That would be an immediate turnoff. (And never fax a "headless" resume.) Even worse is that a generic or "headless" resume also tends to be vague, unfocused, and disorganized.

Q. Will I lose job opportunitites if I state a specific objective?

A. Today the opposite is true. A 180-degree change has occurred in views on the subject of how wide or narrow an objective should be. Nowadays, you should write objective statements that closely match the specific needs of each employer you send your resume to.

In fact, you should try to use the employer's own language (as stated in the help-wanted ad).

Q. What about writing my objective only in a cover letter?

A. These days this is too risky. Although busy departmental heads may still read a few truly outstanding cover letters, even they would prefer to see what they need to know in a single document—your job resume. (And don't forget that separate letters do get detached or even lost in the shuffle. Nowadays, the average pile on a recruiter's desk is from eight to twelve inches high!)

Q. Can't I simply update my present resume in the usual manner?

A. No. You need to do much more than this today. The old idea of simply adding your most recent work experience and dropping off the oldest will hardly be enough. Today, updating your resume means focusing or refocusing it to target a specific employer's needs. Writing targeted resumes with specific objectives is the rule in the new job market.

5

THE "HEART" OF YOUR COMBINATION RESUME: THE SKILLS SUMMARY

A qualifications statement ... is a summary of your strengths and experience as well as an opportunity to sell yourself in a way that cannot be done in other sections of a resume.

It is designed to sell your most marketable abilities and experience.

If well-written, [this summary] can greatly strengthen your perceived worth.

—Tom Washington, President, Career Management Resources [23]

CREATING YOUR SALES PITCH

Since the late '80s, many employers have been complaining that ninety-five percent of all job resumes fail to sell them on the candidate. From this it is obvious that most job applicants still don't know how to market themselves on paper (or else do it badly). Sadly, even the most qualified candidates often fail to do themselves justice because they "undersell" themselves. (Catherine Meehan) This chapter will therefore show you how to develop and add the missing "sell" to your resume.

It is important to realize that a resume *without* that "sell" is not only weak but negative! Why? Because picky and impatient employers will assume that you have nothing valuable to offer. With a resume that creates such a negative perception of you, you would be trying to compete in the job market with a serious handicap. (Robert Half)

So what can you do to position yourself in the eyes of the resume reader as someone who stands out from the pack? In Chapter 4 you learned that selling yourself starts in the first two to four lines of your resume—in a Job Objective. Now you'll see how to add more sell—by writing a Summary of Skills and Experience. More than a sketchy profile or synopsis, a Skills Summary is a dynamic *mini sales presentation*—five to ten bulleted selling points, each designed to back up or support your Objective.

In my view, based on years of resume-writing experience, this Skills Summary is probably the most important section in your entire resume. Its unique function is to demonstrate or "prove" why you are qualified for the position(s) you are seeking. This is crucial in today's job market because a well-written Summary now has to take over the role that a formal cover letter played in the '70s and '80s. In many respects, it is in lieu of that out-dated letter. (This is why you had to learn to trans-fer the selling message of the cover letter to your resume. See page 7.)

Each of your five to ten bullets will be a care-fully worded statement that targets the employer's needs. A series of them will therefore enhance your worth in the eyes of the reader and make you seem like a good "buy." This is so because the total ef-fect of those selling points will be to increase your perceived value and make you stand out from the pack. Isn't that what good self-marketing is really all about?

Thus, in a marketing sense, the Skills Summary is the heart of your resume presentation. If well written, it will have impact. It will not only state your case, but give you a competitive edge.

In a Skills Summary you have a rare opportunity to sell yourself in a way that *cannot* be done in other sections of your resume. And for the purpose of finding and developing your selling points, you can delve into *any* aspect of your past life/school/ work history to find skills or items of work experi-ence, education, or training that might qualify. (Here we freely make use of the best feature of the functional resume to identify and present your strengths—but as *selling points* rather than vague functions you might claim to be able to per-form.)

Such a summary won't be redundant or repeti-tious. You won't be repeating anything you say in your cover note, and in a qualifications statement it is permissible to paraphrase an outstanding achievement—even to repeat it. (Tom Washington) Best of all, you'll find it easier composing a few bulleted statements than having to write a blinding

cover letter. What is more, this summary might be the only portion of your resume that will actually be read by recruiters before the flimsy fax paper begins to curl up in their hands.

Even if you have the most basic or ordinary qualifications, a well-written Skills Summary will help you beat the odds. This is so because the ad-dition of a marketing "top" to Education and Ex-perience will usually convert any basic resume into a self-marketing device that helps get you hired. It is something that all career changers should note. In short, a well-written Job Objective *and* a sup-porting Skills Summary are of crucial importance in making your first impression in today's job mar-ket. Let's take a look at two sample summaries that illustrate the way you need to market yourself in order to impress tough and picky employers.

TWO SAMPLE SUMMARIES: ENTRY LEVEL AND MANAGEMENT

The two summaries on the next page were origi-nally written in the form of cover letters to accom-pany two basic resumes—one for an entry-level position and the other for management. That is what most job applicants did in the '80s.

Those letters commenced with the phrase "I am seeking a(n) . . ." (job objective), and each item in each summary was the subject of a separate sen-tence: "I graduated with . . . ," "I offer . . . ," "I have . . . ," and so on. Each selling point has now been transferred to a Summary section in the re-sume and is highlighted with a black bullet. The formal cover letter now becomes a simple cover note (see page 103) to route the resume.

SAMPLE SUMMARIES (<u>ENTRY LEVEL AND MANAGEMENT</u>)

OBJECTIVE: Entry-level **Accounting/Auditing** position in a Tax or Legal department. Offer experience in Taxation.

SUMMARY:
- B.B.A. degree in Accounting .. Dean's List.
- Candidate for C.P.A. examination in November 1993.
- Internship in a C.P.A. firm; emphasis on Taxation.
- Able to interact effectively with clients and colleagues.
- Mathematical aptitude; analytical skills; detail-oriented.
- Computer skills: PCs . Lotus 1–2–3 . dBase III . Metaphor.
- Able to work well under time and accuracy pressures.
- Leadership positions on campus; president of an association.
- Hardworking .. conscientious .. strong organizational skills.

OBJECTIVE

Senior-level position as **Program Manager/Coordinator** in the Social/Human Services field where my track record of meeting program goals would be an asset. Willing to relocate.

SUMMARY OF QUALIFICATIONS

- M.S.W. degree
- More than 15 years' administrative experience, including present position as Program Director of [deleted] House.
- Experience encompasses a variety of patient populations:
  —Mentally Retarded (adults and children)
  —Physically Disabled (blind and deaf adults)
  —Disadvantaged Inner City Youth
- Rehabilitation experience includes the following programs:
  —Employment and Housing
  —Psycho-Social Rehabilitation
  —Social/Recreational
- Success in obtaining McKinley grant monies through the U.S. Department of Housing and Urban Development.
- Participation in joint projects with other agencies.
- Strong leadership and teamwork skills.

YOUR BEST OPPORTUNITY TO PRESENT YOUR BEST SELF

In a Skills Summary you have an opportunity to record many valuable CAN DO's—items that won't fit into any other section of your resume. (These would ordinarily require a separate cover letter.) In drafting your summary, *you* are in the driver's seat. Throughout this exercise, you will be acting like a professional salesperson preparing a sales presentation or pitch. You are free to decide what to present to the reader and how to word it. (You can even copy or adapt entire sentences from *Winning Resumes*.) Your sole aim is to impress. What you select to emphasize (or omit) is entirely up to you. In doing this, you will *not* exaggerate your CAN DO's, nor will you be attempting to mislead the reader. But you will make every effort to present your facts in a way that is to your own advantage. Begin by summarizing the key or related aspects of your past history—to show the employer that you do have some direct or indirect *experience* or equivalent training, such as volunteer or laboratory experience, or exposure to it.

It is in your summary that you emphasize your successful *track record* (including solving problems in areas that will interest the reader). And that is where you present dollar figures, numbers, or percentages that will impress. Why expect (or rely on) busy readers to search for these at the foot of page 1 or on page 2 of your resume? Or find where your typist may have buried them in the body copy? This is also where you draw attention to your steady *promotions* to positions of increasing responsibility, and your chance to mention that you have previously had supervisory responsibilities (but without mentioning "in Siberia").

As regards the *skills and abilities* you can offer—your best CAN DO's—this should be easy. You already have hundreds to choose from in the checklists on pages 24 to 26, in the forty or so sample summaries on pages 59 to 78, and in every resume in this book. A Skills Summary is also an opportunity to highlight any *awards* or similar items that might impress the reader (such as a mention in a *Who's Who*), but only if these are recent and relate to his or her present needs.

Finally, a summary is your best opportunity to *interpret* or otherwise clarify a zig-zag type of career history (or bowl-of-fruit type of background) in a way that presents you in a favorable light. This is your best chance to state what *transferable skills* you are able to offer from your "varied" life/work experience. It might be of crucial importance if you are moving from one field or career to another.

VALUABLE USES OF A SKILLS SUMMARY

- If you are changing careers, you need to use a summary to identify and present your transferable skills. (Most employers are *not* qualified to do this for you.)
- Since new combinations of skills and experience are being sought by employers (nowadays, many job titles don't mean what they used to), a summary section is the best place to offer them new "mixes" that will match their present needs.
- By offering a selection of CAN DO's in more than one summary, you can prepare more than one resume to target more buyers and explore more job options.
- Writing a good Skills Summary is the best way to prepare yourself for job interviews because it is an exercise in selecting, interpreting, and presenting your facts in a way that will impress.

It is in round 1—the screening stage in which all resumes are merely scanned—that busy employers will greatly appreciate your summary. Why? Because it makes it unnecessary for them to read your entire resume from A to Z in order to find out what they need to know: what you have done to date, what you have learned, what you have achieved, and what your strengths are. All this can be presented in five to ten easy-to-read bullets.

They will certainly notice the effort you make to organize your presentation, interpret the checkered facts of your background, and make it easier for them to evaluate you as a candidate. Thus, in just ten to twenty seconds, many will be impressed with you as someone who is focused, intelligent and does his or her homework. They'll feel you are worth meeting in person. Now let's piece together the "heart" of your winning resume.

VARIOUS NAMES FOR A SKILLS SUMMARY

You have a number of options in deciding what to call your summary:

- SUMMARY (usually for entry- and junior-level positions)
- STRENGTHS (usually for entry- and junior-level positions)
- QUALIFIED BY (for those with qualifying work experience)
- QUALIFICATIONS (for those with solid work experience)
- SUMMARY OF SKILLS AND EXPERIENCE (if the emphasis is on skills)
- SUMMARY OF QUALIFICATIONS (for managers and senior executives)
- SUMMARY STATEMENT (for senior-level applicants)
- QUALIFICATIONS STATEMENT (for senior-level candidates)

These are rough guidelines, *not* inflexible rules. To help you decide what to use, scan the Skills Summaries (pages 59 to 78) to get an idea of what has already worked for someone with a background similar to yours. As a rule of thumb, the first four headings (which are shorter) tend to work well in one-page resumes; the longer headings will also require two to three lines of additional spacing and should only be used in two-page resumes.

Next, what do employers look for in such a summary? Employers want to see your value—what you're offering to do for them. So let's learn to draft five to ten of your CAN DO's—your selling points. They will present your value in the most positive terms. Each will support your Job Objective. (It's largely a matter of selecting only those items that "fit" and coordinating them to create the right effect.)

To help you, the sample summaries on pages 59 to 78 will give you an idea of what yours should look like. Also refer to the Resume Finder (pages 116 to 118).

MAIN POINTS IN A SUMMARY

It should be obvious that if you try to answer most of the employer's questions in advance, you will have helped him or her hire you. That is why a few bullets in your summary should indicate

- Whether your education seems adequate (or equivalent to what they require)
- Whether you have worked at (or near) the right level
- Whether you have special knowledge or expertise
- What your strengths and job-related skills are
- Whether you have had supervisory responsibilities including hiring/terminating staff
- Whether you have been steadily promoted
- Whether you have a track record of success
- Whether you have any noteworthy accomplishments or achievements
- Whether you have been in charge of a large budget or have had P&L responsibility

Note: If you toot your own horn too loudly or excessively, no one will believe you. So don't overdo it. Never use the words *outstanding, exceptional,* or *excellent* more than once. And words such as *strong* and *expertise* should not be used more than once or twice. To exaggerate could be just as disastrous as to undersell or not to sell at all.

Now let's draft your selling points.

DRAFTING YOUR SELLING POINTS

**EDUCATION/
TRAINING:** If you did *not* complete your degree studies, write:
- "Liberal Arts studies; Courses/Workshop/Seminar in ____ ." (Or "B.A. studies; Coursework in ____ and ____ ."—all related to Objective)

EXPERIENCE: Summarize your work experience by adding up the number of years worked (up to 15 years) and listing the main job titles from most important to least important. If your most recent position is the least impressive, state it *last* not first, or even omit it. The exact dates will be given in your Employment History further down.

Examples:
- **"Seven years' experience as Head Cook/Line Cook/Dishwasher."**
"Seven years" gives the impression of solid experience. In fact, you may have worked only three years as Line Cook, two years as Head Cook, and another two as Dishwasher. You are *not* trying to deceive the reader; (s)he is free to check the actual time periods further down the page in the Employment section. You are merely presenting your best self.

- ____ years' broad-based experience in [industry/area] as [job title/job title/job title].

If this is *more* than fifteen years, write:
- More than 15 years' broad-based . . .
Never, never write a figure larger than 15—especially if your age might be a problem. To write "22 years" or "31 years" will invite elimination.

RESPONSIBILITY: If you wish to let the reader know that you have already had supervisory or management-level responsibilities (at *any* time previously) you have various options, as follows:

- **"Seven years' experience as Head Cook/Line Cook/Dishwasher, including supervisory responsibilities."**

- _____ years' broad-based experience in [industry/area] as [job title/job title/job title] including supervisory responsibilities.

- Promotions to positions involving supervisory [or management-level] responsibilities.

**TRACK
RECORD:**
- Track record of success in ____ .
- Proven track record in ____ .
- Verifiable track record ____ .

PROMOTIONS: If you wish to draw attention to your growth and advancement in previous positions, write as follows:
- History of steady promotions to positions of increasing responsibility (including present position as [job title]).
Whenever you seek a vertical move, you need such a supporting statement to inspire confidence in you.

EXPERTISE:

- Expertise in ____ and ____ [areas of specialization].
  A statement like this tells the reader where your strengths lie.

- Areas of experience [or responsibility] include: First Class Hotel, Corporate Dining Room, and Fast-Food Restaurant.
  This describes the *breadth* of your experience. Notice how the order is from most impressive to least.

  Bookkeepers could write:
- Experience includes: Accounts Receivable .. Accounts Payable .. Bank Reconciliations .. General Ledger [etc.]

  Managers could write:
- Experience includes: Sales . Accounting . Payroll . Financial Analysis . Purchasing . Inventory . Marketing . Merchandising . Hiring/Training/Supervising/Terminating staff.

KNOWLEDGE:

- Thorough knowledge of ____.
- Knowledge of ____.
- Knowledge and experience includes ____, ____, and ____.

EXPOSURE:

- Extensive exposure to ____ [if you lack actual experience].
- Exposure to ____ [adds a little to actual experience].
- Participation in ____ [if your own part was small].
- Involvement in ____.

RECOGNITION:

- Outstanding performance appraisals for [year] and [year].
- Recipient of ____ award for ____.
- Letters of commendation from ____.
  There are numerous types of awards you might have received. Mention only one or two that are job-related and will impress employers. But it/they must be recent—in the last few years.

SKILLS AND ABILITIES:

- "Able to handle a heavy workload and meet deadlines."

- "Strong organizational, coordinating, and follow-up skills."

- "Able to develop nonstandard solutions to resolve old problems."

- "Excellent interpersonal and teamwork skills." [Always state that you get on well with others and are a team person.]

- Proven ability to ____.

- Demonstrated ability to ____.

- Able to ____.

- Ability to ____.

- Skill in ____.

- Excellent ____ and ____ skills (and experience).

- Strong ____, ____, and ____ skills. [Refer to Skills Statements, Chapter 2, and elsewhere.]

COMPUTER
SKILLS:
- IBM PC . Lotus 1–2–3 . Microsoft Word . WordPerfect 6.0
  Such a statement is important for numerous positions.

IMAGE:
- Present a positive and professional image.

- Well groomed; professional; mature; dynamic.

The foregoing "how to" is more than you will ever need. But a few more "tips" can be gleaned in many of the Skills Summaries that follow. But which selling points will be best in today's job market?

THE BEST SELLING POINTS TO OFFER IN THE '90s

Today's employers are very payroll conscious and want to see your worth. Your selling points have to impress them as never before, especially those presented by experienced and more senior applicants. Recruiters are looking for evidence of your accomplishments. What have you achieved for others that would also be valuable to them? Have you increased productivity in similar work situations?

Have you managed to cut payroll? Have you succeeded in lowering costs?

That is why more experienced job seekers should try to mention an achievement in both their Job Objectives and Summaries. It will immediately strike the right chord with a picky employer and show what you could also do for his or her company.

The fact that your most outstanding accomplishment might also appear lower down (in the Work Experience section) is not serious because that will indicate *where* you achieved the results. In fact, your best selling points are probably worth repeating—up front, where it matters. (If necessary, paraphrase them so that the choice of words used is different.)

Here are seven samples to illustrate what is required. They emphasize valuable achievements and accomplishments.

OBJECTIVE: A "hands-on" BANKING/BROKERAGE professional with expertise in **Operations/Office Productivity**, strong supervisory skills, and a proven track record in reducing costs seeks a management-level challenge.

SUMMARY OF SKILLS AND EXPERIENCE:

- Strong background in Banking/Brokerage Operations, including nearly four years of supervisory-level experience.
- Effectiveness in restructuring, redefining, and streamlining work processes/functions in a major Wall Street brokerage house.
- Recipient of Quality Performance Attainment Award (1992).
- Expertise in reformulating "reasonable expectancies" for clerical to supervisory-level positions.
- Accomplishments include the <u>reduction of overtime</u> worked by **43%** in one situation, and attainment of service tracking standards with **20%** fewer staff.
- Strong analytical skills; able to identify actual and potential problem areas.
- Hiring, training, supervision, and motivation of personnel.
- Able to <u>cross-train</u> clerical/administrative personnel and raise their morale.

OBJECTIVE: A position as **Medical Office Manager/Secretary** where the ability to take charge would be of value. Have streamlined office procedures and reduced the time taken to see patients in a high-volume traffic situation.

SUMMARY OF SKILLS AND EXPERIENCE:

- B.A. (Science major).
- Certificate in H.P.L.C. (Beckman/Smith-Kline instruments).
- Four years' experience as Acting Office Manager/Medical Secretary in a busy Dermatological practice (Manhattan); one year in a busy OB/GYN practice.
- Able to oversee medical secretaries/assistants and laboratory technicians, as well as clerical personnel.
- Office Management responsibilities include: Insurance Billing .. Collections .. Bookkeeping .. Ordering Supplies and Inventory Control.
- Knowledge of computerized as well as manual office systems and procedures; The Synapse Medical System.
- Strong organizational, prioritizing, and scheduling skills.
- Excellent "people" and patient contact skills.
- Efficient and effective in getting the job done.

OBJECTIVE: ADMINISTRATIVE/MANAGEMENT position where my track record of reducing/eliminating unnecessary expenditures would be of value. Have verifiable records.

SUMMARY OF QUALIFICATIONS:

- Thirteen years' management-level experience in Office Services and Facilities Management.
- Able to plan, direct, and implement cost-reduction programs.
- Track record of reducing expenditures in two situations by ____% to ____%.
- Significant cost savings by implementing cost-effective administrative systems, streamlining existing procedures for more efficient workflow, and improving selection and training of staff to raise productivity.
- Renegotiation of more favorable vendor contracts (prices, terms, and conditions); securing free-maintenance contracts.
- Coordination of corporate relocations—from raw space to finished and decorated offices, including liaison with computer and telecommunications personnel.

OBJECTIVE: A supervisory position in **Medical Billing (computerized)** where my track record of achieving high productivity and efficiency would be of value. Have greatly expedited account tracking procedures. Letters of recommendation.

SUMMARY OF SKILLS AND EXPERIENCE:

- Six years' experience as Medical Billing Supervisor and Office Manager/Administrator in medical environments.
- Expertise in manual and computerized Patient Accounts Billing; also Third Party Insurance Billing and Credit & Collections.
- Successful computerization of medical billing systems in two fast-paced, high-volume situations.
- Troubleshooting skills to remedy actual/potential billing and insurance problems (including related software problems).
- Proven ability to streamline office procedures for greater productivity.
- Evaluation and purchasing of equipment, including negotiating with vendors on quality and price.
- Computer skills (COMPAQ 386/25 .. Novell O/S .. IBM AT .. MS/DOS .. Basic .. Data Entry).
- Hiring, training, supervision, and motivation of personnel.

OBJECTIVE: A middle management position in the SECURITY industry where my track record of increasing the effectiveness of <u>on-site</u> security operations and improving the performance of security personnel would be of value. Ideal position would be in a:
Hotel .. Hospital .. Office Building .. Residential Complex

SUMMARY OF SKILLS AND EXPERIENCE:

- B.A. degree studies; Graduate of a Training Instructor Academy; Secret Military Clearance; NYS Fire Safety Director.
- Eleven years' experience with emphasis on Security Operations in a leading NYC firm providing security services.
- History of steady promotions to positions of increasing responsibility, including positions as Assistant Manager/Supervisor.
- Track record of achievement includes: Securing a bus terminal in a NYC Port Authority building, reducing robberies from parked cars in a major parking garage, and reducing on-site security violations (Fire & Safety) for clients (from 76% to 5%).
- Excellence in hiring, training, and scheduling personnel; able to weld different ethnic groups into an effective unit.
- Foreign language skills (fluent in English and Spanish; working knowledge of Italian).

OBJECTIVE: A position as **Production/Quality Control Supervisor** within manufacturing industry where my track record of achievement in both areas and "hands-on" style would be valued.

SUMMARY OF SKILLS AND EXPERIENCE:

- 11 years' broad-based experience in Manufacturing as: Production Supervisor .. Q.A. Supervisor .. Q.C. Lead Man .. First Piece Inspector.
- Experience includes: Government contracts and inspections; F.D.A. inspections; G.M.P. techniques; S.O.P.
- Successes in lowering the number of rejected units by **20%** (lowered in-house standards that exceeded customer expectations); also raised productivity of staff by **30%** and minimized overtime costs.
- Proven ability to meet production goals on time and within budget.
- Initiative and resourcefulness in solving problems.
- Excellent relations with other departmental heads.
- Bilingual (English/Spanish); able to interpret blueprints.

OBJECTIVE: Position as "Back-of-the-house" **Restaurant Manager/Chef** where my successes in increasing the productivity of staff, streamlining workflow, lowering food costs, and eliminating waste would be valued.

QUALIFICATIONS:

- 12 years as Chef & Sous Chef/Expediter in fast-paced kitchens; supervisory responsibilities in first-class situations.
- Back-of-the-house experience includes responsibility for maintenance, kitchen supplies, receiving of goods, kitchen sanitation, laundry, dishwashing, and supervision of porters.
- Able to oversee cooking for all stations, including cooks, preparation personnel, and waiters; able to train staff.
- Good knowledge of American/Continental cuisine; able to prepare a wide range of fresh soups, pastas, meat, fish, salads, and sandwiches; creating/updating of menus and specials.
- Purchasing of dry, wet, and paper goods to maintain high quality food service while controlling food and supply costs.
- Demonstrated ability to reduce food costs through tighter portion control, reduction of waste, and improved security.
- Able to plan tables, chairs, and settings (banquets/functions) in order to reduce the number of waiting staff required.

6

38 MINI SALES PRESENTATIONS (ENTRY LEVEL TO MANAGEMENT)

Pitching, it is said, is 90% of the baseball game. [Similarly,] the presentation and "sell" of your idea to a producer—known as "pitching"—has become a significant marketing tool.

—John M. Wilson, Writer's Digest

The first five to fifteen lines in any sales or marketing piece are crucial. Because most cover letters are no longer being read, this is where your resume has to deliver a sales pitch. In marketing terms, a well-written summary of your skills and experience is that "pitch." It is a *mini sales presentation* that presents your value or worth on paper—via a series of targeted and bulleted selling points. Such a Summary has impact. If well written, it will usually "increase" your perceived value in the eyes of the buyer: your future employer.

Each of the Skills Summaries presented in the next few pages (and throughout this book) is a winner for two reasons:

1. Every "bullet" is a selling point that backs up (supports) the Job Objective above it.
2. Each Summary has already helped a job seeker get hired.

Whether your own Summary will also be a winner will depend on how well you select, coordinate, and present your selling points. It takes a little practice. (Refer to the previous chapter—to the sections "Drafting Your Selling Points" and "The Best Selling Points to Offer in the '90s." The unique how-to provided is extremely valuable.)

A total of ninety summaries are given in *Winning Resumes*—from entry level to management. Please refer to the "Summary" column in the Resume Finder on pages 116 to 118 to find one or two in your own field (or in a related area). You'll see how they are constructed. (Additional samples appear in every full-length resume presented in this book.) There's a lot you can copy or adapt because similar skills are often included.

To repeat, adding a Job Objective and Skills Summary to "Education" and "Work History" will strengthen any basic resume and convert it into a *marketing* tool. This is your best selling strategy in the '90s when most cover letters are not being read.

Now let's look at a variety of sample summaries—for entry level to management.

OBJECTIVE: Entry-level position as **Account Executive** or **Media Planner** in an Advertising agency.

STRENGTHS:
- B.B.A. degree in Advertising and Marketing.
- Internship in a subsidiary of D'Arcy, Masius, Benton & Bowles.
- Exposure to advertising campaigns, including implementation of the creative process into overall media plans.
- Understanding of the complexities of media planning.
- Presentation skills.
- Able to interact well with people and personalities.
- Able to work well under pressure of deadlines.
- Present an "ad agency image."

OBJECTIVE: A position as **Accounting Clerk (Receivables/Payables)** where my strong reconciliation, customer service, and problem-solving skills would be assets.

STRENGTHS:
- Certificate in Bookkeeping; Liberal Arts credits.
- Ten years' experience as Accounts Receivable Clerk/Accounts Payable Clerk and Royalty Clerk.
- Aptitude for figures.
- Bookkeeping knowledge includes: Cash Receipts and Disbursements . Bank Reconciliations . Billings . Aging of Accounts . Collections . Journal . Royalties.
- Heavy reconciliations experience (manual and computerized).
- Research and problem-solving skills.
- CRT background .. IBM PC .. Lotus 1-2-3.
- Work well under both time and accuracy pressures.

OBJECTIVE: A position as **Accounting Manager/Accountant** in a corporation or Public Accounting firm where my track record, client relations skills, and supervisory experience would be of value.

SUMMARY OF QUALIFICATIONS:
- B.B.A. (Accounting) .. CPA Review Course .. Taxation.
- Eight years' broad-based experience as Accounting Manager in a retail chain; as Staff Accountant in a CPA firm and for an international manufacturer/distributor.
- Have consistently received high praise from external auditors for catching up on backlogs of work and for efficiency.
- Able to supervise all bookkeeping/accounting functions.
- Experience in the computerization of accounting systems.
- Able to prepare Financial Statements.
- Preparation of statistical/financial reports and schedules.
- Forecasting cash flow; budgeting and monitoring expenditures; analysis of variances.
- Computer skills (IBM/Apple PCs . Lotus 1-2-3).
- Preparation of city, inter-state, and federal tax returns.

OBJECTIVE: ADVERTISING: **Account Management** position.

SUMMARY STATEMENT:

- Management of a $35+ million, heavily retail account in a Big 10 advertising agency.
- Involved in planning media for network television and print.
- Strong background in development of collateral materials and print production.
- Able to juggle several projects simultaneously.
- Excellent judgment in developing cost-effective solutions for clients.
- Integral part of Account Planning process.

JOB GOAL: A supervisory-level position as **Administrator/Coordinator** within an AIDS/HIV facility or program where my strong administrative, communications and organizing skills would be assets. Able to train and supervise social work interns.

QUALIFIED BY:

- B.A. degree in Social Work; Attendance at numerous courses/seminars/workshops on AIDS Prevention Education.
- Five years' experience in a Methadone Maintenance clinic including periods as Acting HIV Administrator/Coordinator, as Supervisor of Interns and as Substance Abuse Counselor.
- Case management of up to 70 patients, including persons from minority and disadvantaged backgrounds.
- Populations dealt with include: Substance abusers . alcoholics . homeless persons . victims of rape . battered & pregnant women . emotionally handicapped young adults . and HIV related cases.
- Crisis intervention skills.
- Individual and group counseling skills.
- Liaison with physicians, psychologists, social workers and with county and community social work/legal agencies.
- Proposal and report-writing skills.

OBJECTIVE: A position in **Art/Antiques** where related education and successful experience in an antique center would be of value.

STRENGTHS:

- Strong academic background in Art History.
- Experience in buying and selling art/antiques, including collectibles, old photographs, and daguerreotypes.
- Good eye for art and antiques (all periods).
- Attendance at art exhibits, antique shows, and auctions.
- Ability to advise on the merit and/or potential value of items.
- Photo research skills.
- Good communications skills with both clients and exhibitors.
- Business acumen.

OBJECTIVE: A position as **Bookkeeper (Full Charge)/Bookkeeper** where my broad-based experience and the ability to take charge in a small office and train accounting clerks would be of value.

SUMMARY OF SKILLS AND EXPERIENCE:

- Accounting degree studies; Certificate in Bookkeeping/Accounting.
- Seven years' broad-based experience as Bookkeeper, including experience in a CPA firm; supervisory responsibilities.
- Thorough knowledge and experience of: Cash Receipts/Disbursements .. Accounts Receivable and Payable .. Bank Reconciliations .. Sales Journal .. General Journal .. General Ledger .. Trial Balance .. Payroll .. Payroll Taxes .. Sales Taxes.
- Computerized accounting experience includes: Accounts Receivable .. Cash Receipts/Disbursements .. Payroll .. Inventory .. General Ledger.
- Preparation of schedules (A/R .. Insurances .. Invoices, etc.)
- Knowledge of manual financial statement preparation.
- Computer skills (IBM PC . Apple Macintosh 2x . Microsoft Excel).
- Able to handle heavy workload under time/accuracy pressures.

OBJECTIVE: A position as **Chief Investment Officer** for a Retirement System where my proven track record in the Pension Plan and Investment areas (public and private sector) would be of value.

SUMMARY OF QUALIFICATIONS:

- Background encompasses six years in Pension Plan accounting and administration and five years in area of Investments; includes two separate Plans ($1.5 billion) in a County agency.
- Accomplishments include appointing a new Custodial Bank which, in the first year, saved the County $250,000 and also resulted in additional revenues of $300,000 through a Securities Lending Program.
- Asset allocation experience, including the use of software to assist the Retirement System in creating a diversified portfolio to achieve the projected (actuarial) rate of return. (Vestek and Russell Asset Allocation Models)
- Selection of investor managers, including creation of effective questionaire as a selection tool; also follow-up techniques.
- Able to interpret performance measurement reports in order to evaluate investment managers and ensure that they are performing in compliance with contractual obligations.
- Able to hire, train and supervise professional staff.
- Effective communication with Board of Trustees.
- Preparation and analysis of Financial Statements, including balance sheets, income statements and consolidated statements.

OBJECTIVE: Entry-level position in the BROKERAGE industry (Mutual Funds or Stocks) where my knowledge and selling/trading skills would be assets. Seek sponsorship for Series 7.

STRENGTHS:
- Series 63; exposure to the Series 7 curriculum.
- Chartered Financial Analyst program (present).
- Interested in stock market since age 14 (penny stocks); have invested in blue chip stocks and undervalued issues.
- Knowledge of mutual funds and options.
- Track market movements in: Airlines . Commodities . Banks . Oil . Futures; have been 75% accurate in predictions.
- Monitor Dow-Jones index on a daily basis.
- Cold-calling experience in investment banking; make 250-300 calls per day.
- Successful sales experience (diamonds).
- Self-motivated .. high energy level .. money-driven.

OBJECTIVE: BROKERAGE: **Fixed Income Institutional Sales** position where my "generalist" experience, active account base and proven ability to build and maintain client relationships would be assets. Am a strong closer. (Have Series 3, 63 and 7.)

STRENGTHS:
- Five years' Taxed Fixed Income sales experience on Wall Street in a Primary Dealership.
- Proven ability to sell: Government Bonds . Corporate Bonds . Mortgage-backed Securities (including CMO's) . A.B.S. (asset-backed securities).
- Experience with large/small institutional accounts (Banks .. Money Managers .. Insurance companies .. State agencies)
- Additional experience with: Futures . Options . Synthetics.
- Skill in identifying and/or creating client needs; enjoy high degree of professional credibility with clients.
- Trading skills (able to recognize "relative value").

OBJECTIVE: A position as **Chemist/Chemical Engineer** (R&D) or a suitable position in a Quality Control environment.

SUMMARY:
- B.S. degree in Chemistry and Geology; A grades in Biology-oriented courses.
- Three years' experience as Analytical Chemist in two Pharmaceutical manufacturing environments.
- Experience in wet analytical chemistry methods, UV and IR; familiar with HPLC, GC, TLC and other lab techniques.
- Thorough understanding of qualitative and quantitative measurement; experience in two laboratories.
- Knowledge of Quality Control programs and procedures.
- Knowledge of raw materials, finished products, and Stability Test Procedures.
- Able to achieve results quickly and accurately.
- Supervisory experience in a major laboratory; teamwork and interpersonal skills.
- Excellent written testimonial from an associate professor.

OBJECTIVE: A position as **Clerk/Typist/Receptionist** in a fast-paced environment.

SUMMARY:
- High school diploma—Business major.
- Clerical experience (two years) in an insurance company.
- "Meeting and greeting" experience includes work as Receptionist in a state agency, as Bank Teller, and as Cashier.
- Telephone/switchboard experience (9-line AT&T Merlin).
- Light typing (40 wpm) .. CPT Word Processor .. IBM Terminal .. FAX (Omni) .. Microfilm (Bell & Howell).
- Good "people" skills; pleasant and friendly disposition.
- Willing to learn; punctual.

OBJECTIVE: A position as **Chief Cook/Assistant Chef/Sauté Cook** in a high-volume restaurant.

STRENGTHS:
- Track record of promotions in the B-I-G Organization.
- Experience in Sauté . Broiler . Pantry . Mid-fry stations.
- Training of new hires in each of the above stations.
- Supervision of 10 line and prep cooks.
- Maintenance of Labor and Food Cost percentages/par levels.
- Monitoring of food service standards and quality control.
- Expediting in high-volume situations.
- Able to make hot and cold sauces and salads.

OBJECTIVE: A position as **Data Entry/General Clerk.**

SUMMARY:
- CRT Data Entry studies.
- Temporary assignment as Data Entry/Filing/Updating Clerk in an agency (with in-charge duties).
- Two years' experience as General Clerk in a busy supermarket, including handling large sums of money; exposure to billing and payroll.
- Very quick and accurate in maintaining files.
- Knowledge of: IBM PC 3600 .. Apple IIE .. Light Word Processing .. IBM Selectric II .. Adding Machine.
- Typing skills (35 wpm).
- Self-starter who gets on well with staff and clients.
- Hardworking .. punctual .. excellent attendance .. able to learn quickly and work with minimum supervision.

OBJECTIVE: COMPUTER CONSULTING position where **Systems/Communications** experience in major corporations and ability to complete projects on time and within budget would be of value.

SUMMARY OF QUALIFICATIONS:

- Six years as hands-on consultant to a major airline; successful completion of 5 (five) challenging projects.
- Five years as Systems Group Leader/Senior Programmer/Analyst and Applications Programmer in another major company.
- Expertise in TPF real-time Systems Programming and Networking.
- Heavy experience in Migrating Systems.
- Excellent in Assembler (IBM 370XA) programming.
- <u>Areas of experience include:</u>

System Design & Development	Creative Problem Solving
System Testing & Implementation	Troubleshooting
System Maintenance, Modification, and Enhancement	Debugging
	User Interface/Liaison
System Conversion	User Training
Programming	Documentation

OBJECTIVE: An entry-level position in **Computer Operations .. Data Processing .. Programming.**

STRENGTHS:
- B.S. in Computer Science/Data Processing/Management.
- Coursework in both computer and business subjects.
- Member, Computer Machinery Association.
- Student experience in Programming.
- Strong computer skills (including PCs/CRT Data Entry).
- Leadership and teamwork (Captain, College Sports Team).
- Detail oriented.
- Troubleshooting skills.
- Able to work well under pressure of deadlines.
- Willingness to learn.

COMPUTER HARDWARE AND SOFTWARE:

Hardware:	DEC VAX 8200 .. IBM 4381 .. IBM PC/AT	
Languages:	COBOL .. COBOL II .. BASIC	
Op. Systems:	VAX/VMS .. OS/MVS .. VM/CMS .. IBM PC DOS	
Software:	IBM/CSP (4GL) .. CICS .. VAX/FMS .. VSAM	
Databases:	VAX/RDB .. SQL/DS	
Applications:	Accounts Receivable	Accounts Payable
	Department Budgets	Cash Forecasts

OBJECTIVE: **Computer (PC Network) Administrator:** Novell Local Area Network Administrator with expertise in conversions and upgrades to NetWare/286 (2.15) and heavy Lotus 1-2-3 experience.

SUMMARY OF SKILLS AND EXPERIENCE:

- Novell NetWare Systems Manager training course.
- Four years' "hands-on" experience as Novell L.A.N. Administrator (includes managing 27 computer terminals).
- Participation in many conversions and NetWare upgrades.
- Applications in: Accounts Payable .. Payroll .. General Ledger .. Job Costing .. Accounts Receivable.
- Computer skills (Lotus 1-2-3 .. dBase III+ .. DOS .. S.B.T. Accounting Packages .. Freelance (Design & Graphics) .. Microsoft Word W/P .. PCs .. H.P. VECTRA RS/25C.
- Extensive knowledge of PC hardware upgrading.
- Experience as Coordinator/Liaison between consultant programmers and the needs of the company and individual users.
- Excellent "people" and teamwork skills.
- Foreign language skills (English . German . Spanish . French).

OBJECTIVE: Position as **Counselor/Assistant Supervisor** in the Social/Human Services field.

SUMMARY OF SKILLS AND EXPERIENCE:

- Liberal Arts studies; more than 80 credit hours in C.A.C. program; Orientation training course in a medical center.
- Five years' experience as Counselor/Group Leader (_____ House) and as a Mental Health Worker; also as Night Supervisor in a shelter—inpatients and outpatients.
- Caseloads included: Substance/Alcohol abusers .. Victims of abuse .. Dysfunctional patients .. Personality disorders (B.P.D.) .. Suicide attempts .. Homeless persons.
- Knowledge of JCAH Charting and Documentation, Treatment Planning and Assessment.
- Leading educational seminars and workshops for task-oriented (functional) groups; excellent presentation skills.
- Facilitating Encounter groups (two hours of Group Therapy).
- Individual counseling of inpatients; crisis intervention skills.
- Able to work well with members of multidisciplinary teams (Director, Assistant Director, Social Worker, Psychologist).
- Liaison with Employee Assistance Programs/outside agencies.
- Writing skills (case histories, reports, cover letters, etc.).

OBJECTIVE: A position as **Electronics Technician** where my expertise in the troubleshooting, testing, installation and maintenance of a wide range of control systems (including microprocessor-based systems) would be of value.

SUMMARY OF SKILLS AND EXPERIENCE:

- 10 years' experience in: Electronics .. Telecommunications .. Telephony .. Audio/Video .. Electro-Mechanical Systems.
- Specialization in: - CCTV (Audio/Video)
  - Telephone Switchboard Systems
  - Electro-Mechanical Systems
- Digital experience includes HONEYWELL microprocessor-based Building Control Systems.
- Strong troubleshooting skills to board and component levels.
- Supervision and training of electrical/electronics personnel.
- Extensive training of customers on-site.
- Excellent selling and customer service skills.

OBJECTIVE: A responsible **Engineering Design/Drafting** position. Offer my Electrical and HVAC Drafting experience and ability to design lighting layouts and air ducts.

STRENGTHS:
- B.S. in Electrical Engineering (Design Drafting major).
- Two years' Design Drafting experience, including systems.
- Strong drafting skills and experience (HVAC . electrical . piping . architectural).
- Thorough understanding of statics and circuits, including problem solving.
- Analytical and troubleshooting skills.
- Programming skills (FORTRAN .. 8086 Microprocessor).
- Excellent interpersonal and teamwork skills; reliable.

OBJECTIVE: A position as **Engineer/Electronics Technician** where my experience with high-powered Laser cutting systems, C.A.D. and Knife-cutter systems would be of value. Able to train technicians in four languages.

STRENGTHS:
- Training as Electronics Technician; Class Rank: 2/120
- Three years' experience in U.S. as well as in Western and Eastern Europe.
- Employer's evaluation of performance: "Best technician in Eastern Europe."
- Maintenance/repair of 1000W-2000W invisible (ultraviolet) CO^2 Laser cutting systems; also fine adjustments.
- Maintenance and repair of other cutting systems (knife-cutter).
- Training of engineers and technicians in four languages: English . German . Polish . Russian.
- Troubleshooting and problem-solving experience in West Germany, France, Austria, and the former USSR.

OBJECTIVE: A senior FINANCIAL/ADMINISTRATIVE position where my success in reducing costs and achieving significant tax savings within Service and Manufacturing industries would be of value. Have strong entrepreneurial skills.
"Generalist" background includes corporate:
Finance . Accounting . Taxation . Administration . Law.

SUMMARY OF QUALIFICATIONS:

- More than 14 years' experience as Chief Financial Officer/Controller, Tax Manager, and Legal Counsel in the Manufacturing, Service, and Contracting industries.
- General Management experience includes both short-term and long-range planning to ensure corporate survival.
- Track record of contributing to bottom-line results by reducing costs in Service and Production areas, as well as through implementing more effective financial controls.
- Successful reduction of annual corporate tax liability.
- Able to negotiate and renegotiate contract and payment terms and conditions; excellent business sense.
- Extensive experience in creating and implementing effective financial, budgeting, and accounting systems.
- Preparation of S.E.C. filings, including 10-Ks, 10-Qs, and Proxy Statements.

OBJECTIVE: Senior-level position in HEALTH CARE ADMINISTRATION.

SUMMARY STATEMENT:

- M.P.A. degree in Health Care Administration.
- Thirteen years' experience in the health care industry with a successful track record in planning, program development and project management.
- Wide knowledge of regulatory agencies, hospitals/health care facilities, physicians offices, and insurance carriers.
- Expertise in researching and formulating feasibility studies, conducting surveys, and performing cost-savings analyses.
- Accomplishments include coordinating a psychiatric day hospital program resulting in annual cost-savings of $125,000.
- Strong analytical and diagnostic skills.
- Computer skills (IBM PC .. Lotus 1-2-3 .. Harvard Graphics).

OBJECTIVE: A senior-level position in **Interior/Architectural Design**. Experience includes major hotels, restaurants, and large public and commercial spaces. Proven ability to assume total responsibility for projects—from concept to completion.

SUMMARY OF QUALIFICATIONS:

- B.F.A. degree in Interior Architectural Design.
- Recipient of Browning, Olden & Penfield scholarship.
- Broad-based and successful experience in the design of major commercial spaces—from schematics to installation.
- Able to create diverse environments and achieve dramatic effects and/or striking illusions.
- Expertise in the areas of: Conceptual Design . Color Theory . Drafting & Rendering . Space Planning . Selection of Materials, Furniture & Furnishings.
- Project management and supervisory skills.
- Sensitivity to the needs and perceptions of demanding clients.

OBJECTIVE: A senior-level position in **Corporate/International Law.**

SUMMARY OF QUALIFICATIONS:

- J.D. (Cum Laude), Yale Law School (1985)
- Broad experience in general corporate practice
- Expertise in complex financings
- Significant international experience
- Member of Commonwealth of Massachusetts Bar

OBJECTIVE: A position in **Corporate Law.**

SUMMARY OF QUALIFICATIONS:

- Four years' corporate law experience in challenging Finance/Securities environments; emphasis on contract negotiations and competitive pricing.
- Demonstrated ability to evaluate, assess, and advise on business implications of contract terms.
- Successes in focusing intracorporate entities toward speedy resolution of issues.
- Participation in multimillion-dollar contract negotiations with two stock exchanges, California state government, and Fortune 500 corporations.
- Strong closing skills under pressure timeframes.
- Decision-making skills.
- J.D.; member of California State Bar.

OBJECTIVE: A position in MARKETING where my marketing/promotions experience would be of value and where my continued professional growth would be encouraged.

SUMMARY:
- Experience in Direct Mail . Space Advertising . Telemarketing and Sales Promotion in a Publishing company.
- Exposure to the development of marketing strategies/plans.
- Conducting market surveys to identify potential users.
- Knowledge of lead tracking .. follow-ups .. fulfillment.
- Liaison with media, magazines, ad agency and authors.
- Preparation of reports and statistics for Sales/Marketing managers.
- Able to work under pressure and meet deadlines.
- Organizational, problem-solving and "people" skills.
- Computer skills (IBM PC . Lotus 1-2-3 . R Base).
- Detail oriented .. hardworking .. energetic.

OBJECTIVE: **Producer — Television and Film.**

SUMMARY OF QUALIFICATIONS:

- 12 years' experience in television and film production.
- Experience in developing projects for major corporate clients—from an original concept through completion; encompasses all phases of production and postproduction.
- Proven success in initiating projects, generating story ideas, and in producing, directing, and editing.
- Expertise in field producing and directing.
- Sensitivity to the perceptions and budgetary constraints of clients; experience in preparing budgets.
- Excellent writing skills, both in print and for TV and film production; ability to write for highly technical projects.

OBJECTIVE: A position as **Proofreader.**

STRENGTHS:
- B.A. graduate.
- Intensive proofreading workshop that included hands-on experience of proofreading technical and legal copy.
- Light proofreading experience (mainly catalogues) in a San Francisco bookstore and gallery.
- Familiar with the AMA stylebook.
- Detail oriented.
- Excellent spelling and good command of English.
- Able to work well under time and accuracy pressures.

OBJECTIVE: Freelance work within the PUBLISHING industry. (Fiction)
Areas of interest are: **Manuscript Reading . Book Reviewing . Copyediting . Proofreading.**

SUMMARY:
- Degree in English .. Cum Laude .. Fiction award.
- Editing experience includes: <u>Argus</u> (college literary magazine) .. <u>Star</u> (H.S. literary magazine) .. <u>Ikeys</u> (college newspaper).
- Proofreader/Copyeditor for <u>Durban Gazette</u>, (San Diego, CA)
- Experience as librarian in college and high school.
- Teaching experience (substitute teacher, grade school).
- Writing skills; attendance at writers' workshop.
- Typing (45 wpm) . Macintosh . IBM PC . WordPerfect.
- Proven ability to work under pressure of deadlines.
- Keen eye for detail; able to spot errors in typing, spelling, grammar, and punctuation.

OBJECTIVE: **Retail Manager/Salesman** with a track record of increasing sales in a "soft" market, reducing shrinkage, and contributing to overall store profitability seeks an opportunity. In a major chain of stores I am rated a <u>top 10% manager countrywide.</u>

SUMMARY OF SKILLS AND EXPERIENCE:

- Thirteen years' retail sales/store management experience, mainly in men's wear specialty shops; experience in buying.
- Store operations experience includes: Buying .. Merchandising .. Display .. Stock Work .. Inventory Control .. Cash Receipts .. Bookkeeping .. Housekeeping .. Payroll .. Staffing.
- Thorough knowledge of exclusive men's clothing—from suits to sportswear, and including shoes and all accessories.
- Expertise in European merchandise (brand names such as ____, ____, and ____); also familiar with high-fashion American designer clothing and women's wear.
- Able to satisfy clients requiring custom suits.
- In-depth knowledge of garment construction, fit, and alterations.
- Strong selling skills; familiar with the buying habits of upscale clients; able to train sales staff to sell to the discriminating shopper.
- Able to advise Buyer on fit, color, and quantities.

OBJECTIVE: SALES/MANAGEMENT position within the prerecorded **Video Cassette** industry. Offer a track record of achievement in two start-up companies.

SUMMARY OF QUALIFICATIONS:

- Eight years' successful experience in the Video, Records, and Tapes industry as Sales Manager/Representative for manufacturers of prerecorded videocassettes; as Manager in a high-volume retail store (videos/records); and as Buyer.
- Territory management experience covers the entire southeast region of the U.S.; development of several key accounts.
- Valuable ongoing relationships with key personnel on the Distribution level (V.P. of Sales, Buyers, Sales Managers).
- Understanding of the needs and requirements of authorized distributors and manufacturers; able to predict trends.
- Creation of effective sales/marketing strategies and incentive programs.
- Proven ability to recruit and train superior sales personnel.

OBJECTIVE: **Secretarial/Word Processing** position in a law firm where my related experience and strong organizational and prioritizing skills would be assets. Prefer <u>night</u> shift.

SUMMARY OF SKILLS AND EXPERIENCE:

- Six years' varied experience as Legal Secretary/Word Processor in two law firms, a real estate company, and a major commercial bank. (Part-time assignments.)
- Have assisted <u>five</u> attorneys who specialized in:
    - Litigation
    - Taxes & Estates
    - Real Estate
    - Criminal Law
    - Civil Law
- Word processing experience includes: Correspondence .. Law Briefs .. Affidavits .. Memoranda .. Litigation Documents .. Real Estate Documents.
- Have utilized: WordPerfect (5.0 and 5.1) .. Microsoft Word 4.0 .. N.B.I. .. Datapoint; also Dictaphone and Steno.
- Able to work well under time and accuracy pressures.
- Meticulous attention to detail; very neat.

OBJECTIVE: A position as **Secretarial/Word Processing Supervisor** where my broad-based experience and ability to train and supervise new hires would be of value. Mature and efficient.

SUMMARY OF SKILLS AND EXPERIENCE:

- Degree studies in Liberal Arts; Certificate of Completion as Executive Secretary.
- Thirteen years' secretarial/word processing experience; have trained and supervised numerous typists/clerks.
- Experience includes: Financial and Statistical Reports .. Technical and Legal Documents .. Letters .. Memos.
- Word processing skills/experience: IBM PC . WANG OIS . Microsoft Word 4.0 . WordPerfect 5.1 . Multimate.
- Typing (75 wpm average) .. heavy Dictaphone experience.
- Proofreading and verification of documents.
- Strong organizational and prioritizing skills.
- Able to cope with heavy workloads and meet deadlines.

OBJECTIVE: **Designer/Stylist/Patternmaker.**

SUMMARY:

- Experience as Designer/Stylist (Junior Missy dresses, sportswear).
- Patternmaking experience from first sample through production.
- Thorough knowledge of garment construction, grading, and marking.
- Able to supervise a sample room.
- Knowledge of embroidery and screen printing techniques.

JOB GOAL: A supervisory-level TELEMARKETING position where my track record in Direct Sales/Marketing (business <u>and</u> consumer products) and proven ability to create effective training programs would be of value.

SUMMARY OF QUALIFICATIONS:

- Six years' successful experience in both business-to-consumer and business-to-business telemarketing.
- Expertise in recruiting, training, assigning, and motivating telemarketing professionals, resulting in shorter training time, increased production, and reduced staff turnover.
- Creation of successful contests, incentives, and awards to motivate representatives and recognize achievement.
- Valuable experience in tracking and reporting program results in order to evaluate and increase the effectiveness of programs by segmenting markets by business type, area, size, and so on.
- Script editing and testing; innovative and creative.
- Supervisory skills and experience; excellent "people" skills.

JOB GOAL: Position as **Travel Agent/Airline Employee**. Will relocate.

SUMMARY OF SKILLS AND EXPERIENCE:

- Eight years' travel industry experience, including five years as a Travel Agent (three in an airline).
- Thorough knowledge of SABRE .. SYSTEM-ONE .. PARS.
- Experience in marketing and sales (inside and outside).
- Ticketing and passenger service worldwide; speed and accuracy in dealing with numbers.
- Booking of tour packages for leisure, corporate, and group travel (land/sea/air), including charters, hotels, and car rentals.
- Preparation of weekly ARC sales report.
- Foreign language skills (fluent in English and Spanish; working knowledge of Afrikaans).
- Able to interact effectively with a wide range of people and personalities both in person and via telephone.
- Excellent customer service, problem-solving, and follow-through skills.
- Present a friendly, positive, and professional image.

7

WORK HISTORY + ACCOMPLISHMENTS

Employers rely heavily on your prior career path when making snap judgments about your commitment ("How long did you stay with the company?"), your competency ("Why did you move so often?"), your ambition ("Why did you stay in one job for 32 years?") and the type and amount of responsibility your employer felt safe giving you ("What does your career progression look like?").

—DOUGLAS B. RICHARDSON, career manager and executive consultant [18]

WHAT EMPLOYERS WANT TO KNOW: ELEVEN QUESTIONS

A recruiter tries to match up what you've done before with what he or she needs you to do now. The more similar your past duties and responsibilities are to his or her present needs, the better the "fit." Therefore, in reviewing what you are doing at present (and for other employers), those who read your job resume will be looking for evidence. It is by judging what type of work you've been doing for the past *five* years or so and at what level that they can judge (more or less) whether you'll be able to perform whatever it is they want you to do now. (If your job titles or work experience or dates might be a problem, please refer to Chapter 13, "Fixing Resume Blemishes.")

Here are the main items employers usually look for and why. Most of them should be addressed in your job descriptions.

1. *Your present and previous job titles.* Recruiters will scan your resume to determine whether you are presently holding or have previously held a position similar (in job title) to the one you are applying for and for how long. They will also note whether your job titles indicate growth. Have you steadily advanced or been promoted?

2. *What is the name of your present employer and in which city or town is the business located?* An out-of-state address is often less attractive because conditions and attitudes might be different there. For example, some New York City employers might feel that Californians are too laid back. On the other hand, employers in southern states might be wary about employing a city slicker from the Big Apple. And some New York City employers might prefer out-of-state women, who are supposed to be less aggressive and more polite.

3. *How large or small is your present employer's business or organization?* Is it well known? Is it a Fortune 500 company? Is it an industry leader? Is it one of the biggest . . .

whatever? Is it one of a chain of . . . whatever? Is it a division of a larger group? How big is its annual volume of business? Its gross annual revenues? The size or importance of your employer can impress. It also helps the reader judge what your job title might be worth. Are or were you a little goldfish in an olympic-size pool or a dolphin in a private swimming pool? Did you manage your own business?

4. *What type of business or professional or not-for-profit activity is your present employer engaged in?* What type of product(s) or service(s) do they manufacture, sell, distribute, or provide? This would help a reader decide whether you might also know the type of business he or she is engaged in and whether you are also familiar with the industry in a wider sense. If not, will you be able to adjust?

5. *Whom do you report to?* (The title, *not* the name of the person.) This tells the reader something about the level of your immediate superior. From that, your own level might be judged.

6. *What is your main responsibility?* In other words, what were you hired to do? Is it to word process legal or statistical reports? Is it to do bank reconciliations in an accounting department? Is it to prepare monthly financial statements? Is it to coordinate between departments? Is it to supervise and train new hires in a tele-marketing department? Is it to manage a store, department, division, or territory? Are you in charge of an area or region? Do you have responsibility for servicing key accounts?

How many persons do you supervise? Are they professional, technical, or clerical staff? As much as possible, numbers or the names of clients or geographical areas should be given to help the reader understand the scope of your responsibilities.

7. *What are your main duties?* What specific tasks do you have to perform? Do you have to research and gather information, or is it provided? Whom do you interact with? Do you have liaison with any person, department(s), or outside agencies? Do you have to work under pressure? Are there daily, weekly, or monthly deadlines to be met?

Are you involved in any special projects? Are you in charge of any project? Do you have to prepare and submit any written report(s)? To whom?

8. *What special equipment or materials do you use?* What computer hardware and software? This is very important nowadays!

9. *Forecasts and budgets.* Are you responsible for making cash or sales forecasts? Are you responsible for preparing any budget, or do you only participate or assist your boss in this? What is the dollar amount of that budget? Do you also monitor expenditures? Do you calculate and report on variances?

10. *Do you have Profit and Loss responsibility (or accountability)?* Do you have bottom-line responsibility? More than anything, this would tell the reader how senior your position really is!

11. *What are your achievements? Your accomplishments?* Finally, and most importantly, how well are you performing? What results have you achieved so far? What have you accomplished? Have you made a difference? Have you improved anything? How is it better today than before?

Above all, can you quote numbers or dollar figures to indicate how much you sold or saved for the company? Recruiters like to see numbers or percentages. They are more "real" (objective) than words.

Did you reduce waste or pilferage? How did you do it? Did you streamline any operation? How? Did you shorten a response turnaround time? How? Did you speed up deliveries? What did you do? Did you reduce overtime worked? Did you lower absenteeism? How? Did you reduce payroll costs? Did you raise staff productivity? What method did you use? Did you improve their training? Did you motivate them? Did you increase the company's share of the market for any of its products? How did you do this? Did you revitalize existing products?

Has your employer given you an excellent performance appraisal? Have you won any awards? Have you been elected to any exclusive in-house "club" based on the excellence of your performance? Did you win an all-expenses-paid trip to Hawaii? More than anything, it is *how well* you have performed for another employer that will persuade the next one that you are a valuable person to have on board.

RECORDING YOUR WORK EXPERIENCE

Step One: Decide on a suitable heading for your work experience. Will it be "Previous Experience" or "Professional Experience" or "Employment" or "Student Employment"? Refer to the resume categories and guidelines given in Chapters 8 and 10. (Graduating seniors should consult Chapter 11.)

Step Two: Record the date of your most recent (or best related) work experience: 1993–Present

Step Three: Record a suitable job title or titles (that back up your Job Objective). Refer to the "tips" given in Chapter 13 on adjusting titles.

Step Four: Record the name of your present/ previous employer, the town or city, and the state.

Step Five: Write a brief (one-line) description of what they do (if this is not obvious from the name) or how big or impressive they are.

Step Six: Select only those responsibilities and duties that would support your Job Objective (especially your most related work experience). The first of these should be whom you report(ed) to; the second should indicate the scope or extent of your main responsibility—to show why it is/was important.

Step Seven: Close your description(s) by mention-

ing an accomplishment or two—to show the reader how well you perform(ed). Forty examples are given after sample job descriptions in this chapter.

Accomplishment (or Achievement):

- Streamlined office procedures and reduced unnecessary paperwork. As a result, the work is being done more quickly and with one clerk less. (Savings of $12,000 p.a.)
- Reduced <u>overtime</u> worked by Drivers from an average of 110 hours per week to only 25 hours by restructuring routes and through improved controls.
- Migrated and converted mainframe interest calculation systems to PC. Redesigned these from batch to online, thereby allowing for traffic department to bypass data entry. Reduced *turnaround time* from 2–5 days to 1–2 hours.

USING ACTION WORDS

Use "action" words (verbs) to commence each sentence in your job descriptions, such as the following:

- Report to . . .
- Responsible for (= Am responsible for) . . .
- Review . . .
- Perform . . .

Never write in the first person ("I perform") because a job resume is *not* a letter.

On pages 83 and 84 you'll find two lists of action words to use. Those on the right are more dynamic because they indicate that you are or were improving things at work. For example:

- Cross-trained staff
- Eliminated waste
- Lowered absenteeism rates
- Raised staff productivity
- Renegotiated contracts

This is what today's employers want to hear.

LIKE A FUNNEL

Since you will be recording your work experience in one to four jobs, write less the further back you go in time. Like a pouring funnel that narrows, your details must diminish as you move down the page. (Employers are interested mainly in what you've been doing in the past five years or so.) If you have more than twelve to fifteen years of working experience, end your dates and write the following note: "Details of additional employment will be provided at a personal interview."

ACTION WORDS TO DESCRIBE YOUR WORK EXPERIENCE

Commonly Used

Acted as
Administered
Advised
Analyzed
Approved (invoices)
Arranged (meetings)
Assisted
Attended (closings)
Audited
Authorized (payments)
Calculated
Checked
Coded (data)
Collaborated
Communicated
Compiled
Conceived
Conducted (site visits)
Cooperated
Coordinated
Decided
Defined (tasks)
Drafted
Encoded
Ensured (compliance with)
Entertained (clients)
Expedited (orders)
Exposed to (gained exposure to)
Filled in for
Followed through
Followed up
Handled (a heavy workload)
Implemented
In charge of (was ...)
Input (data)
Interacted with
Interfaced with
Interviewed
Involved in
Learned
Led
Liaison with

More Dynamic

Achieved (annualized savings)
Accomplished
Attained (corporate goals)
Built (relationships)
Consolidated (warehouse)
Constructed
Contributed
Controlled
Converted (manual systems)
Created
Cross-trained
Cut (costs)
Decreased (overtime worked)
Designed
Determined (exact duties)
Developed (fabric ideas)
Devised
Directed
Discovered
Downloaded (a mainframe)
Downsized (an organization)
Eliminated (wastage)
Enhanced
Established
Expanded (customer base)
Evaluated
Forecasted (new trends)
Formulated (policies)
Generated
Get mileage out of (software)
Highlighted (areas of exposure)
Identified (areas of overlap)
Improved
Increased (efficiency of ...)
Initiated
Installed (improved software)
Investigated (new accounts)
Kept (losses below limits)
Launched
Lowered (absenteeism rates)
Maintained (strict security)
Maximized (profitability)

ACTION WORDS TO DESCRIBE YOUR WORK EXPERIENCE

Commonly Used

Made (presentations)
Maintained (responsibility for)
Managed
Monitored (expenditures)
Negotiated
Operated (a scanner)
Organized
Oversaw
Participated in
Performed (Bank Reconciliations)
Pinch hit for
Prepared (financial statements)
Prioritized (work to be done)
Processed (invoices)
Programmed (in Basic)
Promoted (was . . .)
Proofed (bank records)
Provided (support)
Ran (a computer program)
Received (training)
Reconciled
Recorded
Reported
Researched
Responsible for (was . . .)
Scheduled
Screened (callers)
Shopped (the market)
Set up (covers)
Supervised
Tracked
Trained
Used (IBM PC)
Verified (chargebacks)
Visited (clients on site)
Word processed (documents)
Wrote (scripts)

More Dynamic

Migrated (a mainframe system)
Minimized (pilfering)
Orchestrated (efforts of . . .)
Overcame (problems)
Planned
Produced
Raised (staff productivity)
Realized (additional income, cost savings)
Recommended
Redefined
Reduced (turnaround times)
Re-engineered (a company)
Refined (existing systems)
Reformulated (expectancies)
Remerchandised (a store)
Renegotiated (contracts)
Reorganized (workflow)
Restored (profitability)
Restructured (a department)
Retrained
Revamped (store operations)
Reviewed (workflow procedures)
Revised
Revitalized (old product lines)
Saved (money)
Selected (vendors)
Shortened (response times)
Slashed (payroll expenses)
Sourced (mills, suppliers)
Streamlined (office procedures)
Substituted (cheaper generics)
Targeted (new markets)
Troubleshot (problem areas)

1994 – Present   **Accountant** (Junior)
ENGINEERING CONSTRUCTION COMPANY, Houston, TX
—Post and analyze Accounts Receivable.
—Prepare Aging Schedules.
—Code Cash Receipts and Cash Disbursements for EDP system.
—Prepare Project Cost Center man-hour reports.
—Perform Budget Variance Analysis.

1991 – 1993   **Accountant** (Senior)
MAGAZINE PUBLISHING COMPANY, San Francisco, CA
—Responsibilities included both ____ and ____ magazines.
—Reported to the Controller.
—Acted as Controller during a 3-month period.
—Supervised a Junior Accountant and clerical support staff.
Duties included:
—Preparation of Financial Statements for both magazines.
—Monthly closings and year-end adjustments.
—Analysis of General Ledger accounts, and Budgeting and Operating reports.
—Preparation of monthly Cash Flow reports.
—Preparation of automated Payroll, Tax returns, and Pension Plans.
—Attendance at editorial cost and pricing meetings.
—Used PC and Lotus 1-2-3.

Accomplishments:

• Inherited a "messy" situation in Billing and A/R departments; caught up with backlogs of work and achieved the efficiency required for timely and accurate reporting.
• Collaborated with Systems department to refine and modify the existing Billing system.

1993 – Present   **Accounts Payable Clerk**
APPAREL MANUFACTURER, New York, NY
—Report to the Controller.
—Work in a computerized accounting environment.
—Check all incoming vendor invoices and statements.
—Verify the accuracy of extensions.
—Reconcile Accounts Payable.
—Prepare A/P and A/R schedules.
—Write out checks for payment.

Achievement:

• Saved the company money by monitoring discounts.

1991 – Present   **Administrative Manager**
MAJOR FILM DISTRIBUTORS, Los Angeles, CA
—Formulate administrative policies and procedures, including establishing guide-lines and approving expenses.
—Design and implement cost-reduction programs.
—Submit quarterly reports to substantiate results.

• Achieved the following cost savings during past 12 months:

Advertising	**9%**	($121,052)
Air Cargo/Shipping	**24%**	(75,245)
Limousine & Car Services	**13%**	(19,440)
Medical Benefits (negotiated Health Plan)	**16%**	(45,040)
Messenger Services	**12%**	(6,629)
Production Costs	**11%**	(160,712)
Purchases (Office Supplies & Equipment)	**32%**	(47,861)
Travel	**12%**	(122,702)

• By renegotiating maintenance contracts, achieved a 15% reduction in fees.

1990 – Present   **Auditor (Senior)**
"BIG 6" C.P.A. FIRM, Washington, DC

Auditing duties and responsibilities include:
—Plan and execute audits, including:
    Property development company
    Freight forwarding company
    Manufacturing company
    Large importer for the retail industry

—Develop audit programs and schedule and supervise audits.
—Study, evaluate, and report on internal accounting control taken as a whole.
—System review and system note.
—Study, evaluate and report on a large internal audit department.
—Prepare reports on agreed-upon procedures.
—Conduct site visits.
—Review and prepare reports for Audit Managers.

• Recommend system development to reduce costs and paperwork.

1990 – Present **Banking Operations Supervisor**
MAJOR COMMERCIAL BANK, Boston, MA
—Report to the Assistant Vice President, Operations.
—Provide technical support and training to 4 Supervisors.
—Act as liaison between Administration and Operations.
—Review workflow procedures and controls in order to evaluate their adequacy and identify areas for improvement.

Accomplishments:

- Incoming calls (from Branches) regarding missing checks and deposits were previously received in one section and then transmitted to a Processing Department. By consolidating these two functions, achieved a greatly reduced response turnaround time (from 7 days to 24 hours)—and with 20% fewer personnel.
- By streamlining procedures to eliminate unnecessary paperwork, succeeded in reducing overtime worked by clerks by 30%.

1993 – Present **Bookkeeper** (Full-charge)
LARGE MEDICAL PRACTICE, Baltimore, MD
—Prepare General Ledger through Trial Balance.
—Prepare Financial Statement supporting schedules.
—Perform Bank Reconciliations.
—Responsible for Accounts Receivable, Billing, and Collections.
—File State and City tax returns.
—Supervise Assistant Bookkeeper and A/R clerk.

Accomplishment:

- Converted manual A/R and Billings to computerized system.

1991 – Present **Buyer/Purchasing Agent**
MANUFACTURERS OF APPLIANCES, Cleveland, OH
—Responsible for purchasing: chemicals .. electrical supplies .. hydraulic supplies .. instruments .. lubricants .. material handling equipment .. mechanical parts .. plant services .. power transmission products .. metals .. office equipment .. hardware supplies.
—Use "Just-in-time" buying system.
—Manage and maintain an inventory of $3 million.
—Select vendors, evaluate bids, and negotiate procurement contracts.
—Coordinate purchasing of capital items with Engineering Department.
—Use IBM 38 System to generate purchase orders and run reports for planning and forecasting.

Accomplishments:

- By successfully implementing the latest Contract Buying techniques, have reduced the number of vendors from 110 to 61 and have negotiated volume discounts due to greater purchasing "clout." (Savings of up to 20%.)
- Have saved the company $100,000 annually by switching from expensive brand names to generic products.

1991 – Present **Controller**

MANUFACTURERS AND DISTRIBUTORS, Newark, NJ

$15 million annual business volume

—Report to the President.

—Member of management team; involved in policy making.

—Areas of responsibility include: Financial Statements .. Cash Flow Projections .. Budgeting .. Forecasting .. Monitoring of all expenditures.

—Oversee the Accounting Department.

—Manage all administrative functions and Benefit programs.

Accomplishments:

- Reduced average Product Cost 2–3% by renegotiating purchasing agreements and prices, and securing better terms.
- Reduced the Product Line from 270 to 100 items, resulting in reduced overhead and increased profitability.

1990 – Present **Credit & Collections Manager**

MANUFACTURER AND DISTRIBUTOR, Miami, FL

—Report to the Vice President, Finance.

—Investigate and approve new accounts, which range from larger corporate accounts to medium and smaller operations; also U.S. Government accounts.

—Credit approval authority is $100,000.

—Perform extensive credit analysis; review and evaluate accounts on a continuing basis; prepare reports.

—Responsible for collection of $8.5 million in receivables.

—Design and implement more effective systems and procedures to facilitate credit approval and collections.

—Perform extensive financial analysis .. adjustment and reconciliation of accounts .. verification of chargebacks.

—Liaison with attorneys and outside collection agencies.

Accomplishments:

- Reduced number and amount of bad debts by 32%.
- Reduced average collection time from 80 to 65 days.

1992 – Present **Designer** (Sportswear)

APPAREL MANUFACTURER, Los Angeles, CA

—Work with Design Director and team of designers to develop seasonal concepts for: Blouses . Jackets . Skirts & Pants . Dresses.

—Research styling and print ideas.

—Shop print resources.

—Develop special fabric ideas with mills.

—Collaborate with art studios in recoloring prints and developing plaids and stripes.

—Develop trimmings, including novelty items such as crests, buttons, and braids.

—Create embroideries for blouses and jackets.

—Approve lab dips and strike-offs.

—Work with patternmakers.
—Oversee the Design Room.

Accomplishments:

- Coordinated fabrics, styles, embroidery details, and trimmings for first samples of 50-piece blouse line.
- Private Label projects for major department stores and catalog.

1990 - Present **Design Director**
TEXTILE INDUSTRY—PRINT CONVERTER, Manhattan, NY
—Responsible for creating salable product for three different consumer levels: Catalog . Retail Stores . Boutiques.
—Develop and execute designs, from initial concept to final fabric.
—Major clients include: ____, ____, and ____.
—Initiate and build relationships with potential clients.
—Make product and concept presentations to manufacturers.
—Hire, direct and oversee in-house as well as freelance artists.
—Supervise production of piecegoods, coloring and engraving, including on-site supervision of mill production.
—Collaborate with mills to develop new fabrications.
—Forecast fashion trends (patterns, colors, fabrications) and keep abreast of current trends through constant research in the U.S. and overseas.

Accomplishments:

- Designed and produced more than 150 successful designs in fabric and vinyl for products at different price-points.
- Expanded the customer base into new areas (from converting shower curtains and table linens to curtains, drapery, bedspreads, and comforters).

1989 – Present **Engineer**
TELECOMMUNICATIONS CORPORATION, Toronto, Canada
—Responsible for effective operation of an international link.
—Prepare and submit system performance reports to Manager.
—Assist in planning and supervision of the installation; commission new circuits and/or systems.
—Perform major tests on systems in the International Communications Division.
—Assist with the division's budget planning.
—Supervise junior technicians on shifts.

Achievement:

- A failure of international communications system occurred due to faults on two independent (yet identical) tropospheric scatter transmitting paths. Devised a way to interconnect the working sections of each within hours instead of waiting days for replacement parts. The reduced downtime and replacement costs resulted in savings of thousands of dollars.

1992 – Present **Environmental Engineer**
METAL MANUFACTURING COMPANY (2 Facilities), Dover, DE
—Report to the Director of Facilities Engineering.
—Prepare the complex semiannual Pre-Treatment reports (using the Combined Waste Streams formula) for two facilities: Rod Mill and Hot Mill/Pickling.
—Designed Spray Tank to recycle water in pickling line.
—Recommended submerged injection for acid dumping to eliminate emission of brown fumes (nitrous oxide).
—Designed a simple submerged Sensor System to replace a circulating pump, thereby avoiding pump failures and regulating pH within acceptable DEP limits.
—Familiar with the provisions of RCRA, including Record and Pre-Treatment standards.
—Organize shipments of plant waste.
—Acquired knowledge of Water Treatment Plant Operations.

Achievement:

• Took the initiative to design and implement an Acid Hydrolysis process to treat an alkali cleaner (4,000 gallons) in own treatment plants and within the minimum nickel limits, thereby saving the company approximately $30,000 annually. Successfully overcame a coagulation problem.

1992 – 1993 **Financial Analyst/Capital Markets Accountant**
COMMERCIAL BANK, Chicago, IL
—Assisted a Senior Financial Analyst.
—Calculated principal and interest payments due on Bonds.
—Booked dividends on Common Stock.
—Received intensive training covering all aspects of specialized securities.
—Handled approx. $400 million in Asset Backed Security Bonds (ABS).
—Acquired a thorough understanding of the nature of cash flows.
—Managed an additional $350 million in Mortgage Backed Securities (MBS).
—Learned the nature of prepayment speeds and how to calculate the value of Bonds with different prepayment speeds (PSA).

Accomplishment:

• Was promoted very rapidly and given some of the responsibilities of my superior officer.

1990 – Present **Finance and Credit Analyst**
FACTORS CORPORATION, New York, NY
—Supervise and maintain the credit files of manufacturers and wholesalers of Men's, Women's, and Children's apparel and home furnishings.
—Areas of responsibility include setting credit limits, and analyzing and revising credit files.
—Supervise investigators and collectors.

• Have kept losses below maximum allowed.

1991 – Present **Chief Financial Officer**
TRANSPORTATION SERVICE, Denver, CO
—Responsible for day-to-day management of Finance, Administration, and Operations—the latter jointly with a V.P.
—Main responsibilities are to ensure timely and correct billings; to improve the cash flow situation; to renegotiate contracts with labor unions, insurance companies, and for the delivery and maintenance of a fleet of 75 motor vehicles.
—Oversee a staff of 110 (operations, accounting, clerical).
—Produce quarterly financial reports and statements.
—Interact frequently with government agencies.

Accomplishments:

• Reduced total expenditures $125,000 in first nine months by reducing insurance costs and through effective use and scheduling of manpower and motor vehicles.
• Reduced monthly cash commitments significantly by initiating a more favorable Fleet Purchasing/Leasing Program.
• Realized additional income from unused warehouse space.

1992 – Present **Labor Analyst**
MAJOR HOTEL CHAIN, Las Vegas, NV
—Work in the area of Operations Management Services.
—Assist with the development, implementation, and maintenance of effective labor control and business forecasting systems.
—Analyze descriptions of functions performed, organization charts, and project information to determine more precisely the exact duties and responsibilities of various employees and individual work units.
—Identify areas of overlap in duties and responsibilities.
—Establish work measurement programs and make sample observations of work to develop standards of manpower utilization.
—Make recommendations for reorganizing work units as well as individual job duties to increase efficiency and eliminate excess processing steps and labor costs.

Accomplishment:

• As a result of labor studies conducted in Front Services, Front Office, VIP Services, Guest Services, Reservations, and Retail Operations, annualized cost savings of $350,000 have been achieved.

1992 – Present **Lawyer (Corporate)**
MAJOR LAW FIRM, Washington, DC
—Significant transactional experience with emphasis on financings, including complex private placements and equipment lease financings, other secured/unsecured financings, loan workouts, and mergers and acquisitions.
—Securities law experience, including preparation of registration statements and related documentation in connection with public securities offerings and mergers, as well as SEC compliance work.
—Bank regulatory experience and involvement in advising both business and not-for-profit corporations.

1991 – Present **Manager—Restaurant**
FAST FOODS AND BAR (One of well-known chain of restaurants), Seattle, WA
Assigned to troubleshoot and turn around a high-volume situation and bar that had been running in the red for three years; seating for 280; American cuisine; gross sales of $1.4 to $2 million annually.
—Analyzed food and liquor costs (grosses) to pinpoint potential areas of loss or wastage.
—Estimated daily sales and forecast staff requirements in order to reduce the labor cost %.
—Started up "pull & prep" sheets in order to improve portion control and reduce or eliminate waste.
—Established "par" levels (standards).
—Kept a perpetual inventory of "ins" and "outs" to eliminate free pouring.
—Maintained strict security on all deliveries and requisitions.
—Ensured high food service and quality control standards.

Accomplishments:

• Restored the outlet to profitability.
• Food Costs: Achieved 41% net.

Liquor Costs: Achieved 24% net.
Labor Costs: Achieved 30% (gross).

1987 – Present **Manager—Retail**
RETAIL STORE CHAIN, Dallas, TX

<u>Store in the Stage Coach Mall</u> (1990 – Present)
—Successfully revamped and reorganized a rundown 3,900-sq.-ft. store with a high shrinkage problem.
—Rehired and retrained new staff of 8.
—Remerchandised the store according to customer profiles.
—Improved all aspects of day-to-day store operations.

<u>Store in the Highwayman's Mall</u> (1987 – 1990)
—A two-level store on 16,000 sq. ft.
—Reponsible for store operations; supervised 23.
—Implemented improved controls and security.
—Expedited movement of merchandise to selling floor.

<u>Accomplishments:</u>

- Reduced shrinkage from 9.8% to 3.9% by implementing tighter controls and security.
- Increased monthly sales by 40% (on average) by streamlining and coordinating merchandising in order to have goods on sale within 24 hours.

1992 – Present **Marketing Analyst**
MARKETING RESEARCH FIRM, Los Angeles, CA
—Identify marketing opportunities for consumer packaged goods companies, mainly X CORP.
—Handle: "Sniff" deodorants and "Ouch" hair removal products.
—Develop and present bimonthly segmental analyses based on: Pricing .. Sales Volume/Share .. Distribution .. Causal Support.
—Analyze such data to advise where Sales Representatives should try to acquire a greater share of shelf space for X products.
—Computer software utilized: Lotus 1–2–3 . Metaphor . Scanfact . Scanfact PC . Harvard Graphics.

<u>Achievements:</u>

- Developed techniques to measure the cost effectiveness of in-store promotions for two products.
- Created new programs for more efficient data retrieval that enabled client to receive its reports six days earlier.

1990 – Present **Medical Administrator** (Hospital Supply)
MAJOR HOSPITAL, Chicago, IL
—Responsible for day-to-day management and administration of a department that processes requests for supplies of ____.
—Areas of responsibility include: staffing .. budget preparation .. in-service education .. staff evaluation .. quality assurance.
—Oversee 3 Supervisors and 25 auxilliaries/technicians.
—Evaluate staff and create and implement motivational programs to increase their efficiency and reduce absenteeism.

Accomplishments:

• Initiated and conducted a <u>Productivity Time Study</u> project to analyze the time taken by staff to produce specific items. Set performance standards for evaluating the efficiency of individuals. Resulted in an overall increase in productivity of 8–11%.

• Initiated and conducted a <u>statistical survey</u> to determine the percentage of unsatisfactory units produced and calculated a Quality Index for each employee. Due to timely identification of those responsible for errors, additional training was provided and disciplinary measures taken. Error rate dropped from 15% to near zero, resulting in elimination of frustrating delays and downtime.

1992 – Present **Medical Secretary/Assistant Office Manager**
MEDICAL PRACTICE, Columbus, OH
—Work in a large and busy Ob/Gyn practice (20-25 deliveries per month); high volume of patient traffic.
—Perform duties of Office Manager during her absences.
—Operate in a fully computerized office (IBM compatible equipment—The Synapse Medical System).
—Schedule and coordinate patient appointments for Office Visits/Surgery/Labs.
—Duties include: Patient Billing .. Patient Accounts .. Claim Forms .. Insurance Billing .. Collections .. Bookkeeping.
—Assist with minor office surgery.
—Commenced as <u>Medical Assistant</u> (1987).

Achievement:

• By effectively screening patients (per telephone and in person), have enabled doctors to use time more productively.

1993 – Present   **Paralegal** (Litigation)
LAW OFFICE, Portland, OR
—Work in a small law office (five attorneys).
—Assist in all phases of litigation.
—Conduct both legal and nonlegal reasearch.
—Attend depositions and compose detailed summaries of proceedings.
—Examine and select materials at document productions.
—Organize and index documents obtained during discovery.
—Maintain court papers and memorandums.
—Prepare court exhibits.
—Attend trials.

1988 – Present   **Program Director**
REHABILITATION FACILITY, San Francisco, CA
—Report to Executive Director.
—Responsible for management and administration of a large housing program for psychiatrically disabled persons.
—Program includes housing of 175 psychiatrically disabled men and women in residential settings (from 24-hour supervised residences to scattered-site independent apartments).
—Responsible for operating budget of $3.2 million.
—Write grant proposals to secure funds from federal, state, and city agencies, as well as from private foundations.
—Oversee a staff of 55 (Social Workers . Rehabilitation Counselors . B.A. graduates specializing in Mental Health).
—Interact extensively with other agencies.

Accomplishment:

• Raised nearly $500,000 from private sources.

1992 – Present   **Programmer/Analyst**
INFORMATION SYSTEMS, Philadelphia, PA
—Report to Director of Information Systems.
—75% of duties involve: Analysis . Design . Coding . Programming.
—Lead a training team that assists end users on site in various cities.
—Collaborate with two other Programmer/Analysts.
—Client base includes: NYSE .. ____ Stock Exchange .. NASD .. ____ Insurance .. ____ Bank .. Brokerage Houses .. AB&C Advertising .. City of ____.

Accomplishments:

• Designed, coded, and set up a major Autoquote System that assisted the sales force by speeding up the turnaround time for bids. It became possible to do in one hour what had previously taken the Estimating Department 2–3 weeks.

1993 – Present   **Public Relations Officer**
THE FAMINE RELIEF PROJECT, New York, NY
—Responsible for day-to-day management and administration of the New York office.
—Liaison with other offices worldwide.
—Duties include project management, special events, and fundraising.

Achievements:

• Managed the participants in a Film Project concerning Famine Relief in Africa.
• Organized special events to publicize and promote The Famine Relief Project, including Announcement and Award Ceremonies at the United Nations.
• Organized successful Benefit Movie Premiere and Reception; enrolled new donors and raised pledges; responsible for all publicity. Obtained good media coverage.

8

CONSTRUCTING THE TOOLS YOU NEED TO FIND A JOB IN THE '90s

If buildings were constructed like most resumes, King Kong would have destroyed the world.
  —DR. JEFFREY ALLEN, *How to Turn an Interview into a Job* [1]

Many employers complain about carelessly organized, unfocused, or poorly written resumes.
  —ROBERT WENDOVER, "How Recruiters Judge Resumes" [24]

Let's organize your job search equipment. In this chapter, there is very little for you to read but much to refer to. You'll see how to construct the most important tools you will need for finding work in today's job market: job resumes, cover notes, salary history, references, fax cover sheet, and thank-you letters. You will also be shown how to target help-wanted ads.

Starting at the top of your job resume, there are many ways to present your name, address, and telephone number(s). On the next two pages are eleven different headings to help you save one, two, or three lines of valuable resume space.

To construct the body of your resume, you'll need to organize your data into suitable resume categories (or sections). Again, you are given many options. For example, there are four names to use for your Skills Summary and just as many for Work Experience. In short, you'll learn how to structure this important document.

ELEVEN DIFFERENT LAYOUTS
(For One-Page and Two-Page Resumes)

JOHN R. DOE
100 Smith Street #4-B
Edison, NJ 08818
(908) 000-0000

This popular, *centered* layout requires a total of 4½ lines. There's a 1½ space between the Name and the Address. Note also that there are *two* spaces between JOHN and R. and another *two* spaces before DOE.

MARY-ELLEN DOE

100 Smith Street #4-B
Edison, NJ 08818   (908) 441-0000

This alternative layout saves you an entire line!

If you want employers to leave *messages*, type your answering machine/service number after your address:

LESLIE M. DOE

100 Smith Street #4-B
Edison, NJ 08818   Messages: (212) 544-0000

If you are still attending *college*:

JOAN GRADUATE

Permanent Address: School Address:
21 Larch Hill Road   2049 S. Carrolton
Livingston, NJ 07039   New Orleans, LA 70148
(201) 239-0000   (604) 681-0000

If you are planning to *relocate*:

RALPH RELOCATOR

New York Address: Atlanta Address:
1033 Lincoln Place #4-F   Del Monte Apartments #J-2
Brooklyn, NY 11213   330 Brown Lee Road
Res: (718) 385-0000   Atlanta, GA 30311
Bus: (212) 608-0000   Messages: (404) 699-0000

If you need to save *two* lines:

Where *two* telephone numbers are given, a good layout is

SALLY SUPERVISOR

1541 Ward Avenue #4   Res: (718) 440-0000
Bronx, NY 10463   Bus: (212) 555-0000

This layout saves *two* lines, is neat and has eye appeal. (1½ space between Name and Address; ½ space *after* Address.)

JANE ELEGANT

210 Simpson Boulevard, Boston, MA 02116 • (617) 820-0000

This layout is both elegant and very economical. Only *two* lines are required instead of four! (There is a 1½ space between the Name and the Address.)

But if the street address is too long, shift the phone number:

MARK RICHARDS

(718) 554-0000   4711 Great Eastern Street, Middle Village, NY 10077

If you like this heading but have *two* phone numbers:

SUSAN JONES   66 East 114th Street #14-R, New York, NY 10046

Res: (212) 481-0000; Bus: (201) 667-0000

If you prefer a *centered* heading:

MARK RICHARDS

4711 Great Eastern Street • Middle Village, NY 10077 • (718) 554-0000

A centered address uses an extra line:

SUSAN JONES

66 East 114th Street #14-R, New York, NY 10046
Res: (212) 481-0000; Bus: (201) 667-0000

RESUME CATEGORIES
(ONE-PAGE RESUME)

Here are a selection of alternative categories for use in compiling a one-page resume for most types of work. The wide range of options available will help you be creative in presenting your unique "ingredients" and write more than one resume. Many items of similar information (such as several awards) will usually justify the use of a separate category.

The *order* in which you present them can vary. It depends mainly on what will interest employers the most and should therefore appear first.

Note: Job seekers with several years' work experience and/or those with impressive achievements will usually require a two-page resume. Because the design and construction of a two-pager differs so greatly from a one-pager, this is dealt with in another chapter devoted entirely to the subject of two-page resumes and who should use them. (See pages 132 to 156.)

RESUME CATEGORIES

(One-Page Resumes)

OBJECTIVE: State the level and type of the position you seek. Offer your *three* strongest skills. Offer value. (See Chapter 4.)

SUMMARY: Record your skills, strengths, and achievements. (See Chapters 5 and 6.)

STRENGTHS: Record your skills, strengths and achievements.

QUALIFIED BY: Show what qualifies you for the job.

QUALIFICATIONS: Interpret what you're offering.

PERSONAL SKILLS: Suitable only for actors and junior clerical positions.

EDUCATION: NAME OF SCHOOL or COLLEGE, City, State
... **Degree in** ... [major/minor]   [date of graduation or anticipated graduation]
Certificate of Completion in [subject]   [date of graduation]
Related coursework:
[course A, course B]
Honors & Awards: •   G.P.A. = 3.5; Cum Laude
Projects:
Special Papers:
Activities:

(See Chapter 11 for suitable samples.)

HONORS & AWARDS: (See p. 175)

COMPUTER SKILLS:
Hardware:
Software:
Applications:

(See page 69.)

STUDENT PROJECTS: NAME OF COLLEGE, City, State
• Description of best project (Give grade if A or B)
• Description of another project (individual or class)

(See Chapter 11 for suitable samples.)

INTERNSHIPS: (See pp. 160 and 169)

EXPERIENCE: If related to your Job Objective. (See Chapter 1.)

EMPLOYMENT: If *not* related to your Job Objective. (See Chapter 11.)

STUDENT EMPLOYMENT: If unrelated but to help fund tuition costs. (See Chapter 12.)

TESTIMONIAL: Extract(s) from letter(s) of recommendation. (See pages 67, 113–14 and 216).

TEACHERS' COMMENTS: Extracts from letters that mention your skills and strengths.

INTERESTS: Have you climbed Mt. McKinley in Alaska? (Only long-term interests.)

ACTIVITIES: Leadership activities (might be better under Education).

MEMBERSHIPS: Never record anything political, activist, or religious.

LANGUAGE SKILLS: Fluent in _____ and _____; working knowledge of _____.
French (speak, read, and write); Italian (conversational).
Bilingual (English/Spanish).

TRAVEL: Names of countries visited; names of destinations.

PERSONAL: [Date of Birth], [Marital Status], Excellent health (if not excellent, omit).

REFERENCES: Available upon request; Furnished upon request.

PORTFOLIO: Available upon request.

VIDEO CASSETTE: Available upon request.

DEMO TAPES: Available upon request.

SHOW REELS: Available upon request.

CLIP FILE: Available upon request.

DISCOGRAPHY: Available upon request.

TAPES: Available upon request.

COVER NOTE

Accompany your job resume with a brief cover note—to route it to the right party or department. The sample letter on page 104 has already been used successfully by thousands of job seekers. (They were hired.)

The letter itself contains no "sell" because that has already been transferred to the Summary section of the resume. It only tells the reader why you are writing, where you heard about the position, and who should be reading your resume.

More importantly, it is in this note that you should state your *salary requirements*—if, and only if, this is required of you. Otherwise, omit. (Note that a *range* of $5,000–6,000 should be given—not wider.) The phrase "depending on the scope of my duties, benefit package," and so on, will make it possible for you to raise your top figure later at the job interview, especially if the benefits package being offered is less than you're getting at present.

SALARY HISTORY

A formal salary history is often requested in help-wanted ads. It should be recorded on a separate sheet of paper. Because this is often used to screen out applicants, you must be very careful how you write it. As a rule, state only your *base* salary and omit your bonuses, incentives, commissions, or benefit packages. (This gives you the option to *understate* your total earnings or not to disclose any item at the subsequent interview. Such a strategy is sometimes necessary because high earnings are a turn-off to payroll-conscious recruiters.) A sample salary history is given on page 105.

A Very Special Note: In the new job market, the entire issue of salary has become a sore point with many job seekers. Employers are determined to reduce their payroll and cut benefits. So, while they continue to offer challenging positions, they are usually for less money. Unfortunately, many job seekers define a "good" job as a well-paying one and have not yet adjusted their expectations to the changed world we are living in. The reality is that in the new global economy even the most prestigious companies will simply export jobs or use off-shore facilities if domestic labor costs are too high. This poses a threat to all highly paid professionals. (*The Wall Street Journal*, March 17, 1993) And don't overlook the fact that due to automation, a two-year degree is the new requirement in many industrial and laboratory jobs—not a four-year degree as before. This means a lower starting salary.

I mention this because leading employment experts have expressed the view that many worthwhile positions on their books remain unfilled because applicants demand more than companies might be willing to pay. [42] Unfortunately, some might have unrealistic notions of what they ought to be paid. What do they base their salary expectations on? In a free market economy, prices, salaries, and wages are determined by supply and demand. That is why in today's buyer's market, some employers are suggesting that former IBMers were highly overpaid. (*U.S. News & World Report*, June 28, 1993)

It is therefore important for some job seekers to rachet down their expectations in their covering notes. They should also be careful not to disclose more than is necessary in their formal salary histories.

COVERING NOTE TO ROUTE YOUR RESUME
(As Used By Thousands of Successful Job Seekers)

MARTIN P. SMITH

48 Colonial Road #2-D • New Haven, CT 60617 • Messages: (203) 637-0000

Date

Name (or The Advertiser)
Title
Company Name   **Attention:**_____ Department
Street Address (or Box No.)
City, State, Zip Code

Position:_____

Dear _____:

I am applying for the above position as advertised in the _____ of ____/____/____ and enclose a copy of my most recent resume for your consideration and review. For your convenience, a summary of my skills, strengths, and achievements is presented in the resume.

All in all, I feel confident that I would be a good "fit" for the position and a strong asset to your company. I look forward to meeting with you. In any event, I will phone you early next week to confirm that you have received my resume and cover note.

Sincerely,

Martin P. Smith

SALARY REQUIREMENTS
(Only If Requested; Otherwise, Omit)

This would range from $31,000 to $36,000, depending on the scope of my duties and responsibilities, benefit package, and incentives. [Do *not* give a range of more than $5,000–6,000.]

Encl. Resume

(Salary history)

Note: Please do *not* address this letter to "Dear Hiring Executive" or "Good Morning." It's easy enough to phone the company's human resources department and ask who's in charge of a specific search. Then address your correspondence to that person. It might impress that party to see that you already know his or her name! [13] And if you don't hear from them within 4–6 weeks, don't hesitate to mail your resume again. They are *not* likely to notice this.

JOHN (JANE) EXECUTIVE

Salary History

Position		Salary
THE GREEN & GOLD CORPORATION		
Chief Financial Officer and V.P.	– Present	$70,000
WHITE, BLUE & BROWN, INC.		
C.F.O. and Controller	– 1990	$60,000
	– 1987	$57,500
BLACK & SMITH LIMITED		
Controller	– 1986	$50,000
	– 1985	$46,500
BROWN AND JONES, INC.		
Senior Accountant	– 1984	$42,500

Note: Above figures are base salaries only and do *not* include benefit packages or other compensation.

THE THANK-YOU LETTER—THE MOST IMPORTANT LETTER TO WRITE

It is a well-known fact that within the first sixty minutes after your job interview, up to 85 percent of what was said will have been forgotten! But what about the fact that employers might also forget your name, who you were, and what you looked like? After all, no one took an instant Polaroid photo of you at the interview.

That is why the most important thing you can do after meeting with an employer is to write him or her a "please remember me" letter, which is usually referred to as a "thank-you" letter. It can clinch it for you.

There are *five* good reasons for writing one to every employer you meet with: The first reason for writing a thank-you note within twenty-four hours is to make them recall you and your name. Call it an exercise in name recognition. When a decision has to be made, you will be remembered more clearly than the other candidates.

The second reason is that the employer likes to know that you are still interested in him/her and his/her company or firm. The third reason is to give you an opportunity to mention any achievement or accomplishment of yours (or ability) that will help you do the job well. (It might have been overlooked at the interview.) The best type of information to give is to state how you solved a similar problem for a previous employer. (Refer to the advice given on page 30.)

The fourth reason for writing a follow-up letter is to make a favorable impression as a person who follows up things that need to be done. It's like following up a sales lead, and is a valuable skill to demonstrate.

The fifth reason is to confirm how interested you are in the position. Enthusiasm for the challenges of the job counts for a lot! And your politeness and good manners will also be appreciated. That is the thank-you bit. Everything else about the letter is *sales*!

All things being equal, writing such a thank-you letter on the *same* day as the interview will maximize your chances of being appointed. (So don't forget to ask for his or her full name and address.) A sample thank-you letter is given on page 107.

EMILY ENERGETIC

176–50 71 Road, Kew Gardens, NY 11367 • (718) 544-8000

Date

Name
Title
Company Name
Street Address
City, State, Zip Code

Dear _____:

Thank you for seeing me on ____ regarding the _____ position. Since your company is in a start-up situation, the duties of the position are challenging, and I am very enthusiastic about the possibilities of being involved in broader areas.

When my present [previous] employer needed to look for new business, I initiated and executed a very successful telemarketing project that increased our customer base by 25 percent. I feel confident that I could put such skills to work in your company as well because of my relationship-building skills with people in the industry.

All in all, I came away very impressed by [company name], and would like to thank you again for your time and your courtesy.

Sincerely,

[Sign your name]

STATIONERY

To write your *cover notes*, use first-class bond paper with a 25% cotton fiber content such as:

24lb French linen embossed (white)
24lb Strathmore Bright White (laid)
24lb Alpine Nuance Irish linen (white)
24lb Eaton Bright White (laid)

To print your *resumes*, use top quality bond paper such as:

24lb Strathmore White (actually off-white)
24lb Strathmore Ivory (laid)
24lb French linen embossed (off-white)
24lb Fox River Circa 83 Lamplighter Ivory

All these papers will give you an excellent finish on any good copier. However, should you wish to have them laser-printed, consult a laser-printing professional for the best kind of paper to use. (The process is different.)

For mailing a one-page resume and cover note, my own preference is that the letter be white and the resume off-white. I always suggest *different* colors to those mailing a two-page resume. Why? Because having three pages in the same color might give the reader the impression that it's a three-page resume which is usually a no-no (except for senior executives).

A pastel color such as light gray French linen embossed is also elegant, and believe it or not, some very eyecatching and successful resumes have been printed on white, gray, or natural parchment! (60 lb Parchtone) Readers have been intrigued by the marbled texture of the paper.

A very important item of stationery is a black, *fine-tip pen*. Why? How will you create the black bullets for your resume? How will you make five to ten of them for your Skills Summary and a further three to five to highlight your accomplishments? The answer is to type either a small "°" or a larger "o" and then to ink them in carefully. But, please don't overdo the use of bullets. They are intended to highlight your selling points—*not* your job duties. (There, I've given away a trade secret!)

And *envelopes*? All this talk of matching envelopes is so much poppycock. They will only impress the wastebasket. (The only exception is in the case of top-level executives.) A far better idea is for your resume to arrive *unfolded*—looking as sharp as the day it was printed. Use plain white or brown Manila envelopes for this purpose, size 9″ x 12″. For those who demand the best, there is Survivor Stock #R1460. It comes only in white, size 9″ x 12″, but has enough eye appeal to charm any secretary and it has a velvety, textured silk finish.

REFERENCES

Prepare a separate sheet of paper to list two to four of your business and professional references. It's much more professional to be prepared for the interviewer than to fumble in your pockets or handbag for those slips of paper. Record your particulars as follows:

JOHN (JANE) SMITH

<u>References</u>

First and Last Names of Referee
Job Title
Name of Company, Firm or Institution
City, State
(000) 000-000

TWO PAIRS OF WALKING SHOES

Shoes are part of your wardrobe. So why don't I head this section "Wardrobe"? Because in today's labor market the success of your job search campaign may well hinge on how much walking and talking you do. Of course, I do expect you to look sharp at all times. How else can you expect people to refer you to their friends or to someone who is hiring?

Try to leave some leather on the pavements of your city or town. I am a strong believer in dropping off resumes in person. You never know who you'll meet, and employers respect this direct and confident approach. You can so easily be the warm body they're looking to hire! This is how Peter F., a former marine, was hired as Operations Manager of a Big 10 advertising agency and Betty S. managed to get three job offers in one week!

MEETING YOUR FUTURE BOSS

White-collar workers should consult John Molloy's *Dress for Success* books (for males and females) to get an idea of what would be the most appropriate items to wear. The general rule is dress conservatively.

Let me add my own two cents' worth. No heavy perfume. No heavy makeup. No chunky jewelry. And not a ton of overpowering after-shave lotion or cologne. A diamond in one's nose might look a little too "foreign" and a stud in a man's ear might send the wrong signal to an interviewer.

Above all, be friendly, energetic, and enthusiastic. Practice the Great American Handshake—not a "bone crusher" like they do in Texas nor the Chassidic or Oriental "deadfish" variety. Nor should your hands be wet and clammy. Are you nervous? Why? Can't you do the job? Job opportunities get lost because a handshake fails to communicate energy and confidence.

Never display anger. Never be resentful. Never be cynical. Don't complain. Don't criticize others and certainly not your previous employer. Don't be "bossy." Don't highjack the interview. Don't interrupt. Don't slouch. Try to sit as close to the interviewer as possible—upright at the edge of his or her desk. And don't look at your watch. It's rude!

For the benefit of newcomers to America, the secret of success is to S-M-I-L-E. An employment interview is a teeth-to-teeth confrontation between you and the interviewer. A smile shows you are confident. It helps to disarm an aggressive interviewer. So, relax and don't be intimidated. The interviewer is probably just as nervous as you are. Always remember: a barking dog will back off if you show no signs of fear. A straight-in-the-eye smile will similarly disarm many a tough employer. Above all, never put yourself down (see p. 213).

TELEPHONE

Frankly, every job searcher should first spend one or two weeks in some telemarketing "boiler room." There you'll learn to work from a script in selling subscriptions for a newspaper or whatever. And using the phone daily to make cold calls will cure you of the "stage fright" people experience when having to call an employer.

After you've done some selling, you'll understand that it's foolish to try to "wing" it without a prepared script, and you'll probably know what to say when you phone an employer between 8 A.M. and 9 A.M. or between 5 P.M. and 7 P.M. That's when the secretary isn't there to screen your call.

Be persistent and don't hesitate to play on the employer's emotions: "Mr. Jones, do you remember when you were looking for the first entry-level position and everyone told you you didn't have any 'experience'? I'm in that catch-22 situation right now, just like you once were."

And do record a professional message on your answering machine!

FAX COVER SHEET

This is the last job-search tool presented. (Although resumes have been faxed for ten years or so, I have not seen this type of cover sheet in any other resume manual!)

Although today's employers are interested mainly in a good job resume—more than any other document or sheet—the sample provided shows you how to help recruiters match up what you're offering against what they require. (This may be copied from help-wanted ads or internal postings, or from what you've been told or advised.) But before completing the "I offer" section, first read "Drafting your Selling Points" on pages 57–59. It shows you how to word those items. Also, look at the items in related Skills Summaries (pages 59 to 78).

If your age might be a problem, be careful. For example, you should write "More than 10 years' experience," but never mention a figure larger than that.

Above all, don't overstate your qualifications. They'll say you're overqualified! Try to be a perfect "fit."

Note: Wherever possible try to *avoid* having to fax your resume. As we have noted, fax printouts are awful and difficult to handle. Rather, deliver your printed resume by hand or messenger service, or follow up your faxed resume with a mailed one that is (laser) printed on quality "rag" paper.

FAX COVER SHEET

(PAGE ____ OF ____)

TO: _____ ATTENTION: _____

FIRM: _____

DEPT: _____ POSITION(S) INTERESTED IN:

TEL: _____ _____ / _____

FAX: _____

MY BEST ACHIEVEMENT(S):

_____

_____

_____

YOU REQUIRE: I OFFER: [Be a good "fit."]

1. _____ 1. ____ graduate; OR ____ Studies (To graduate:
                                 _____; ____ Credits)

2. _____ 2. ____ years' experience in ____
                                 OR More than ____ years' experience in ____
                                 OR Nearly ____ years' experience in ____

3. _____ 3. Expertise in:_____.
   _____   Knowledge of:_____
   _____   Award for:_____

4. _____ 4. Strong_____skills

5. _____ 5. Able to_____

6. _____ 6. Able to_____

FROM:_____

ADDRESS:_____

_____

TEL:_____(DAY)

[WARNING: DO NOT OVERQUALIFY YOURSELF!]

(See page 39, "Answering Help-Wanted Ads")

Part Three

WINNING
RESUMES
FOR THE '90s

9

ONE-PAGE RESUMES THAT MARKET YOUR TRANSFERABLE SKILLS

YES, the individual creates unemployment to the degree that he or she is stuck at the kitchen table not knowing his or her own abilities, or where to plug them in.

—TOM JACKSON, *Guerrilla Tactics in the Job Market* [3]

HOW TO CONSTRUCT A COMBINATION RESUME FROM "PARTS"

Let's learn to market your transferable skills. We'll see how a successful combination resume was constructed from the hundreds of winning "parts" provided in this book.

Julie Edwards (not her real name) had previously worked as a trader in a Chicago brokerage house. However, after six weeks of pounding the pavements of New York's Wall Street area, she decided to look for other work—as an administrative assistant or office manager.

However, her resume was still presenting her as a trader/broker, and Julie needed to market her other skills so as to project a different image to employers. What she had to offer outside her own field was not her past experience as a trader but her transferable office skills. Her resume's focus had to be changed.

First, she scanned the Skills Checklists on pages 24 to 28 and easily identified thirteen of her own skills and strengths. Next, she checked the sample Job Objectives on pages 48 and 49. She used these to draft her own. It was purposely wide.

She then scanned a few Summaries (see pages 7 and 145–146). These helped her select ten skills sentences to back up that objective. These "bullets" or selling points made up her Skills Summary.

Julie's next step was to present her administrative/office management duties and play down her trading activities. (She even adjusted a job title or two to reflect the duties she was choosing to emphasize. More on this subject later.)

Her final touch was to add even more value—a few words of praise written by a previous employer. (Why not?) Julie's combination resume helped her find employment in an entirely different field—as Medical Office Manager—even though her actual credentials were far from perfect.

A WINNING COMBINATION RESUME

The combination format allows you to select and present any combination of your skills and experience. Here's how Julie did it.

JULIE EDWARDS

OBJECTIVE: A position as **Administrative Assistant .. Office Manager .. Sales Liaison**. Offer strong "people," liaison, coordinating and problem-solving skills. Efficient and effective.

SUMMARY:
- A.A.S. degree in Administration and Accounting.
- Experience in Sales office operations/administration.
- Research, record keeping, and file maintenance.
- Aptitude for figures .. able to reconcile accounts and prepare statistical reports.
- Knowledge of routine Bookkeeping/Auditing procedures.
- Strong organizational, liaison, and follow-up skills.
- IBM PC .. Lotus 1–2–3 .. Multimate .. Light typing.
- Work well under pressure .. able to get the job done.

EXPERIENCE: **Administrator/Sales Liaison**
1990–1992   LEONARD P. BLAKE, INC., Chicago, IL
- —Provided administrative support to six traders.
- —Performed record keeping and general office duties.
- —Maintained daily statistical records; posted balances.
- —Updated computerized data; heavy phone contact.
- —Responsible for office equipment; ordered supplies.

1988–1989   **Administrative Assistant/Acting Office Manager**
UNITAS CAPITAL GROUP, INC., Chicago, IL
- —In charge during absences of the Office Manager.
- —Posted daily transactions; balanced inventory positions.
- —Researched and resolved discrepancies.

1987–1988   **Administrative/Accounting Clerk**
REPUBLIC TRUST COMPANY, Milwaukee, WI
- —Acted as client liaison and audited accounts.

EDUCATION: MILWAUKEE COMMUNITY COLLEGE, Milwaukee, WI
A.A.S. in Business Administration and Accounting (1986)

TESTIMONIAL: Written by Vice President (Previous Employer):
"Julie handles a crisis calmly and efficiently. She's a great team worker and thoroughly professional. Her 'people' skills are excellent." (Original letter available)

MORE SAMPLE RESUMES—ENTRY LEVEL TO MANAGEMENT

This chapter contains a selection of sample resumes. Each is a one-page combination resume. (A further selection of two-page resumes will be found in the next chapter, on pages 132 to 156. Some of you might need a longer presentation.)

Resumes for recent *college graduates* and career changers can be found in Chapter 11, on pages 157 to 175. (These are designed for those job seekers with little or no work experience.)

A final selection of *multiple resumes* appears in Chapter 12, "Targeting Jobs with Different Resumes." Here you will see how two to four different resumes can be constructed from the *same* education and work experience.

Each sample resume is a *marketing* tool. It has a "top" that sells—even without a cover letter. If you need to do so, it can be faxed, as is.

Although these samples cover many fields, your own type of work might not be addressed. Please don't worry. All you have to do is refer to the previous two pages and see what Julie Edwards did.

To summarize:

1. Discover your skills by doing the exercises on pages 21 to 23.
2. Look for a suitable Job Objective on pages 48 and 49.
3. Find a suitable Skills Summary on pages 59 to 78.
4. Search for a "bottom" (Experience) on pages 81 to 96.

With so many "parts" to copy or adapt, you can easily construct your own job resume—or two or three. It's almost like doing a jigsaw puzzle! To locate those sample "parts," turn to the Resume Finder on the next few pages.

(Only half of the resume samples presented in this chapter are of job seekers with a four-year college degree. The rest have either an Associate's degree or job-related courses to offer. Due to automation and software packages, a two-year degree is the requirement for many jobs today.)

THE RESUME FINDER: HOW TO FIND THE SAMPLES YOU NEED TO WRITE YOUR WINNING RESUME

On the next few pages is a Resume Finder. It will help you locate all of the resumes and resume "parts" that appear in the pages of this book, and will save you many hours of searching for something suitable to copy or adapt.

Column 1: Alphabetical list of job types.

Column 2: This gives you the number of the page(s) where an *entire* resume sample appears—from entry level to management. That will give you the Big Picture. A number in parenthesis (#) indicates that the resume is in a *related* field.

Column 3: Here you are advised where to find the *basic* skills that are often required of a particular type/level of position.

Column 4: In the fourth column you'll see where to find sample Job Objectives that can be copied or adapted in writing your own.

Column 5: To help you compile your selling points for a Skills Summary, please refer to a wide range of targeted summaries that have already worked for others.

Column 6: The last column refers you to suitable Job Descriptions for describing the duties and responsibilities you perform.

Note: Although a very wide range of samples is presented (by type and level of position), your own field or type of work might not be covered. In such a case, please select a field or type of work close to it and work from there. It's easier than you think!

Before writing a one-page resume, always refer first to the wide range of options available to you on pages 101 and 102. To construct a two-page resume, always refer to the model resume on pages 136 and 137, and to the additional options on pages 138 and 139.

RESUME FINDER

(SEE ALSO THE RESUME CATEGORIES AND OUTLINES ON PAGES 101–02, 136–37, AND 138–39.)

TYPE OF WORK/FIELD	RESUME	SKILLS	OBJECTIVE	SUMMARY	EXPERIENCE
Accountant (entry level)	—	24–26	45/47/54	54/(66)	85/131
Accountant/Auditor	131	24–28	47/48/64	(54)/64	85/88/131/204
	(147–8)	—	131/147	131/147	86/141/147–8
Accountant (Financial)	147–8	24–28	48/66/72/147	66/72/147	90/147–8
Account Executive/Sales	(130)/167	24–25	49/(76)/130	130/(167)	130/(167)
Accounting Clerk	(119)/121	24–25	48/64/121	64/(119)	85/(119)/121
Accounting Manager	(147–8)	24–28	48/64	64/(66)	(85)/86/(147)
Accounts Payable/Receivable Clerk	119/121	24–25	48/64/121	64/119/121	85/119/121
Administrative/Executive Assistant	7/(145–6)	24–26	7/46/143	7/(77)/145	81/145–6/188
Administrative Assistant/Office Manager	114–145–6	24–28	46/114/145	114/145/190	81/145–6/190
Administrative Manager	(145–6)	24–28	48/60/72	(54)/60/145	81/86/145–6
Administrator/Coordinator (Healthcare)	(151–2)	24–26	48/65/72	65/(70)/72	(151–2)
Administrator: M.I.S.	153–4	24–28	47/48/(69)	(69)	81/153–4
Administrator: Social/Human Services	(151–2}	24–28	48/49/54/72	54/(60)/72	(94)/(151)
Advertising Account Executive	(167/174)	24–28	64/(167)	64/(167)	(167)/(174)
Advertising Manager	—	24–28	65	65	—
Architectural Designer	—	24–28	73	73	—
Arts Administrator	(145–6)	24–28	47/48/65	65	(145)/(171)
Auction House Assistant	171	24–25	65/171	65/171	171
Banking & Brokerage Operations Supervisor	—	24–28	46/59	59	87
Bookkeeper	121/141–2	24–26	47/48/66	66/121/141	87/121/141–2
Broker (Securities)	11–12	24–26	11/45/67	11/67	11–12
Buyer/Purchasing Agent	—	24–28	49	—	87
Chef/Cook/Baker	—	24–26	62/68	62/68	(92)
Chemist/Chemical Engineer	—	24–28	47/67	67	40/90/156
Clerk (General)	(119)	24–25	48/68/119	68/119	(119)/(126)
Clerk/Typist/Receptionist	(126)	24–25	48/68/126	68/126	126
Communications/Advertising	188	24–26	48/75/188	75/(167)	(167)/188
Communications/Fund-raising	(167)	24–26	48/49/(167)	(167)	96/(167)(188)

TYPE OF WORK/FIELD	RESUME	SKILLS	OBJECTIVE	SUMMARY	EXPERIENCE
Computer Administrator (Network)	(153–4)	24–28	48/(69)/70	(69)/70	(81)/153–4
Computer Consultant	(149–50)	24–28	69/(153)	69/(70)/(153)	81/(153–4)
Computer Operations/Data Processing	—	24–25	47/(68)/69	(68)/69	81
Controller	(147–8)	24–28	64/(66)/(72)	64/(66)/(72)	(85)/88/(147–8)
Counselor (Social/Human Services)	151–2	24–26	70/151/(175)	70/151/(175)	151–2
Counselor/Supervisor (Children)	123	24–26	(70)/123	(70)/123	123
Counselor (trainee)	160/175	24–26	158/160	160	160/175
Credit Analyst	—	24–26	(169)	(72)	(88)/(90)/91
Credit & Collections Manager	(147–8)	24–28	(45)/(48)	—	(7)/88/(91)
Customer Service Representative	122/194	24–25	48/122/194	122/194	9/122/130/194
Data Entry Clerk	119	24–25	48/68	68	(119)
Design Director	—	24–28	—	—	(88)/89
Designer (Fashion)	196	24–26	77/196	77/196	88/89/196
Efficiency Analyst/Industrial Engineer	—	24–28	49/(59)/(62)	(60)/(61)/62	(91)/(94)
Electronics Technician (Laser systems)	—	24–26	49/71	71	—
Electronics Technician	—	24–26	49/71/(168)	71/(168)	(168)
Engineer (Communications)	—	24–28	49/(71)	(71)	89
Engineer (Environmental)	—	24–28	47/67	67	90/156
Engineering Design/Drafting	168	24–25	71/168	71/168	168
Film/Video/TV (entry level)	172/186	24–26	(45)/172/186	172/(185)/186	172/186
Film/Radio/TV Producer	192	24–28	(45)/75/192	75	192
Financial Analyst	9/169	24–26	9/45/46/169	9/66/169	9/88/90/(169)
Financial Manager	(147–8)	24–28	48/60/66/72	(60)/66/72	(86)/(88)/91
Financial Officer (C.F.O)	—	24–28	48/60/66/72	60/66/72	(86)/(88)/91
Graphics Designer/Art Director	128/197	24–25	49/128/197	128/197	128/197
Import Manager	124	24–28	124	124	124
Interior Designer	—	24–28	73	73	—
Investment Officer (senior)	—	24–28	66	66	—
Labor Analyst	—	24–28	49/(59)/(62)	(59)/(62)	91/(94)
Lawyer	—	24–28	73	73	92/(134–5)
Marketing Assistant	169/174	24–26	(49)/74/174	74/174	93/146/169/174
Marketing/Product Manager	155–6	24–28	(45)/49/155	155	(93)/155–6
Market Researcher/Data Analyst	166/174	24–26	74/166/174	74/166/174	93/169/174
Medical Administrator	—	24–28	48/49/(70)	(54)/60/(70)	(91)/94
Medical Accounts Biller	—	24–26	(60)/61/(70)	(60)/61	(94)

TYPE OF WORK/FIELD	RESUME	SKILLS	OBJECTIVE	SUMMARY	EXPERIENCE
Medical Office Manager/Secretary	190	24–28	60/61/190	60/(61)/190	(81)/94/188/190
Microbiologist/Biotechnologist	170	24–25	74/170	74/170	170
Office Coordinator/Liason	185	24–26	48/49/185	185	185
Office Manager	114/190	24–28	48/60/114	60/114/190	81/94/114/190
Paralegal/Lawyer's Assistant	120/173	24–26	120/173	120/173	95/120/173
Personnel Officer (entry level)	161	24–26	158/161	161	(161)
Production/Quality Controller	—	24–28	49/(59)/62	(59)/62	—
Program Manager	(151–2)	24–28	48/49/54/151	54/151	95
Programmer/Analyst	149–50	24–26	47/61/149	61/(69)/149	81/95/150/163
Proofreader	—	24–25	75	75	(188)
Promotions—Music Industry	193	24–28	48/193	(167)/193	(167)/193
Public Relations Officer/Promotions	(188)	24–26	47/48/(193)	(75)	96/188
Publishing Assistant	(188)	24–25	75	75	188
Radio Announcer	192	24–26	(45)/192	—	192
Restaurant/Hotel Manager	—	24–28	45/49/62	62/(68)	92
Retail Manager	125/127	24–28	49/76/125	76/125	93/(127)
Retail Salesperson	—	24–26	76	76	125/127
Sales (Direct)	127	24–26	127/(167)	127/(167)	127/(167)
Sales Manager (Film & Video)	(155–56)	24–28	49/76	76	(81)/(130)
Sales Representative (Outside sales)	130/167	24–28	(49)/76/130	76/130/167	12/130
Sales (Securities)	11–12	24–26	11/45/67	11/67	11–12
Secretarial Supervisor	—	24–26	48/77	77	(81)
Secretary (Senior)	143–4	24–26	46/143/(145)	143/(145)	(81)/143–4/(145–6)
Secretary/Word Processor	126/182	24–25	7/48/77/126	7/126/182	126/182/(185)
Security Officer	—	24–28	48/61	61	—
Social Work Trainee	160/175	24–26	158/160/175	160/175	123/160/175
Social Worker	(151–2)	24–28	48/54/65/151	54/65/151	(95)/151–2
Stylist/Patternmaker	—	25–25	77/(196)	77/(196)	88/(89)/(196)
Systems Analyst	(153–4)	24–28	69/153	69/(153)	81/95/(149)/153
Teacher	129	24–28	(49)/129	129	129
Telemarketer (Supervisor)	—	24–28	78	78	—
Translator/Interpreter	183	24–26	183	183	183
Travel Agent	—	24–28	49/78	78	—
Word Processor/Secretary	126/182	24–25	7/48/126	77/126/182	7/126/182

EVELYN BROWN

402 Magazine Street #9-D • Newark, NJ 07105 • Messages: (201) 690-0000

OBJECTIVE: A position as **Data Entry/Accounting Clerk** where my strong inputting, computer, and reconciliation skills would be of value. Accurate and able to get the job done on time.

STRENGTHS:
- A.A.S. degree (includes Accounting courses).
- Knowledge of Accounts Receivable/Payable .. Billings .. Invoicing .. Cash Disbursements .. Payroll.
- Nearly six years' experience in both manual and computerized accounting environments.
- Reconciliation skills; able to balance financial records.
- Strong data entry skills and experience.
- Computer skills (IBM PC .. Data General .. DataEase .. WordPerfect 5.1)
- Able to work well under pressure and meet deadlines.
- Excellent teamwork and interpersonal skills.
- Bilingual (English/Spanish).

EXPERIENCE:
1992–Present

ALPHA MOVING & STORAGE, INC., Newark, NJ
Biller/Order Entry Clerk
—Input customer accounts into computer files.
—Prepare and mail billing invoices.
—Maintain accounts; heavy interaction with customers to resolve discrepancies.
—Order Entry duties (DataEase software).

1990–1991

JOHN CUNNINGHAM LTD, Warehouse, L.I.C., NY
Assistant to Bookkeeper/Data Entry Clerk
—Duties included: Accounts Payable .. Payroll .. Journal .. Cash Disbursements.
—Posted transactions.
—Prepared and mailed invoices manually.

1988–1989

UNIVERSITY ACCOUNTING OFFICE, New York, NY
Accounting/Reconciliations Clerk
—Reconciled statements of student financial records.
—Maintained records of student checks.
—Updated Financial Aid records.

EDUCATION:

HERBERT LEHMAN COLLEGE, CUNY, Bronx, NY
A.A.S. degree (1993) ... Accounting courses.

A-B-C BUSINESS SCHOOLS, New York, NY
Bank Teller Certificate (1990)

JOAN MACMILLAN

48 West 225 Street #7-C • New York, NY 10463 • (212) 562-0000

OBJECTIVE: Position as PARALEGAL in a Real Estate Department (or firm).

STRENGTHS:
- B.A. degree and Paralegal Certificate (ABA approved).
- Five years' experience as Real Estate Paralegal/Mortgage Loan Administrator/ Administrative Assistant.
- Preparation of closing documents; attendance at closings.
- Heavy liaison with banks, attorneys, and realtors.
- Strong organizational, prioritizing, and coordinating skills.
- Writing, editing, and proofreading skills.
- Able to work well under pressure of time constraints.

EXPERIENCE: WHITE, GREEN, BLACK & GOLD, Law Firm, New York, NY
1992–Present **Paralegal** — <u>Real Estate</u>
—Prepare closing documents for: Condominiums . Co-Ops . Single-family residences . Commercial properties.
—Represent the lender at closings.
—Review title reports/surveys; arrange for title representation.
—Coordinate closing dates with lending institutions.
—Heavy client contact, via telephone and in person.
—Execute all required follow-up correspondence.
—Prepare and file UCC Financing Statements.
—Process recorded instruments.

Administrative Assistant— <u>Real Estate Department</u> (1990–1991)
—Performed most of above duties until qualifying as Paralegal.

1988–1989 FIRST NATIONAL BANK OF NEW YORK, New York, NY
Mortgage Loan Administrator — <u>Real Estate Department</u>
—Processed loan applications, withdrawals, and credit denials.
—Followed up on closing documents (insurance, title reports, surveys, and escrow agreements).
—Interacted one-on-one with the bank's clients.
—Heavy telephone contact with attorneys.

1986–1988 FLUSHING HOUSING CORPORATION, Forest Hills, NY
Assistant to Executive Director
—Prepared reports required for board meetings; attended.

EDUCATION: ADELPHI UNIVERSITY, New York, NY
<u>Paralegal Certificate</u> (January 1989)
  Included: Real Estate law . Contracts . Legal Research . Westlaw
QUEENS COLLEGE, NEW YORK, NY
B.A. in Communication Arts (1990)

SUSAN P. MASON

3210 Wrightsboro Road, Dallas, TX 75240 • (214) 590-0000

OBJECTIVE: **Accounting/Bookkeeping** position where my ability to train and supervise clerks and strong reconciliation, problem-solving, and customer service skills would be of value.

STRENGTHS:
- Completion of Accounting courses in a Business School; CRT Data Entry skills; WANG Word Processing; Typing.
- Nine years' experience in Billing, Invoicing, and Reconciliations, including both manual and computerized records.
- Ability to research, investigate, and resolve problems related to client and customer billings; very accurate.
- Effective interaction with departments and/or affiliates.
- Able to handle a heavy workload and meet deadlines.
- Experience in training and supervising accounting clerks.

EXPERIENCE: [Deleted] NETWORK TELEVISION, Dallas, TX
1992–Present **Billing Representative**
—Report to Supervisor/Manager, Station Compensation Dept.
—Process billing orders received from affiliate stations.
—Verify details (program, sponsor, agency, time aired).
—Input data (CRT); recheck on next day's Daily Report.
—Interact with agencies to resolve disputes re amounts, playdates, non-aired commercials; research/follow-up.
—Check monthly invoices and reports received from M.I.S.
—Balance all billings for the entire month.
—Review affidavits from affiliates and make adjustments.
—Collaborate with Credit & Collections.

1986–1991 SHOWTIME/THE MOVIE CHANNEL, New York, NY
Billing Coordinator (1990–1991)
—Processed the billings of <u>two</u> companies.
—Interacted per telephone with regional offices and affiliates to assist in resolving problems in customers' accounts.
—Input details of customer contracts; also cash received.
—Calculated city and state sales taxes.
—Extensive coordinating, problem-solving, and liaison work.

Accounts Receivable Clerk (1986–1989)
—Calculated and verified payments and discounts.

1983–1985 P.O.P MANUFACTURING CO., New York, NY
Accounts Payable Clerk

EDUCATION: LA GUARDIA COMMUNITY COLLEGE: <u>Accounting Courses</u> (1984–5)
SOBEL COMMERCIAL SCHOOL: <u>Business Certificate</u> (1983)

ANTONIO GARCIA

200 East 23 Street #5-A, New York, NY 10003 • (212) 677-0000

OBJECTIVE: A position as **Customer Service Representative.** Offer my strong problem-solving and "people" skills. Am very organized. Clerical/Administrative skills.

STRENGTHS:
- Coursework in Business Administration; intensive in-house training programs.
- Nearly four years' successful Customer Service experience in two major companies (G.H.I. and Con-Edison).
- Knowledge of medical terminology.
- Coding (ICD-9 .. CPT .. GHI).
- Thorough knowledge of Medicare Parts A and B, as well as N.Y. City and Federal Health Insurance contracts.
- Able to handle a heavy volume of work (up to 120 calls per day).
- CRT data entry skills.
- Numerous letters of recommendation from satisfied clients.

EXPERIENCE: **Subscriber Relations Representative**
1992–Present   GROUP HEALTH INCORPORATED, New York, NY
   —Interact with Subscribers and Providers over the phone and in person.
   —Answer questions relating to Claims and Contracts.
   —Identify/resolve problems (or refer to proper department).
   —Heavy research and follow-up.
   —Handle 100–120 calls per day and a heavy workload of clerical/administrative work.
   —Code claims (20–25 per hour).
   —Acquired a sound knowledge of Medicare Parts A and B, as well as N.Y. City and Federal Health Insurance contracts.

1989–1991   **Customer Field Representative**
   CONSOLIDATED EDISON COMPANY OF NEW YORK, N.Y.C.
   —Visited the homes of customers.
   —Answered questions about billing and meter reading.
   —Handled complaints.
   —Completed and filed reports.
   —Performed Data Entry using IBM PC.

EDUCATION: G.H.I. IN-HOUSE TRAINING PROGRAMS (4–6 Weeks)
   Medical Terminology; Coding; Contracts
   CON-EDISON IN-HOUSE TRAINING PROGRAMS
   Field Training (4 Weeks); Customer Satisfaction (6 Weeks)

   BRONX COMMUNITY COLLEGE, City University, N.Y.C.
   Business Administration Studies (1987–1989)

MARTIN SANTUCCI

1045 Cordova Street • Pasadena, CA 91109 • (213) 752-7777 (Day)

OBJECTIVE: A position as **Counselor** (Paraprofessional) with emotionally or physically handicapped children (ages six through teens).

SUMMARY:
- Five years' counseling experience in a Mental Health clinic and in an After-School program.
- Experience with children ages 6 through 12 years.
- Cases included children from broken homes .. victims of abuse .. neglect .. drugs .. domestic violence; also those who were emotionally or physically handicapped.
- Excellent working relationships with Social Worker, Clinic Coordinator, Supervisors, and Director.
- Preparation of follow-up reports.
- Ability to interact well with parents in English/Spanish.
- Able to assist children with Academic Skills problems.

EXPERIENCE: THE CHILDREN'S AID SOCIETY, Pasadena, CA
1990–Present —Clinic at 79 Bolivar Avenue

Senior Counselor (1993–Present)
- —Report to the After-School program supervisor.
- —Work with children (7- to 8-year-old boys and co-eds).
- —Assist with: Gym .. Library .. Field Trips .. Games Room .. Arts & Crafts .. Group Discussion.
- —Interact with parents.
- —Prepare follow-up reports.

Counselor/Paraprofessional—Dictorial Program (1992)
- —Promoted to assist children in an After-School Program.
- —Worked with children ages 6 through 12 years.
- —Assisted them with Reading and Math problems.

—Mental Health Clinic at Garcia Street (1990–1991)
- —Cases included children from broken homes, emotionally and physically handicapped children and victims of child abuse, neglect, and drugs.
- —Interacted well with Social Worker, Clinic Coordinator, Supervisor, and Director.
- —Assisted in Group Therapy sessions.

OTHER
EMPLOYMENT:
1988–1989 Clerk, BROWN BROTHERS, Pasadena, CA

1987–1988 Clerk, CHEMICAL BANK, San Diego, CA

EDUCATION: PASADENA COMMUNITY COLLEGE, Pasadena, CA
A.A.S. degree—Human Sciences Major (1990)

MARY PHILLIPS

1226 Sierra Way • Piedmont, CA 97435 • (415) 436-5555

OBJECTIVE: A position as **Import Manager/Senior Bookkeeper.**

STRENGTHS:
- Four years' experience as Import Manager in a fast-growing and fast-paced firm that imported women's sportswear.
- Thorough knowledge of Import documentation . Letters of credit . Dealing with customs brokers and freight forwarders . Rate negotiations . Claims processing . Costing . Allocation and distribution of incoming goods . Warehouse and inventory control . Invoicing.
- Timely resolution of problems under pressure covering all aspects of importation, distribution, trucking, and routing.
- Aptitude for figures; IBM PC skills.
- Able to deal effectively with brokers, forwarders, banks, and warehouses; able to pacify impatient customers.

EXPERIENCE: **Import Manager**
1990–Present
FINANCE-TO-INDUSTRY CORP, INC., San Francisco, CA
Finance company (liaison between importers and banks)
—Service client requirements concerning letters of credit . financing . documentation; resolve related problems.
—Deal with banks (L/Cs, wire transfers and foreign currency).
—Open letters of credit for clients; process all amendments.
—Invoice clients; forward statements (L/Cs, open bills).

1986–1990
Traffic/Import Manager
T. JOHNSON PRODUCT DEVELOPMENT, INC., New York, NY
Importers of Women's Sportswear
—Handled a $15 million traffic flow of imported goods.
—Prepared cost estimates for importation and distribution of goods.
—Opened letters of credit; negotiated customers' L/Cs with banks.
—Oversaw computerized and manual routing of goods to clients.
—Responsible for warehouse and inventory control.
—Supervised invoicing operations.
—Negotiated rates with freight forwarders, customs brokers, truckers, and warehouses.

1985
Bookkeeper
BROWN & JONES, CPAs, New York, NY
—Responsible for computerized Accounts Receivable/Payable.

1983–1984
Textile Designer
WONDER FABRICS, Converters, New York, NY

EDUCATION: STATE UNIVERSITY OF CALIFORNIA—**B.S. degree** (1983)
SAN FRANCISCO ART INSTITUTE—<u>A.A.S.</u> (1981)

SARAH JOHNSON

210 Kilgrow Boulevard • Detroit, Michigan 48225 • (313) 365-1000

OBJECTIVE: A position in RETAIL MANAGEMENT where my accomplishments in major department stores would be valued.

STRENGTHS:
- Bachelor's degree in Clothing/Textiles (Pi Delta Phi).
- Experience as Department Manager/Salesperson in leading retail stores.
- Completion of Executive Training Program.
- Track record of exceeding sales objectives and achieving outstanding departmental growth.
- Able to identify customer needs and win their confidence.
- Proven ability to train and supervise sales personnel.

EXPERIENCE: **Manager**
1991–Present ALEXANDER'S, Boy's Furnishings Department, Detroit, MI
- Responsible for day-to-day operations of a $6 million area.
- Supervise and schedule three salespersons and stockperson.
- Implement creative merchandising ideas to display goods.
- Track merchandise from point of entry to selling floor.
- Monitor current versus out-of-date purchase orders, delivery dates, cut-off dates, and the type of goods ordered.
- Responsible for markdowns . transfers . RTVs.
- Perform customer service and problem-solving functions.
- During my tenure, the volume of business has exceeded every planned percentage increase. I achieved the highest sales increase of any department within the group.

1989–1990 **Assistant Department Manager**
BLOOMINGDALES, Housewares Department, New York, NY
- Responsible for merchandising a $4 million floor.
- Analyzed sales figures to identify trends and best sellers.
- Participated in developing sales/marketing strategies/plans.
- Negotiated with vendors.
- Made presentations at merchandising meetings.
- Supervised sales personnel; maintained inventory control.
- Contributed to increased departmental sales and profits.

1988 (3 months) Executive Training Program.

1988 **Salesperson**
SAKS FIFTH AVENUE/MASON'S BOUTIQUE, Dearborn, MI
- Was ranked among the top producers in both.

EDUCATION: MARYGROVE COLLEGE, Detroit, MI
B.A. in Clothing and Textiles (1987)

SONIA LAMBERT

79–06 50th Avenue #B • Woodside, NY 11126 • (718) 333-6666

OBJECTIVE: **Secretarial/Word Processing** position. Able to process a wide variety of documents—neatly and accurately. Work well under pressure.

STRENGTHS:
- Ten years' secretarial experience in various industries (Engineering . Medical . Retail . Municipal).
- Word Processing includes: Professional Write .. WordPerfect .. Lotus 1–2–3 .. WordStar.
- Typing skills (55–60 wpm); Dictaphone experience.
- Typing experience: Correspondence .. memos .. medical and budget reports .. manuals .. purchase orders.
- Detail-oriented and accurate; good knowledge of spelling.
- Excellent attendance; punctual; very hardworking.

EXPERIENCE:
1990–Present THE APEX GROUP OF COMPANIES, INC., New York, NY
Secretary—<u>Engineering Department</u>
—Word Processing using WordPerfect 5.1.
—Type inspection reports and interoffice memos.
—Telephones . fax . photocopying . filing.

1985–1989 ST. LUKE'S-ROOSEVELT HOSPITAL, New York, NY
Secretary—<u>Medical Department</u>
—Word Processing using WordPerfect and Lotus 1–2–3.
—Scheduled meetings.
—Performed routine office duties, including: Answering telephones .. photocopying .. fax .. filing.
—Typing included: Manuals .. medical reports .. purchase orders .. payroll (120).

1982–1985 B. J. ALTMAN'S, Department Store, New York, NY
Secretary—<u>Accounts Payable Department</u>
—Used Lotus 1–2–3.
—Typed memos to departmental heads and monthly vendors' reports; also scheduled meetings.

1979–1981 FLUSHING MEADOWS HOUSING CORPORATION, Queens, NY
Typist/Clerk—<u>Chief Superintendent's Office</u>
—Typed letters to tenants and departmental heads.
—Performed light bookkeeping duties.

EDUCATION: NEW YORK UNIVERSITY—<u>Certificate in Microcomputers</u> (1987)
QUEENS COLLEGE—<u>Introduction to Computers</u> (1980)
TAYLOR BUSINESS SCHOOL—<u>Secretarial Skills</u> (1979)
NYC COMMUNITY COLLEGE—<u>Liberal Arts Courses</u> (1978)

LUIS BASURTO

1143 Fulton Street, Atlanta, GA 30326 • (404) 843-0000

OBJECTIVE: Position in DIRECT SALES/CANVASSING.

STRENGTHS:
- Track record of consistently exceeding weekly and monthly sales quotas in two situations; promotion to Lead Representative.
- Experience includes selling cable-TV and retail sales.
- Completion of two intensive sales seminars.
- Successful experience in managing own territory.
- Excellent listening skills; able to identify client needs.
- Strong cold calling, canvassing, and closing skills.
- Customer service, liaison, and follow-up skills.
- Bilingual (English/Spanish).

EXPERIENCE: **Lead Representative**—Direct Sales
1990–Present   CABLE-TV COMMUNICATIONS, INC., Atlanta, GA
- Responsible for managing a territory.
- Generate and follow up on leads for cable-TV sales.
- Advertise and promote the company's products and services.
- Develop new accounts.
- Schedule installations.
- Collect subscriber fees.
- Make daily reports to Sales Manager.

Accomplishments:
- Consistently exceeded weekly quotas; won competitions; received cash awards.
- Successfully opened 500+ new subscriber accounts.
- Promoted to Lead Sales Representative.

1988–1989   **Department Manager/Salesperson**
STATIONERY SUPPLIES, INC., Atlanta, GA
- Responsible for day-to-day management and sales in the Paper Products department.
- Supervised employees and motivated them to sell more.
- Duties included: Ordering .. Display .. Sales reports.
- Consistently exceeded monthly sales quotas.

1985–1987   **Trading Floor Clerk**
JONES & JONES, INC., Brokerage House, Nashville, TN
- Recorded and delivered daily stock orders.
- Interacted heavily with brokers.
- Compiled and reviewed brokers' trades with other firms.

EDUCATION: CABLE-TV COMMUNICATIONS SALES SEMINARS
Professional Selling Skills (2 Weeks); Creative Selling (2 Weeks)
SCHOOL FOR TELEVISION ARTS—Commercial Art Courses

JEAN DU PLESSIS

71–10 Highgate Street, • Stamford, CT 06105 • (203) 876-0000

OBJECTIVE: A position as **Graphics Artist/Designer/Illustrator**.

SUMMARY:
- B.F.A. degree .. Courses in Computer Graphics .. Gold Medal Award (H.S.)
- Experience as Optical Scanner Operator for a major publisher and as Assistant Designer in a graphics production department.
- Good color sense.
- Excellent drawing skills (freehand illustration .. rendering).
- Paste-ups and mechanicals (computerized) .. Marker comps.
- Computer skills (Macintosh . Photoshop . QuarkXpress . Powerpoint . Pagemaker 3.0 . Superpaint . IBM PC . Microsoft Word; exposure to Persuasion and Harvard Graphics.)
- Photography.
- Able to work well under pressure of deadlines; teamwork skills.
- Portfolio (includes freelance illustration .. slides .. logos).

EXPERIENCE: **Optical Scanner Operator**
1992–Present   MAGNUM HOUSE PUBLISHING, Juvenile Books, New York, NY
- Use Mac Quadra 700 computer and Howtek Scanmaster III+.
- Scanning .. Retouching .. Color Adjustment.

1991 (6 months) **Assistant Designer**
A.Z. GRAPHICS, INC., Production Department, New York, NY
- Company produced slides for executive presentations.
- Used Macintosh to prepare slides from client information received via modem.
- Software used: Powerpoint (Macintosh) . Microsoft Word (IBM PC); obtained exposure to Persuasion and Harvard Graphics.

EDUCATION: SCHOOL OF VISUAL ARTS, New York, NY
B.F.A. degree (1993) .. <u>Major:</u> Illustration
Courses in Computer Graphics:
- Computer as Design Tool (Pagemaker . Superpaint . Macintosh)

NEW SCHOOL OF SOCIAL RESEARCH, New York, NY
- Courses in QuarkXpress and Photoshop

OTHER EMPLOYMENT: <u>Office:</u> Set up filing system; ordered supplies. (2 Years)
<u>Client Relations:</u> Assisted in hosting art receptions. (1 Year)
<u>Front Desk:</u> Coordinated deliveries; supervised messengers. (1 Year)

BETTY FISHMAN

401 Linwood Drive #4Z • Fort Lee, NJ 07024 • (201) 583-0000

OBJECTIVE: A teaching position in a HIGH SCHOOL with responsibility for the learning disabled in a Special Education department. [Or "Areas of interest are . . ."]

LICENSES AND CERTIFICATIONS
- Permanent New York State Certification in Special Education (9/83)
- Health Conservation in Day Schools (7/85)
- Neurologically Impaired Emotionally Handicapped in Day Schools (6/84)
- Children of Retarded Mental Development in Day Schools (6/83)

EDUCATION

FORDHAM UNIVERSITY, New York, NY
Master of Science degree in Special Education (1983)
> Completion of 30 additional credits in History and Art to qualify for the 2nd Differential.)

BROOKLYN COLLEGE, City University of New York, NY
Bachelor of Arts degree in Art History (1977)

TEACHING EXPERIENCE 1979–Present

RICHMOND HEIGHTS JUNIOR HIGH SCHOOL, Staten Island, NY
Teacher (H.C.) (1984–Present)
- Teach science, mathematics, art, reading, and social science subjects.
- Prepare lesson plans.
- Conduct classes using artistic materials to stimulate motivation.
- Oversee student activities.
- Perform clerical/administrative duties.

Art Teacher (C.R.M.D., N.I.E.H., and H.C.) (1982–1984)

Mathematics Teacher (1979–1982)

ADDITIONAL SKILLS AND EXPERIENCE
- Able to teach Arts & Crafts.
- Mathematics tutor (Grades 6–12).
- Bilingual (English/Spanish) .. Studied at University of Puerto Rico.
- Camp Counselor (Camp LUBO, White Lake, NY—1975–1978).
- Travel and study in Angola, Namibia, and South Africa.
- Business experience in retail stores.

TOM MACNEIL

139 West Brunswick Road, Chicago, IL 35001 • (412) 888-0000

OBJECTIVE OUTSIDE SALES position where my strong customer service, relationship-building skills, and proven track record in outside sales would be of value. Will travel.

SUMMARY
- Successful experience as Sales Representative/Territory Manager/Customer Service Representative for major manufacturers of Shopping Bags and Roofing Systems.
- Proven ability to maintain and develop an existing account base of $800,000 (retail and resale) in the Illinois area and customer base of nearly $1,000,000 in NY/IL.
- Track record of increasing sales in a new and highly competitive territory by 8% in only 6 months.
- Valuable contacts in the Retail and Packaging industries.
- Thorough understanding of Manufacturing; able to communicate effectively from client to mill to management.

EXPERIENCE
1991–Present

GOOD BAG MANUFACTURING CO., Chicago, IL
Second largest bag/laminated bag manufacturer in U.S.
Sales Representative/Territory Manager (IL and NYC) (Present)
- Territory includes Chicago and Metropolitan New York.
- Service two territories by working two weeks alternately.
- Products sold include Paper and Plastic Shopping Bags.
- Sell to major Department Stores and Retail Paper Distributors.
- Successfully maintain an account base of $1 million.
- Increased sales by 8% in the tough New York marketplace.

Customer Service Representative (Chicago) (1991–1992)
- Serviced the needs of Retail and Resale customers.
- Customer base included direct accounts such as _____ and _____ , as well as 125 Retail Paper Distributors — $600,000+ in total.

Assistant to Plant Manager
- Worked in the Plant; coordinated Orders and Production schedules to increase efficiency and ensure timely delivery.

1989–1990

BRONX ROOFING SYSTEMS, Bronx, NY
Sales Representative
- Called on industrial and commercial customers.
- Supervised installation crew; follow-up; customer service.
- Improved the company's Sales Demonstration format.

1988

Previously worked as Assistant (intern) to a Marketing Director.

EDUCATION AMERICAN UNIVERSITY, Washington, DC
B.A. in Marketing/Advertising/Public Relations (1988)

ACTIVITIES Member of Freemasons and Rotarians.

JOAN WIGGINS

7820 N.W. 56th Street • Miami, FL 33166 • (305) 591-0000

OBJECTIVE   A position in the field of AUDITING.

SUMMARY
- B.B.A. degree in Public Accounting.
- Have completed all four Parts of C.P.A. Examination.
- Nearly three years' Auditing experience in an Audit Unit with responsibility for monitoring contractual compliance; additional experience in a Financial Aid Office.
- Analysis of budgets and variances, including recommending amendments where necessary; exercise judgment.
- Computer skills (Lotus 1-2-3 . MultiMate . IBM PC).
- Excellent teamwork skills; interact effectively with peers.
- Able to compose own correspondence.
- Recipient of excellent Performance Evaluations.
- Well-groomed and professional image.

EXPERIENCE
1990–Present

Accountant
DEPARTMENT OF HOUSING PRESERVATION AND DEVELOPMENT, Dade County, FL
- Review the processing of fiscal documents, claims, tax bills and accounting receipts and reimbursements.
- Perform field audits to monitor contract compliance on 15–20 Community Consultant contracts and for cost reimbursement purposes.
- Analyze complex budgetary estimates and authorizations and recommend amendments where necessary.
- Prepare reports and correspondence affecting various community organizations.

1989–1990

Trainee Accountant
FINANCIAL AID OFFICE, Miami University, Miami, FL
- Responsible for resolving students' financial aid problems.
- Researched and coordinated data from the Computer Department and various Administrative offices.
- Input data concerning financial aid forms.
- Assisted students to complete financial aid awards.
- Helped prepare annual Federal and State reports.

Summers
(1986–1988)

Accounting Clerk
UNIVERSITY EXTENSION SERVICE - Community & Rural
- Reviewed budgets for Summer programs.
- Participated in developing a Purchasing System.
- Prepared annual report for U.S. Department of Agriculture.

EDUCATION   C.P.A EXAMINATIONS (4 X Parts) (1994)
UNIVERSITY OF MIAMI— **B.B.A. in Public Accounting** (1990)

10

WHEN A TWO-PAGE RESUME WORKS BETTER

Q. Should my resume be no longer than one page?
A. Epitaph for the One-Page Resume Theory: Once and for all, let's put this overaged turkey of a theory to rest.
—William E. Montag, President, career counseling and outplacement firm [15]

Unless you're Lee Iacocca, brevity isn't your answer.
—John Lucht, executive search consultant [5]

ONE PAGE VERSUS TWO: EXPLODING A BIG RESUME MYTH

Today it is a well-established fact that the "ideal" resume length of the '80s—the-one-page-resume-to-be-used-for-all-jobs-and-at-all-levels—is probably the biggest and most damaging myth of resume writing. You might find this surprising because you've probably been told, time and again, that busy employers simply won't read two pages. But the fact is that they *will* read a well-written two-pager that is "airy" (has lots of white space) and that tells the reader all he or she needs to know about you. They prefer them to a skimpy one-page resume that either says too little about your skills or is much too crowded. More than anything, all resumes *must* be easy to read.

It actually takes *less* time to sell an employer with a good two-page resume than it would take them to read a boring and crowded one-pager. Many perfectly well-qualified job seekers have had to learn the hard way that one-pagers don't always achieve the same results as a two-page approach.

It is still true that for most entry-level jobs, and in applying for positions in the first years of your working life, a one-page resume will probably be the most suitable. But as you acquire more experience, many of you will *outgrow* one-pagers and require two-pagers instead. They certainly work better for experienced secretaries seeking advancement to Administrative Assistant/Executive Secretary, or if you're an accomplished supervisory-level job seeker. Otherwise, an employer might conclude that if you've managed to squeeze so many years of experience on one page, what you're offering can hardly be valuable. He or she may decide, rightly or wrongly, that you've probably been doing the same thing year after year. To summarize, unless you're a junior-level job applicant, a two-page resume may be the key to a successful job campaign.

DON'T S-T-R-E-T-C-H YOUR ONE-PAGE RESUME—REDESIGN IT!

Is a two-page presentation only a longer version of the same format you've been using since entry level? Is the only or main difference the fact that your Experience section should now be presented before Education? No. No. No. Job resumes can't be stretched out like stringy cheese. They have to be redesigned and reconstructed. A two-page presentation *will* differ, both in form and in content, from any shorter resume you may have written previously. Only then will it help you come across as a more senior applicant or give you a "supervisory" or "managerial" image.

Why have well-written two-pagers often worked better than good one-pagers? What special "magic" can there be in a two-page resume? In dressing for a job interview, a tailored, two-piece "presentation" will often work better for you. You'll come across as being more professional, more "qualified," and even as more *senior*. In the same way, a two-page resume also looks different and is a more effective and impressive presentation of your value to a prospective employer. This is so because the process of reconstructing your resume will also increase your *perceived worth*—if only because a two-pager generally has more "body" than a flimsy one-pager.

But its content will also be different. Why? Because you're now engaged in marketing yourself for a promotion, advancement, or for a supervisory or management-level position.

ESSENTIAL COMPONENTS OF AN EFFECTIVE TWO-PAGE RESUME

The secret of a two-page presentation is to get your primary selling message across on the first page (Tom Jackson). If you do that, you won't lose more than 20 to 30 percent of your readers after page 1. But by then you should have sold them!

The "heart" of your new presentation will be a Summary or Qualifications Statement on page 1: ten to fifteen lines that present your main selling points. The usual heading for this section is one of the following:

- SUMMARY OF SKILLS AND EXPERIENCE
- SUMMARY OF QUALIFICATIONS
- SUMMARY STATEMENT
- QUALIFICATIONS

Next, you'll present your most related work experience (usually your present and previous positions). If you run out of space on page 1, try to squeeze in your *best* experience (and an accomplishment or two).

In this way, your selling message will now be concentrated on page 1 and you'll get this across *before* the reader gets to page 2 (which, as a rule, presents less marketable or unrelated information). This is why carefully constructed two-pagers have been so successful in marketing value to employers. They are cleverly designed marketing pieces— *not* longer versions of basic one-page formats.

WHEN A TWO-PAGE RESUME REALLY HELPS

In helping you decide whether a two-page resume would be best in your case, I draw on my experience of writing thousands of successful resumes (one-pagers, two-pagers, two-pagers with a title page, and folding brochures). This includes feedback I received over a nine-year period from successful clients who had previously used one-page resumes without success.

What follows are *eight* criteria for deciding whether you, too, will benefit from using a two-page presentation. It could make a big difference in the impression you make on paper.

1. If you're an *exceptional college graduate* with outstanding achievements, preferably of a supervisory or managerial nature (one student founded, managed, and supervised a successful Hotline and Clinic for Women), or if you've already published something job-related or have engaged in research projects that would interest an employer, a two-pager might do you more

justice because you have already demonstrated that you are more than entry level.

2. If your brief work history has been one of very *rapid growth* and accomplishment (including steady promotions to supervisory-level responsibilities), you might also have outgrown your one-page resume and now need a stronger one to market you more effectively for advancement to more *senior* positions.

3. If you've had more than five years of working experience *and* have been given steadily increasing responsibility (such as secretaries who perform *higher-level* administrative duties or bookkeepers who assist or take over as office managers), a two-pager might be the best way of presenting you as an office manager or as an administrative assistant/executive secretary. Add an achievement or two to show how well you've performed.

   Employers will look at your recent job titles, so include the job title you're seeking in the first two job descriptions you present. For example, Administrative Assistant/Secretary or Office Manager/Bookkeeper. (See pages 7, 60, 114 and 201.)

4. If you're aiming for your first *management-level* position and have already had suitable supervisory experience (such as substituting for your manager during his/her absences, or acting as Supervisor or as Assistant or Acting Manager), a two-pager will help you come across as more managerial. (You'll write a good Summary of Skills and Experience and add bulleted accomplishments after each job description.) Your two-page resume will be perceived as having more weight than a one-pager, with its entry-level look. (See pages 145 and 146.)

5. Nearly all *supervisors, managers,* and *senior executives* will require resumes that are two pages long. In particular, senior executives will usually need two to three pages *and* a title page in order to present themselves effectively. A one-page resume could be disastrous unless you're in the Lee Iacocca league.

6. If you've had extensive experience but in different fields, use a two-page resume (or two one-pagers) to present different selections of facts in a focused manner. Use page 1 for your Job Objective, Summary of Skills and Experience, and one or two items of directly related work experience. (Place unrelated items on page 2.)

7. If you're an *immigrant* or someone whose education and work experience has been mainly in another country, use a Summary on page 1 to present what you know or can do—but don't reveal *where* you learned it. Give your best work experience near the foot of page 1, but do try to make it less "foreign," even if you have to omit the country! On page 2 you'll reveal more of your "foreign" past, but try to Americanize all foreign job titles, company names, and names of educational institutions.

8. In general, experienced job seekers with *something to "hide"*—a shortcoming or potential turnoff—should try to present their best selves on page 1 and record their least attractive (or less marketable) details on page 2.

RESUME CATEGORIES AND MODELS

On pages 136 and 137 is an outline or model of a two-page combination resume. (It's almost like filling in the blanks!) In addition to general layout, there is much to guide you in preparing your own two-pager. On pages 138 and 139 you'll find additional resume categories for a two-page resume. These might be helpful in organizing your data more effectively. For example, your working experience might be *direct* (Professional Experience) or only *related* (Related Experience). If totally unrelated to your Job Objective, it would be Additional Employment.

If some of your jobs have been omitted, you should use Summary of Previous Experience or

Highlights of Previous Employment. Attorneys prefer the heading "Legal Experience" to cover their work as attorneys, but "Business Experience" or "Other Professional Experience" for their non-legal experience.

Senior-level teachers need to divide their work experience into Supervisory/Administrative Experience and Teaching Experience. Those whose formal education is weak (or unrelated) will benefit by using categories such as In-Company Training Programs. (See also page 156 and 201.)

SAMPLE TWO-PAGE RESUMES

On the pages that follow you'll see how Deirdre Lovell transformed a bland and lackluster one-pager into a winning two-pager—an effective marketing tool. Thereafter, a further seven two-pagers will illustrate the difference between "stretching out" a one-page resume and remodeling it. In each case, you'll become aware of the crucial (sales/marketing) role of the Summary and see how accomplishments have been indented and bulleted.

MODEL TWO-PAGE RESUME

PROFESSIONAL OBJECTIVE

A [level] position in **Area/Department/Field** [type] where my experience in [track record/accomplishment] and strong [skill area], [skill area], and [skill area] skills would be of value.

SUMMARY OF SKILLS AND EXPERIENCE [or **SUMMARY OF QUALIFICATIONS**]

- Degree [or degree studies in] .. [most related course(s)] .. [honors/awards] .. [Additional job training/courses/seminars/workshops].
- [Number spelled out] years' experience as [best job title/second best title/third best title], including supervisory/management-level responsibilities.
- Expertise/specialized knowledge in the areas of [area] and [area].
- Recipient of [corporate recognition or award].
- Achievements/Accomplishments include:_____, which increased/reduced ____ and/or earned/saved $____ p.a.
- Thorough knowledge of ____ and ____.
- Excellent ____ and ____ skills.
- Able to_____.
- Able to_____.
- Strong interpersonal, communications, and teamwork skills.
- Computer skills [such as IBM PC .. Lotus 1-2-3 .. WordPerfect 6.0].

PROFESSIONAL [or **RELATED**] **EXPERIENCE** [or **BACKGROUND**]

1993 –
Present

Present Job Title
[NAME OF COMPANY/INSTITUTION, City, State]
 [Description of what it does and how impressive or big it is.]

- Report to [title only of immediate superior].
- [Describe main duties and responsibilities in 3–5 lines.]_____
_____
_____
_____
_____

Accomplishments:
- [Describe result(s) achieved. Give numbers/percentages.]_____
_____
- _____
_____

(continued)

PROFESSIONAL [or **RELATED**] **EXPERIENCE** [or **BACKGROUND**] (continued)

1987 –   [NAME OF PREVIOUS EMPLOYER, City, State]
1992   [**Last Job Title:** <u>Division/Area/Branch/Department</u>] (1990 – 1992)

- [Describe main duties and responsibilities in 2–3 lines.]_____
_____
_____

<u>Accomplishments:</u>
• [Describe result(s) achieved. Give numbers/percentages.]_____
_____

[**Previous Job Title**] (1987 – 1989)

- [Describe main responsibilities in 1-2 lines.]_____
- _____

<u>Accomplishments:</u>
• [Describe result(s) achieved. Give numbers/percentages.]_____
_____

1983 –   Job Title
1986   [NAME OF EMPLOYER, City, State]
            • [Describe main responsibilities in 1 line.]_____

[*Note:* Because employers are *not* interested in what you did more than ten years ago, end this section with the following line:]

Have also worked as ____ and ____. Details will be furnished at a personal interview.

ADDITIONAL [or **UNRELATED**] **EMPLOYMENT**

1982 –   [<u>Job Title</u>]
1983   [NAME OF EMPLOYER, City, State]

EDUCATION AND TRAINING

[IN-HOUSE TRAINING PROGRAMS/COURSES/WORKSHOPS]

[NAME OF EDUCATIONAL INSTITUTION, City, State]
[**Degree**] in [job-related major] [date, unless too long ago]

PROFESSIONAL AFFILIATIONS/MEMBERSHIPS/ACTIVITIES

Member, _____
Member, _____

CATEGORIES FOR TWO-PAGE RESUMES

Your data has to be presented in an organized manner to support your Job Objective. Ask yourself: What will the reader want to read first? Your direct (most related) experience *must* appear on page 1. Anything additional or unrelated should be presented on page 2. (Anything you may have to "hide" is recorded on page 2.) The following categories are commonly used:

PAGE I

OBJECTIVE
PROFESSIONAL OBJECTIVE
POSITION OBJECTIVE
CAREER OBJECTIVE

LICENSES AND CERTIFICATIONS

SUMMARY STATEMENT
SUMMARY OF SKILLS AND EXPERIENCE
SUMMARY OF QUALIFICATIONS
QUALIFICATIONS

COMPUTER HARDWARE AND SOFTWARE

PREVIOUS EXPERIENCE
PROFESSIONAL EXPERIENCE

[Must be directly related to your Job Objective.]

PROFESSIONAL BACKGROUND

[Covers a wider range of positions; is more general.]

RELATED EXPERIENCE

[When your experience is not directly related to your Objective.]

LEGAL EXPERIENCE [Attorneys]

SUPERVISORY/MANAGERIAL/ADMINISTRATIVE EXPERIENCE [Teachers]

SUMMARY OF PREVIOUS EXPERIENCE

[Use this when you wish to omit many previous positions.]

HIGHLIGHTS OF PREVIOUS EMPLOYMENT

[Use if you wish to highlight selected positions only.]

PAGE 2

ADDITIONAL EMPLOYMENT
[This is for unrelated work experience.]

OTHER PROFESSIONAL EXPERIENCE
[Use for high-grade additional experience that is unrelated.]

BUSINESS EXPERIENCE [Attorneys]
TEACHING EXPERIENCE [Teachers]
PERFORMING EXPERIENCE [Arts]

SALES TRAINING
MANAGEMENT EDUCATION AND TRAINING
IN-COMPANY TRAINING PROGRAMS
EDUCATION AND TRAINING
EDUCATIONAL BACKGROUND

PROFESSIONAL AFFILIATIONS AND MEMBERSHIPS
COMMUNITY ACTIVITIES
PROFESSIONAL ACTIVITIES
[Use to boost your professional experience]

PERSONAL DATA

REFERENCES

(Refer to additional categories on page 102.)

DEIRDRE LOVELL

75 Second Avenue #10-F
New York, NY 10033
(212) 844-0000

OBJECTIVE: Seeking a position where I may use my experience as Full Charge Bookkeeper.

EXPERIENCE: PARK AVENUE REALTORS, INC., New York, NY
6/92 – Present   Position: Bookkeeper
Duties include: Bookkeeping functions through Trial Balance for four companies.

3/90 – 1/92   THE [deleted] AID SOCIETY, New York, NY
Position: Bookkeeper
Duties included: Accounts Payable, Claim Processing, Accounts Receivable, Donations.

5/87 – 11/89   ACE PLUMBING & HEATING CORP., New York, NY
Position: Full Charge Bookkeeper
Duties included: Posting, Journals, Accounts Payable, Accounts Receivable, Bank Reconciliation, Posting to General Ledger, Trial Balance, Payroll, Financial Analysis and Reports.

10/84 – 10/86   GLOBAL TRADING COMPANY, New York, NY
Position: Bookkeeper
Duties included: Accounts Receivable, Accounts Payable, Billing, Posting, and Deposits.

3/80 – 5/81   JOHN SMITHERS & COMPANY, New York, NY
Position: Clerk
Duties included: Clerical, Billing, Order Control.

EDUCATION: Madison Business & Data Processing Institute (11/89–3/90)
Haussman Computer Associates, Inc. (12/86–4/87)
Cope Vocational Institute (11/83–6/84)

SKILLS: Hardware: IBM PC, Tandy 6000 Multi-user, Database System
Software: Lotus 1–2–3, Multiplan

DEIRDRE LOVELL

75 Second Avenue #10-F
New York, N.Y. 10033   (212) 844-0000

JOB OBJECTIVE

Position as **Full Charge Bookkeeper/Bookkeeper** where broad-based experience and knowledge of advanced computerized accounting systems would be of value. Mature, cost-conscious, and efficient.

SUMMARY OF SKILLS AND EXPERIENCE

- Certificate in Advanced Computerized Bookkeeping; Diploma in Computer Programming; Bookkeeping Certificate.
- Nine years' successful and diversified experience as a bookkeeper in both computerized and manual environments.
- Experience includes 2½ years as Full Charge Bookkeeper.
- Employers have included: Real Estate Investment .. Contractor .. Import/Export .. and a major Non-Profit organization.
- Thorough knowledge of Bookkeeping/Accounting through Trial Balance.
- Computer skills (IBM PC . TANDY 6000 Multi-User System . Database System . Lotus 1–2–3 . Multiplan . Sunbelt).
- Analysis and preparation of financial and statistical reports.
- Able to handle a heavy workload and meet deadlines.
- Positive and professional image.

PROFESSIONAL EXPERIENCE

1992 – Present   **Bookkeeper**
PARK AVENUE REALTORS, INC., New York, NY
—Hired to do the books of <u>four</u> investment companies through Trial Balance.
—Use a One-Write System.
—Interact with clients and managing agents to obtain information.
<u>Achievements</u>:
- Successfully reorganized the existing bookkeeping systems; created new ledgers and implemented improved controls.

1990 – 1992   **Bookkeeper**
THE [deleted] AID SOCIETY, New York, NY
—Reporting to the Comptroller, worked in a large and fully computerized financial area with 14 full-time employees.
—Duties included: Accounts Payable .. Accounts Receivable .. Claims Processing .. Donations .. Analysis of Accounts.
—Heavy data input using IBM PC; Lotus 1–2–3 spreadsheets.

(See over)

PROFESSIONAL EXPERIENCE (continued)

Bookkeeper, THE [deleted] AID SOCIETY

Achievements:
• Through efficient organization and prioritization of work, was successful in reducing the amount of overtime worked.
• In a Letter of Recommendation, the Comptroller wrote: "Ms. Lovell is a conscientious and capable Bookkeeper. She can be relied upon to complete her work accurately and in a timely manner. She is intelligent and more than able to handle the responsibilities assigned to her." (Original letter available at an interview.)

1987 – 1989   **Full Charge Bookkeeper**
ACE PLUMBING & HEATING CORP., New York, NY
  Contractors & Renovators
—Reported to the President.
—Responsible for all Bookkeeping functions through Trial Balance.
—Specific duties included: Posting to General Ledger . Accounts Receivable . Accounts Payable . Bank Reconciliations . Journal . Trial Balance.
—Prepared Payroll and Payroll Taxes (city, state, federal).
—Prepared Sales Tax spreadsheets; completed W2 forms.
—Financial analysis and reports.

1984 – 1986   **Bookkeeper**
GLOBAL TRADING COMPANY, New York, NY
  Importers & Exporters
—Reported to the President.
—Duties included: Accounts Receivable .. Accounts Payable .. Billing .. Deposits .. Posting.

Previously worked as Accounting Clerk in JOHN SMITHERS & COMPANY. Details will be furnished upon request.

EDUCATION AND TRAINING

11/89–3/90   MADISON BUSINESS & DATA PROCESSING INSTITUTE, N.Y.C.
                    Diploma in Advanced Computerized Bookkeeping
                .. Included Lotus 1–2–3 . Multiplan Software; TANDY 6000
12/86–4/87   HAUSSMAN COMPUTER ASSOCIATES, INC., N.Y.C.
                    Certificate in Data Processing/Cobol Programming
                .. Achieved a Grade of 95% .. IBM PC . Database System
11/83–6/84   COPE VOCATIONAL INSTITUTE, N.Y.C.
                    Bookkeeping & Secretarial Certificate

KATHLEEN O'HARA

110 Berrian Road   Res: (203) 329-1000
Stamford, CT 06905   Bus: (212) 970-4000

JOB OBJECTIVE

A position as **Senior Secretary/Personal Assistant** to a top executive. Able to handle confidential matters discreetly and interact effectively with senior executives.

SUMMARY OF SKILLS AND EXPERIENCE

- More than 14 years' experience as Secretary/Personal Assistant to senior executives in prestigious firms such as Golden Brothers, Inc. and Anderson, Thompson & Maclaine.
- Strong organizational, coordinating, and follow-up skills in arranging meetings, both domestic and overseas.
- Able to assist in drafting contracts and related agreements, including litigation documents.
- Able to compose own letters, memorandums, reports, etc.
- Typing skills (85 wpm) .. WordPerfect 5.1 .. IBM PC.
- Experience in maintaining personal checking accounts, making social arrangements, and entertaining visiting executives.
- Work well under time and accuracy pressures.
- Well-spoken, well-groomed, and professional.

PREVIOUS EXPERIENCE

1992 – Present   ANDERSON, THOMPSON & MACLAINE, New York, NY
                       "Big 6" CPA firm

                       Confidential Secretary/Executive Assistant
                       to Executive Partner

                       —Responsibilities include organizing meetings of Management Committee and out-of-town and international meetings.
                       —Prepare minutes and draft standard agreements (domestic and international), as well as related documents.
                       —Entertain visiting senior executives, including chairmen.
                       —Maintain personal calendars and private checking accounts.

(continued)

PREVIOUS EXPERIENCE (continued)

1984 – 1991   GOLDEN BROTHERS, INCORPORATED, New York, NY
                       Commodity Traders (Division of B-I-G International)

Senior Secretary/Executive Assistant   (1988 – 1991)
to Director of Copper (Worldwide)
—Coordinated meetings of the Trade Committee.
—Compiled monthly domestic/overseas Copper positions.
—Acted as liaison with Golden Brothers offices overseas.
—Composed own correspondence (nontrading).
—Drafted standard contracts from transaction slips.
—Used WordPerfect 5.1 on IBM PC.

Secretary/Administrative Assistant   (1984 – 1987)
to Senior Vice President, Cobalt Trading
—Duties included heavy dictation and telexes.
—Maintained an appointments calendar.
—Updated cobalt positions.
—Liaison with overseas customers and GoldBro offices.
—Kept detailed expense reports for tax and/or reimbursement.

1982 – 1984   JONES, SMITH & HARDWICK, INC., New York, NY
                       Wall Street Brokerage House

Executive Secretary
to Vice President, Domestic Purchases
—Duties included heavy phone contact with steel mills.
—Typed contracts for each Buy/Sell transaction completed.

Details of additional employment will be furnished at a personal interview.

EDUCATION AND TRAINING
              THE LEARNING ANNEX, New York, NY
                    WordPerfect 5.1 (1991)
              CITY COLLEGE, City University of New York, NY
                    Liberal Arts studies in English/Economics (1983 – 1984)
              KATHERINE GIBBS SECRETARIAL SCHOOL, New York, NY
                    Secretarial/Business Studies Certificate (1982)

CATHERINE TAYLOR

510 N. Michigan Avenue
Chicago, IL 60611
(312) 661-0000

PROFESSIONAL OBJECTIVE

To assist a senior executive in a fast-paced environment as his/her highly organized and capable **Executive/Administrative Assistant.** Will help you achieve your corporate objectives. "Thanks for a sterling performance" wrote my previous boss.

SUMMARY OF SKILLS AND EXPERIENCE

- Nine years' experience as Personal/Executive Assistant to senior executives in fast-paced Sales/Marketing offices.
- Areas of achievement include: Reorganizing sales offices; liaison work; producing promotional materials; telemarketing; negotiating.
- Active involvement in building relationships with corporate clients and in expanding the existing client base.
- Strong organizational, administrative, and follow-through skills.
- Able to oversee projects; efficient and effective in getting the job done; meticulous attention to detail.
- Writing skills include business proposals, sales brochures, marketing literature, and executive correspondence. Typing (55 wpm).
- Computer skills (IBM PC . Lotus 1–2–3 . WordPerfect 5.1).
- Professional image; well-groomed; high energy level.

PREVIOUS EXPERIENCE

1992–Present **Executive Assistant to President & Sales Director**
U.S. COMPUTER SERVICES, INC., Chicago, IL
    International Sales & Service Organization
Hired to assist the President in streamlining and focusing U.S. sales and engineering efforts.
Responsibilities have included:
—Reorganizing the Sales Office and improving Service procedures.
—Acting as liaison between Senior Management, Sales and clients.
—Analyzing the user market to target prospective clients.
—Drafting business proposals; writing the President's correspondence.
—Assisting in contract negotiations and also in developing ongoing relationships with clients.

Achievements:
- My boss achieved a 20% increase in his client base, due, in part, to my contributions as his Assistant which included implementing a successful telemarketing project.
- Received the President's "highest recommendation."

(continued)

CATHERINE TAYLOR   **Page 2**

1990–1992   **Administrative Assistant to V.P./Sales Director**
                 STATE-OF-THE-ART COMPUTERS, INC., New York, NY
                     Consulting, Sales & Service
                 Hired to assist in reorganizing Sales Office/Department procedures.
                 —Implemented improved systems for filing and correspondence.
                 —Reviewed procedures for submitting proposals, bids, and contracts.
                 —Revised, wrote, and edited sales and marketing literature.
                 —Used IBM PC to generate daily reports and promotional materials.
                 —Initiated promotions and public relations activities.
                 —Wrote executive correspondence.
                 —Performed a wide range of administrative duties, including overseeing the office and
                 interviewing job applicants.
                 Achievements:
                 • My efficiency and strong organizational skills helped the Vice President achieve his
                   sales goals; also wrote effective sales letters that contributed to the overall team effort.
                 • Developed a computerized tracking and follow-up system for processing new leads.

1984–1989   **Assistant to National Sales/Marketing Director**
                 PROMOTIONAL CONCEPTS, INC., New York, NY & Los Angeles, CA
                     International Exhibits & Graphics Production
                 Hired to assist in opening and expanding a new sales territory and to monitor day-to-
                 day office operations.
                 —Assisted Senior Management to develop Bonus and Commission structures; also in
                 setting quotas for national sales team.
                 —Participated in sales development; attended contract negotiations.
                 —Assisted in writing business proposals.
                 —Facilitated the approval of design and artwork for final production.
                 Achievements:
                 • Was entrusted with executing the National Sales Manager's directives during his fre-
                   quent absences abroad.
                 • Learned to negotiate and participated in closing deals.
                 • Was given more creative and challenging work.

EDUCATION

                 NORTHWESTERN UNIVERSITY, Evanston, IL
                 B.B.A. degree in Finance/Marketing (1983)
                 ... Additional studies in French and Italian

                 Letters of Recommendation Available Upon Request

JENNIFER LIM

350 Sacramento Street   Res: (415) 222-0000
San Francisco, CA 94111   Bus: (415) 321-0000

PROFESSIONAL OBJECTIVE

Senior-level position as **Financial Accountant** where my Finance and Accounting education, experience in healthcare environments, and ability to analyze and control expenses would be of value.

SUMMARY OF QUALIFICATIONS

- M.B.A. in Finance: coursework in Advanced Financial Analysis, Investment Analysis, and Quantitative Analysis; B.A. in Accounting
- Ten years' experience as Senior Accountant/Staff Accountant/Auditor in major institutions; additional two years as Reimbursement Accountant working on Institutional Cost Reports and related government reports; history of steady promotions.
- Excellent research and analytical skills for financial/statistical reporting and for analyzing investment accounts and income statement variances.
- Thorough knowledge of manual and computerized accounting, including preparation of Financial Statements and Schedules.
- Computer skills (Lotus 1–2–3 .. McCormack & Dodge Software).
- Communications skills—orally and in written reports.

PROFESSIONAL EXPERIENCE

1990–Present   SAN FRANCISCO MEDICAL CENTER, San Francisco, CA
                Financial Accountant
                —Report to Directors of Reimbursement and Financial Planning.
                —Assist in preparing the Institutional Cost Report.
                —Prepare related Government Tax Forms and Reports.
                —Compile material required for mandatory State audits.
                <u>Achievements</u>:
                - Performed special projects designed to analyze and contain departmental expenses; recommendations have resulted in annualized cost savings of $100,000.

1980–1989   NEW YORK GENERAL HOSPITAL, New York, NY
                Senior Accountant—<u>General Accounting Division</u>   (1985 – 1989)
                —Prepared monthly financial statements and schedules (6 pages).
                —Analyzed income statement variances.
                —Performed analysis of investment and other asset accounts.
                —Reconciled computerized billing, pledge, and check issuance reports.
                <u>Achievements</u>:
                - Participated in designing and implementing improved control procedures for the newly automated General Ledger system.
                - Actively involved in computerization of Financial Statements.

(continued)

JENNIFER LIM

PROFESSIONAL EXPERIENCE (continued)

> **Staff Accountant** (NEW YORK GENERAL HOSPITAL)   (1982 – 1984)
> —Prepared income statements and hospital service revenue schedule.
> —Analyzed Patients' Accounts Receivable, Hospital Service Revenue, and Third Party Contractual Allowances.
> —Recorded and analyzed investments, payroll, and contributions.
> —Analyzed cash accounts, long-term liabilities, and receivables.
>
> **Cash Accountant**   (1980 – 1982)
> —Reconciled operating cash accounts and investment accounts.
> Achievements:
> • Initiated and implemented improvements in the system for processing Accounts Receivable, Accounts Payable, and Foreign Collections, resulting in more effective control procedures.

1979   EASTERN CHEMICAL PRODUCTS, Long Island City, NY
Cash Auditor
—Audited branch disbursements, sales, and expenses.

EDUCATIONAL BACKGROUND

> BARUCH COLLEGE, City University, New York, NY
> M.B.A. in Finance (1986)
> Completed coursework included:
> —Analytical Methods in Finance
> —Advanced Financial Analysis
> —Investment Analysis
> —Corporate Budgeting
>
> HOFSTRA UNIVERSITY, Hempstead, NY
> B.A. in Accounting and Business Administration (1978)

MEMBERSHIPS

> New York Healthcare Financial Management Association
> Asian Finance Society

References Furnished Upon Request

RONALD PINSHAW

115 Newbury Street #44
Boston, MA 02116   (617) 266-0000

PROFESSIONAL OBJECTIVE

> **Computer Systems Programming/Support** position where my broad-based experience, wide knowledge of state-of-the-art software, and strong analytical, problem-solving, and training skills could help execute projects on time and within budget.

SUMMARY OF SKILLS AND EXPERIENCE

- B.S. degree in Computer Science .. Courses in Hardware & Software Development for Business/Personal applications.
- Experience in Systems Programming/Support within a major Insurance Company and Consulting/Sales experience as Senior Computer Specialist within Radio Shack/Tandy Corporation.
- Proven ability to analyze system requirements and advise users on the most appropriate Hardware/Software.
- Troubleshooting skills to diagnose system/programming bugs.
- Excellence in providing user support and user training.

SOFTWARE/ LANGUAGES

Clipper .. FUNCky Library .. CLIP 2 (HLLAPI) Library .. FoxPro .. ANSI C .. Borland C++ .. BLINKER .. dCLIP .. Attachmate 3270 EXTRA .. MS-DOS .. Microsoft Windows .. Microsoft Visual Basic (Windows Version) .. CodeBase 4.5 for Visual Basic .. Quarterdeck QEMM .. Quarterdeck DESQview .. AmiPro .. Harvard Graphics .. Various DOS–based utilities .. Banyan Vines .. basic TSO/SPF .. basic JCL .. COBOL .. COBOL QuickJob .. PL/I .. FORTRAN

HARDWARE

IBM PCs .. IDE Technology .. ProSlot Technology .. Banyan Vines Networking System .. Attachmate 3270 Gateway.

PROFESSIONAL EXPERIENCE

1990–Present   THE [deleted] INSURANCE COMPANY, INC., Boston, MA
Systems Programmer — <u>Product & Service Systems</u>   (Present)
—Work with a multi-user, Banyan Server–based Disability/Major Medical Insurance system for processing underwriting applications and updates (UAS).
—Program analysis, coding, documentation, testing, debugging and implementation on all phases of UAS enhancements.
—Perform similar duties on all phases of a system called Plan Information Data Base for issuing policy contracts.
—Provide support for speedy resolution of operating problems.
—Develop operations manuals and train users.
<u>Achievement:</u>
- Analyzed and fully developed a reporting system that supplies upper management with daily/monthly reports showing Underwriter/New Business performance.

PROFESSIONAL EXPERIENCE (continued)

Systems Technical Support (... INSURANCE CO.)   (1990–91)
—Provided technical support to the New Business Health Division (50 persons); 30,000 applications received annually.
—Reviewed and analyzed new products and modifications for system upgrading of all external files.
—Participated in preparing test strategies for new products.
—Developed test patterns for both new and existing products by utilizing system environment (65 databases).
—Monitored the success of all test functions.
—Maintained documentation for new products and for system upgrading.
—Trained users.
—Performed extensive troubleshooting of production problems.
—Prepared operator manuals.
—Improved my knowledge of software (Clipper, FoxPro, QEMM, Cobol, HLLAPI, Automator and DOS–based utilities).

1982–1989   RADIO SHACK/TANDY CORPORATION, Queens, NY
Senior Computer Specialist/Assistant Manager
—Based in a store that was in Top 10 of 7,000 countrywide.
—In charge of all in-house computer training.
—Responsible for educational and retail sales in the Computer Division; acted in a Sales/Customer Support role.
—Analyzed system requirements of customers.
—Assisted with installation and PC support.
—Troubleshot customer hardware/software problems.
Achievements:
• Received numerous awards for Outstanding Performance.

Computer Trainer/Computer Specialist — Queens District
—Analyzed customers' system and software/hardware needs.
—Trained users on-site; also trained computer salespersons.

1982 – 1984   ST. JOHN'S COLLEGE, Queens, NY
Student Faculty Assistant

EDUCATION AND TRAINING

THE [deleted] INSURANCE COMPANY — Outside Classes
Clipper 5.0 .. ANSI C .. C++ .. basic TSO/SPF .. basic JCL
RADIO SHACK/TANDY CORPORATION TRAINING PROGRAMS
In-House Software & Hardware Development Training (annual)

ST. JOHN'S COLLEGE, Queens, NY
B.S. in Computer Science/Data Processing (1984)

JAMES JEFFERIES

227 Huntington Street #5   Res: (718) 789-0000
Brooklyn, NY 11216   Bus: (718) 443-8000

PROFESSIONAL OBJECTIVE

Senior-level position in the SOCIAL/HUMAN SERVICES field where my extensive experience as an Alcoholism Counselor and expertise in alcohol and substance abuse would be of value.

SUMMARY OF QUALIFICATIONS

- Master's degree in Adult Education (coursework included different modalities of treatment). Additionally, attendance at numerous seminars/workshops on alcohol and drug abuse.
- New York State Certified Alcoholism Counselor (1990).
- Ten years' experience in a Rehabilitation/Outreach Center and in a hospital, covering both inpatients and outpatients.
- Populations handled include physically and emotionally disabled persons, cases of chemical dependency and psychiatric illness, and emotionally handicapped adults.
- Able to deal with hard-to-reach, involuntary and multi-problem clients, as well as disadvantaged families.
- Excellent screening and interviewing skills; sensitivity in dealing with patients from different ethnic backgrounds.
- Diagnostic and treatment skills (short- and long-term).
- Design, implementation and assessment of behavior plans and treatment plans.
- Experience of mental status evaluations, including vocational and educational assessment and evaluation.
- Assessment of community referral and follow-up procedures.
- Effective liaison with members of multidisciplinary teams.

PROFESSIONAL EXPERIENCE

1990–Present   THE [deleted] RESCUE HOUSE, Brooklyn, NY
                Outreach/Rehabilitation facility
            Senior Alcoholism Counselor   (1992 – Present)
—Report to the Director.
—Deal with indigent and homeless, chemically dependent adult males (drug and alcohol abusers).
—Conduct a structured 90-day program for 25 clients at a time.
—Interview, screen and assess intake.
—Prepare written psycho-social evaluations.
—Refer clients for medical and psychiatric evaluations, if necessary.
—Prepare treatment plans based on individual needs.
—Conduct group therapy sessions thrice daily, five days per week.
—Provide individual counseling, including hard-to-reach and multi-problem cases.

(continued)

PROFESSIONAL EXPERIENCE (continued)

Cont'd. **Senior Alcoholism Counselor** (THE [deleted] RESCUE HOUSE)
—Provide vocational counseling as well as on-going follow-up and after-care on completion of the 90-day treatment period when the Center becomes a halfway house assisting in the rehabilitation of clients.
—Use Alcoholics Anonymous and other self-help groups.
—Make referrals to other agencies such as the Office of Vocational Rehabilitation Services, Medicare and SSI.
—Counsel families; develop suitable referral plans for them.
—Work as a member of a multidisciplinary team.

Alcoholism Counselor (1990 – 1991)
—Completed the required 150-hour C.A.C. program of training.

1983–1989 INTERFAITH HOSPITAL, Jamaica, Queens, NY
Detoxification Center (Methadone & Chloralhydrate)
Patient Coordinator
—Conducted a 21-day program for inpatients.
—Performed intake interviewing and assessment.
—Screened and evaluated cases.
—Conducted group therapy.
—Referred clients to other programs for ongoing outpatient treatment.

Additional employment in teaching. Details upon request.

CONTINUING EDUCATION

1990 N.Y.F.A.C. APPROVED ALCOHOLISM COUNSELOR TRAINING

1990 ALCOHOLISM COUNCIL OF GREATER NEW YORK
Basic Alcoholism Training Program

1989 UNIVERSITY OF GEORGIA, Athens, GA
Alcohol & Drug Studies (Residential Treatment)

1987 RUTGERS UNIVERSITY, New Brunswick, NJ
Alcohol Studies Program

EDUCATION

FORDHAM UNIVERSITY, New York, NY
M.S. in Adult Education & Human Resources (1989)

DELAWARE STATE COLLEGE, Dover, DE
B.S. in Elementary Education (1980)

PETER LONDON

20 East 20th Street #4
New York, NY 10004

(212) 720-0000

PROFESSIONAL OBJECTIVE

Senior Administrative M.I.S. position in the HEALTH CARE field where my expertise in <u>Computer Applications</u> and success in significantly exceeding collections targets in hospital environments would be of value.

SUMMARY OF QUALIFICATIONS

- —— years' administrative experience in major New York hospitals, including position as Associate Director, Fiscal Services.
- Extensive experience in computerization, including the design and implementation of ambulatory financial computer systems covering up to 350,000 annual visits to NYC municipal hospitals.
- Experience as a Systems Analyst involved in projects dealing with financial and computerized operations—hardware and software.
- Installation of smoothly functioning computerized Cashiering . Billing . Accounts Receivable systems; also A/R backlog reduction programs.
- Able to weld people from diverse backgrounds into effective operational groups.

PROFESSIONAL BACKGROUND

1980 – Present
NEW YORK CITY HEALTH & HOSPITALS CORPORATION, New York, NY
Associate Director, Fiscal Services, O.P.D. (1985 – Present)
_____ Hospital (1,500 beds)
—Installed the Shared Medical Systems (SMS) ambulatory computerized Billing and Accounts Receivable system.
—Designed and implemented cashiering policy and procedures (both manual and automated) to support computerized operations.
- Exceeded fiscal year collections target by $1,500,000 annually for 1985, 1986, and 1987.

Senior Systems Analyst—<u>Revenue Management Division</u> (1983 – 1984)
—Coordinated the implementation of a computerized Billing and Accounts Receivable system for NYC Emergency Medical Services.

Ambulatory Patient Accounts Manager (1982)
_____ Hospital Center (1,000 beds)
—Installed the Shared Medical Systems ambulatory computerized Billing and Accounts Receivable system.
—Designed and implemented billing procedures (manual and automated) to support the computerized operations.
- Exceeded the fiscal year's collections target by $1.8 million.

(See over.)

153

PETER LONDON

PROFESSIONAL BACKGROUND (continued)

NEW YORK CITY HEALTH & HOSPITALS CORPORATION

Cont'd.   **Systems Analyst** — Revenue Management Division   (1980 – 1981)
—Collaborated with outside consultants to reduce Accounts Receivable.
—Designed and implemented the Acute Care Ambulatory Model System and Model System manual.
—Developed monthly ambulatory Billings and Revenue forecasts by hospital.

1978–1979   BETH ISRAEL MEDICAL CENTER, New York, NY
Administrator/Coordinator
—Conducted a management study of and systems improvement to the Central Accessioning Laboratory.

EDUCATIONAL BACKGROUND

BERNARD M. BARUCH COLLEGE, City University of New York, NYC
M.B.A. degree Program in Health Care Administration (Present)
. . . Have completed 60 of the 68 credits required.
COLUMBIA UNIVERSITY, New York, NY
B.A. degree in Political Science (1977)

. . . Continuing education through attendance at healthcare seminars.

PUBLICATIONS

"A Study of the Utilization and Staffing of the Surgical Suite," Abstracts of Hospital Management Studies, December 1979

PROFESSIONAL AFFILIATIONS

Member, American Management Association
Member, Healthcare Financial Management Association

Note: In this example the job seeker has worked mainly for one employer but has been assigned to various divisions and hospitals. After each successful project he has been promoted. His four job titles therefore indicate increasing levels of responsibility. Above all, his work experience seems to be varied.

Similarly, those who have worked mainly for the same employer but within different departments or divisions (or who might have been transferred to other companies within the *same* group) should try to break up those work experiences and even use the names of different companies. In that way you will be able to indicate that your experience is broad based and not limited. (See also page 205.)

NEVILLE SOMERS

92 Plainfield Drive
Sayreville, N.J. 07840   (201) 854-0000

PROFESSIONAL OBJECTIVE

Senior management position as **Product/Marketing Manager** within the Specialty Chemicals industry. Offer my proven ability to direct Product/Sales Managers to achieve increased sales and profits.

SUMMARY OF QUALIFICATIONS

- More than 10 years' Product/Marketing Management experience in the specialty chemical divisions of major corporations; proven ability to lead and direct product development programs—from an initial concept through selling of product to end users.
- Track record of accomplishment in all facets of marketing and management for the sale of a variety of product lines.
- Success in revitalizing sales of mature lines of products, as well as identifying new markets for existing lines.
- Negotiation of major sales contracts ($10–15 million annually).
- Expertise in identifying user needs .. research and development of new product programs .. and licensing of new products.
- Effective in supervising key accounts, including training an effective sales force and implementing distributor training programs.
- Hiring and training of sales engineers and product managers.

PROFESSIONAL BACKGROUND

1986–Present   ____($400 MILLION SPECIALTY CHEMICAL COMPANY), Jersey City, NJ
                              Subsidiary of a $10 Billion International Oil Company

Market Development/Marketing Manager   (1990–Present)
—Areas of responsibility encompass: Copper Plating chemicals .. Zinc Plating processes .. Conversion Coatings.
—Design and implement creative marketing and product sales plans.
—Facilitate and improve the quality of communication between groups involved in the growth and fluctuations of each product.
—Review product sales reports from a national sales force of 45.
—Follow up and motivate individual salespersons; accompany them on their sales calls to customers.
Accomplishments:
- Revitalized the sales of a mature line of Copper products that has generated approximately $2,500,000 in operating profits (75% of the total for the entire division).
- Identified the market and introduced a new line of Zinc plating chemicals that attained sales of $1,400,000 in only two years.

(See over.)

155

NEVILLE SOMERS

PROFESSIONAL BACKGROUND (continued)

Product Manager (1986 – 1989)
—Responsible for Tin and Copper products.

1977–1985　BARLOW-JOHNSON CHEMICAL COMPANY, Newark, NJ
Fortune 500 company (annual sales of $2.1 Billion)
Sales/Marketing Manager (1983 – 1985)
—Worked in the specialty chemicals division which marketed a line of chemical additives for the rubber and plastics industries.
Accomplishments:
• Managed the development of and launched a new line of epoxy hardeners that generated sales of $1,100,000 within two years.
• Implemented training programs for salesmen of plastic additives; increased departmental sales from $6,250,000 to $8,300,000.
• Instituted an aggressive pricing program and used lower-cost materials, thereby increasing profits generated by a mature line of wire drawing compounds.

Laboratory Manager/Product Line Supervisor (1977 – 1982)
—Provided field technical service for latex paint additives.

1973–1976　DURAND CHEMICAL CORPORATION, Newark, NJ
Manufacturers of Industrial Coatings and Adhesives
Technical Service Chemist (1974 – 1976)
—Formulated industrial maintenance coatings and adhesives.

Sales Representative (1973)

SALES/MANAGEMENT TRAINING PROGRAMS
AMERICAN MANAGEMENT ASSOCIATION
New Concepts in Marketing (1993); Marketing for the '90s (1990)
Telemarketing (1989); Negotiating Skills (1988)

EDUCATIONAL BACKGROUND
FAIRLEIGH DICKINSON UNIVERSITY, Graduate School of Business, NJ
M.B.A. in Marketing (1986)
SETON HALL UNIVERSITY, NJ
B.S. in Chemistry (1976)

PROFESSIONAL MEMBERSHIPS
- Member, American Electroplaters Society
- Member, Society of Plastic Engineers

II

FOR COLLEGE GRADUATES AND CAREER CHANGERS

Making presentations, problem solving, and working with people are the critical skills necessary to make it in business.
—Dr. Bruce W. Mattox, Jr., Chairman of the division of business and economics at Carson-Newman College. [BusinessWeek's *Careers*, 9/87]

This chapter is designed to help recent college graduates and career changers—all those who have to market their recent education. In the new job market of the '90s, thousands of entry-level positions have disappeared. Thus, in a recent survey of graduating seniors (reported in the *New York Times*), 60 percent said they were anxious about their chances of finding work in the field of their choice. You might even be wondering whether it was worth $20,000–50,000 and the effort to acquire that "sheepskin."

Of course it was, but in a buyer's market your degree certificate or diploma won't sell itself! Formal education and "school experience" has to be marketed, and you'll need to do it well—in a variety of combination resume formats. You'll find many samples in the pages that follow.

Unfortunately, many graduates are *not* doing this, and 85 out of every 100 job resumes are (a) not doing the writers justice and (b) do *not* qualify as effective self-marketing devices. Why? Mainly because their resume-writing, letter-writing, and job-search strategies are still geared to the seller's market of the '80s.

USING OUTDATED JOB SEARCH STRATEGIES IN THE '90s

As many as 95 percent of recent graduates still use a conventional work history or "chronological" (dates in reverse order) resume. Unfortunately, this widely used format draws attention to your *lack* of direct work experience in your field! That, as you know, is your Achilles' heel.

Second, the chronological format is *not* designed to enable you to present your skills and abilities—your CAN DO's. In which section of the resume will you do this? (For this you would need a "functional" resume.)

Third, to market those skills, you are probably using a formal cover letter to sell yourself to employers—the traditional approach. But, as we have already explained, this twin-paper strategy is now outmoded and you would be wiser to transfer those selling points to a Summary section in your job resume. (See example of Phillip Smith on pages 8 and 9.) Nowadays, your first impression has to be made in your job resume—*not* in the cover letter as before. These letters should *not* be sent to personnel departments, who do most of the hiring for entry-level positions.

Fourth, the old strategy of omitting a Job Objective and stating this in your cover letter (to keep your resume "flexible") is also outdated. Fifth, you might be making the mistake of "saving up" some of your best selling points for the job interview instead of including them in your resume.

"But if I do that I'll have nothing else to talk about," is an anxiety response I often hear. "Don't worry," I reply. "You'll *need* those selling points to get you to those interviews. They are designed to *pre-sell* you to the reader."

Most, if not all the foregoing strategies won't work in a highly competitive job market because they ignore the importance of the first five to fifteen lines in your resume, where your "sales pitch" should be delivered. So, how should you market yourself to picky employers in the '90s? You should use the flexibility of the combination resume format to present your unique strengths in a single document; that is, *all* of your selling points:

skills + life/school/work experiences
+ achievements.

Today, it is generally agreed that this format is best if you are going after your first job, or are changing career fields—*not* the functional resume approach.

Best of all, with today's combination format (which has very little in common with the old "combined" or "hybrid" formats you'll find in some resume books), any number of different and imaginative resume variations are possible. To illustrate this, let's do a case study. We'll see how Cathy Windell (not her real name) was able to compose not only one but two different resumes—to emphasize different skills, her major and her minor, and various experiences or aspects of the same experience, both in school and at work.

TWO DIFFERENT RESUMES: TO EMPHASIZE A "MAJOR" AND A "MINOR"

Two million graduates annually would like to find work in the field of their choice, but this is becoming increasingly difficult. In fact, 60 percent (or more) of graduating seniors would improve their chances of success by learning how to explore more options. To do this effectively, you will have to start by (a) strengthening your "main" resume and (b) writing an additional one, focused differently.

HOW CATHY WINDELL PRESENTED HER CAN DO'S IN TWO RESUMES

Cathy Windell (not her real name) had recently graduated with a degree in psychology. Her minor was in business. She now wished to explore a few of her job options.

Cathy's first choice was to work with patients in the field of Social/Human services. An alternative (or corporate) option was in a human resources or personnel department. She began by drafting two Job Objectives:

1. An entry-level position in the SOCIAL/ HUMAN SERVICES field
2. An entry-level position within a PERSONNEL/HUMAN RESOURCES department

Cathy also composed a third Job Objective—a wider one to cover other job options:

An entry-level position within a company or firm where my "people," problem-solving, and organizational skills would be of value.

Cathy's next step was to compile *two* lists of her CAN DO's. From these she drafted *two* versions of a Skills Summary to support each of her first two Job Objectives. (Every selling point or "bullet" selected for each Summary had to back up its own objective—to "prove" why she was qualified.)

MAIN DIFFERENCES BETWEEN CATHY'S TWO FOCUSED RESUMES

There are differences in emphasis between versions A (see page 160) and B (see page 161) of Cathy's resume. You will learn a great deal by comparing them line by line.

JOB OBJECTIVE: The two versions offer different job-related skills (Cathy's CAN DO's) to address the needs of different employers.

SKILLS SUMMARY: The "bullets" in version A have a definite "flavor." They mention different patient populations that social workers have to deal with. The B version tones down the social work aspect. All of Cathy's CAN DO's are now more "corporate." Notice how various personal qualities are stressed.

EDUCATION: In version A, the related *courses* would interest employers in the Social/Human Services field. B focuses more on what interests corporate recruiters.

Version A stresses Cathy's *special papers* that would interest those who deal with deviant behaviors. The corporate version (B) stresses *leadership activities* that the business world wants to know more about.

INTERNSHIP: For the benefit of interviewers in the Social/Human Services field, a detailed account of Cathy's activities as a counseling intern in a clinic is presented. (The hospital gave this valuable job description to all interns.) Corporate interviewers would be more interested in what she did in a "unit" (B version). (Personnel officers can relate to interviewing and evaluating skills.)

EVALUATION/APPRAISAL: This might be the best "selling point" in both resumes. It tells employers *how well* Cathy performed. Version A gives a lengthy extract from a supervisor's letter that would be appreciated by other social workers. The corporate version (B) is brief. It mentions the word *excellent* and Cathy's "people" skills, not patients.

WORK HISTORY/EMPLOYMENT: In Cathy's A resume, her internship is emphasized. Her other work experience as a tutor and as a secretarial assistant has already been referred to in her Summary. A three-line description of this is more than adequate! For corporate recruiters, *dates of employment* are given.

CATHY WINDELL [Version A]

OBJECTIVE: Entry-level position in the **Social/Human Services** field where my ability to interact well with individuals/groups and strong communications and follow-up skills would be assets.

SUMMARY:
- "A" grade for internship as Counselor in an Alcohol and Substance Abuse unit at St. James Hospital; also internship (as a high school student) in a home for the aged.
- Experience as a tutor of learning disabled students.
- Participation in group therapy sessions.
- Communications skills in addressing student groups.
- Secretarial/clerical skills and experience (IBM PC . typing).
- Caring . persevering . professionalism.

EDUCATION: UNIVERSITY OF DENVER, Denver, CO
B.A. in Psychology (Dec. 1991)
Coursework included:
- Introduction to Counseling Techniques
- Counseling Techniques for Alcoholism and Drug Abuse
- Dysfunctional families
- Abnormal Psychology

Special Papers: Wrote a 12-page report on internship in Alcohol and Substance Abuse Unit; also papers on Obsessive-Compulsive Behavior and Dysfunctional families.

INTERNSHIP: BUSH MEMORIAL HOSPITAL, Denver, CO
7/91–8/91 Treatment and Rehabilitation Program for Chemical Dependency
—Worked as trainee **Counselor** under supervision of a C.A.C.
- Group therapy sessions
- Family therapy
- Aftercare planning
- Daily supervision
- Lectures and Workshops
—Co-led a women's group (weekly).
—Made and documented psychosocial assessments.

EVALUATION: Written by Supervisor (C.A.C.):
(extract) "Ms. Windell has related well to staff and patients. In supervision, she has been able to identify and work through countertransferential issues. She has been able to explore specific interventions and extrapolate to aftercare issues. Her performance was excellent." (Original letter available upon request)

STUDENT EMPLOYMENT: From 1989 to present, work part time as Tutor of learning disabled children. Give talks to students on campus. Also employed as Secretary/Administrative Assistant (1987–1988).

CATHY WINDELL [Version B]

OBJECTIVE: An entry-level position within a **Human Resources/Personnel** department where my "people" and interviewing skills, office experience, and knowledge of statistics would be of value.

SUMMARY:
- "A" grade for Internship .. excellent performance appraisal.
- Interviewing skills; able to screen and evaluate applicants.
- Communication skills (addressed college students on campus).
- General office skills and experience (IBM PC, typing, filing); worked as Secretary/Administrative Assistant in an agency.
- Fast learner .. ability to set and achieve goals.

EDUCATION: UNIVERSITY OF DENVER, Denver, CO
B.A. in Psychology and Business (1991)
Related coursework:
-Statistics I and II
-Interviewing and Counseling Techniques
-Managerial and Organizational Concepts
-Business Management
Leadership Activities: Was Group Leader/Facilitator for a 3-month project involving a company in Chapter 11; Gave talks to college students .. Co-led a women's self-help group.

INTERNSHIP: **Student Counselor**
7/91–8/91 BUSH MEMORIAL HOSPITAL, Denver, CO
—Intake interviewing and screening (under supervision).
—Learned to make psychosocial evaluations.
—Attended lectures and workshops.
—Co-led a women's self-help group (weekly).

APPRAISAL: Written by Supervisor of Interns:
(extract) "Cathy Windell served as Counseling Intern from 7/8/91 to 8/7/91. **Her performance was excellent.** She has related well to staff." (Original letter available upon request)

WORK
HISTORY: Tutor (Mathematics and English)
1989–Present X-Y-Z HIGH SCHOOL, Denver, CO

Summer 1989 Assistant Manager and Waitress
THE SIZZLING SOSATIE, Chicago, IL
—In charge during absences of the Assistant Manager.

1987–1988 Secretary/Administrative Assistant
(Part/Full-time) DU PLESSIS & EDWARDS, INC., Chicago, IL
—Acquired office skills (IBM PC, typing, filing).

"FUN HOUSE MIRROR" IMAGES AND OTHER DISTORTIONS

Nearly all career changers, returning-to-work homemakers, and recent college graduates have a common resume-writing problem: too little or no *direct* work experience. The purpose of this section is therefore to show you how to present additional skills and/or information in lieu of formal work experience. In particular, the sample resumes in this chapter will demonstrate the use of a variety of ingredients to create a *perception* of work experience.

A "BIOLOGICAL BOOKKEEPER"

In practice, many job seekers with "too little" or no direct work experience will probably write a chronological type of resume because it looks "normal" even if it does emphasize the "wrong" work experience. What career changers usually do is add an item or two of recent education, training (such as a paralegal certificate), or volunteer experience to their previous work history resume. They don't try to remodel or reshape it. The result? Their "updated" resume seems irrelevant to employers in their new field.

Similarly, recent college graduates are often too eager to demonstrate to employers that they have already worked in the "real" world. And so they pad their resumes with a series of *unrelated* work experiences.

The result? A half-baked resume in which half the page (or more) will *not* interest prospective employers. Thus, a biology graduate who had funded her tuition costs by working as a bookkeeper now devoted 70 percent of her resume to describing her bookkeeping activities and only 30 percent to biology. She therefore came across as a "biological bookkeeper." Similarly, an outstanding engineering graduate presented herself as an Office Supervisor (60 percent) and Electrical Engineer (40 percent). She struggled to find a job!

In today's job market, all such amateurish efforts will be screened out. To a busy reader, that distorted, two-dimensional piece of paper *is* you. Fortunately, there's a lot you can do to improve your presentation and image. You can learn to impress readers in the first five to fifteen lines of your resume (Job Objective and Skills Summary) *before* they even get to the sparse details of your work experience.

THE VALUE OF HANDS-ON (OR LAB) EXPERIENCE

After graduating as a Computer Programmer, Richard S. prepared a new resume. He wrote a brief Objective, a two-line description of the programming course, and added a six-line description of his previous (but unrelated) employment. The result? A very bare-looking resume.

To fill up the blank space and try to give an impression of some work experience, Richard successfully used a three-pronged strategy. *Step one:* He recorded his new diploma and detailed descriptions of courses he'd completed. (He adapted these from a college manual.)

EDUCATION: (NAME) UNIVERSITY, School of Continuing Education
           Diploma in Computer Programming (May 1991)
           .. An intensive hands-on program (16 credit courses).
             Honors: G.P.A. = 3.9
             Coursework:
                 Programming I & II: Included ...
                 Advanced Programming: Topics included ...
                 Cobol I & II: Major topics included ...
                 VSAM & IDCAMS: Accessing VSAM files ...

And so on. These descriptions filled half a page!

Step two was to take advantage of the fact that the program included *hands-on* training. Since this was practical (though unpaid) experience, these "duties" were also adapted from his college manual.

EXPERIENCE:
1990–1991

Trainee Programmer (or Student Programmer)
(NAME) UNIVERSITY, School of Continuing Education.
—Performed detailed programming in both COBOL and Assembler languages using concepts of structured programming.
—Wrote, tested, and debugged programs.
—Working in an IBM mainframe COBOL environment, designed, wrote, and compiled several programs of growing complexity.
—Participated in building on a semester-long COBOL project that stressed structured and modular programming strategies.
—Wrote, debugged, and executed programs using VSAM files and created and modified own files.
—Debugged COBOL programs through understanding IBM abend codes and associated core dumps.
—Programmed various applications in Assembler language.

Richard's final touch was to offer employers his "portfolio."

PORTFOLIO:
- Updating a Sequential Master File.
- Payroll Report.
- Sales Report.

These steps filled an empty-looking resume.

THE VALUE OF YOUR SPECIAL PAPERS, PROJECTS, AND ACTIVITIES

You can avoid distorting your resume presentation. You don't need to emphasize your unrelated work experience at Joe's Pizza Parlor. As a general rule, only internships and volunteer work may be job related. Other forms of work experience—either full-time, part-time or temporary—will only impress if they were ways of helping you fund tuition costs, if you were able to cope with a lot of work-study pressure, or if you had a chance to use skills related to the job you're seeking (such as leadership, selling, or customer service or other "people" skills).

Instead of highlighting your *paid* work experiences, the most interesting information (from an employer's perspective) might be what you did *without* any remuneration: your term papers, thesis, special college projects, or extracurricular activities. These are often more job related!

Even if you have little or no *direct* work experience, it's still possible for you to add some "red meat" to your college resume by describing special papers you wrote, projects you executed, and activities you participated in—either alone or as a member of a team. Always include them. They might be more interesting than your degree certificate.

PAPERS

The papers you wrote might demonstrate good research, writing and analytical skills (if your grades were As or Bs). And they can be excellent "conversation" pieces. For example, when one Wall Street executive noted a paper mentioned in a resume, that interviewer wanted to know more: "I'm really curious to learn how the Tokyo Stock Exchange differs from the New York and American exchanges. What were your main conclusions?"

PROJECTS

Projects tend to be job related. Since they are often completed under the supervision of an Adjunct Professor, they are the nearest thing to on-the-job experience.

Describing your projects also helps you fill up those wide-open spaces in your resume and will sound very good to the reader—like actual professional experience. (And if your grades are *good*, state them!)

ACTIVITIES

The nature of your campus activities might demonstrate good interpersonal, communications, organizational, liaison, coordinating, follow-up, teamwork, and leadership skills. Were you elected to various offices? Were you Captain of any team? Did you represent any group? Did you organize or coordinate any activity? Such skills are valuable in the occupational world. (See Chapter 2.)

How should you present and market all of this to employers? The best place to include them is under EDUCATION, as subheadings titled Special Papers, Special Projects, and/or Activities. But if they are many in number and/or are impressive, a special category might be even better.

To summarize, your internships, thesis, special papers, projects, and activities might be the best part of your entire resume presentation! Study the way these have been presented in the next few pages. See how they add "body" and "sell" to a resume. Each of those job seekers started with a bare-looking resume but ended up with a *marketing* device that worked.

FROM DISTORTED IMAGE TO WINNING PRESENTATION

In the sample resumes that follow, we will see how recent college graduates and career changers created a positive impression in their resumes. In each case, 90 percent of the presentation is job related and only 10 percent (or less) refers to other employment—either what they did to help fund tuition costs, or positions they held *before* making a career change.

Cynthia: Her internship is job-related *experience*. Look at the powerful impression her resume creates by addressing the reader in a Summary and adding related courses and details of two job-related projects. (Don't save such items for the job interview!)

Beverly: There are always openings in sales and Beverly tries to enter this tough but lucrative field. See how she presents her case to *media* bosses. (An account executive services existing clients and usually earns a base salary. A sales rep has to secure new clients and therefore earns more—in commissions.)

John: His previous resume devoted 60 percent to unrelated work experience. Now this employment section is 10 percent. Instead, his Summary, Courses, and Student Projects are all job related and create *synergy*—three sections that mutually reinforce a positive impression.

James: See his activities section and how his leadership skills are highlighted by concentrating the evidence in one category. Also note his bulleted achievement.

Suzanne: She only has a two-year degree, but it involved an additional research project. See how her thesis and coursework are presented and how she mentions her knowledge of state-of-the-art techniques.

Lillian: Although her academic attainments were unimpressive, her "people" and organizational skills are highlighted in one impressive area of the resume. And her internships sound like "real" work experience.

Naomi: This career changer was interviewed by all of the major networks. After listing her strengths, see how she presents college projects—as if she had "worked" for the Departments of English and Media Communications. And notice how her achievements stand out. Naomi's previous (unrelated) employment deserves a three-liner—not more!

Robert: Those who have worked for years in a nonlegal environment and now qualify as paralegals need to do much more than add this certificate to the education section of their old resumes. They now need to highlight *different* items to support a new Job Objective. Notice how the job-related coursework is now high-lighted, followed by a Related Skills section to address the needs of a law office. (Previous employment, if unrelated, should never occupy more than 10 to 20 percent of any job resume.) See resume of Joan MacMillan on page 120.

Stacey: Note the four projects (team and individual) that she executed for an Adjunct Professor. They sound like "real" work experience.

Debora: This career changer thought she had "nothing to offer" in her new field except for her present degree studies. Not true. All of the other sections (Field Work, Special Papers, and References) also help in promoting her cause. They are everyday items. Only her academic achievement is "special." (Debora's previous employment is now a footnote.)

CYNTHIA LEWIS

20 Parkside Avenue • Cambridge, MA 02157 • (607) 584-0000

OBJECTIVE   Position in **Marketing Research/Data Analysis**.

STRENGTHS
- Degree in Psychology and Sociology; emphasis on research.
- Research internship in a major hospital.
- Marketing research projects at college.
- Questionnaire techniques, including: administration .. scoring .. statistical analysis .. and interpretation of results.
- Knowledge of Population Demographics to identify user markets.
- Computer skills (IBM PC .. SYSTAT).
- Excellent interpersonal and teamwork skills.

EDUCATION   BOSTON UNIVERSITY, Boston, MA
B.A. in Psychology and Sociology (Double Major) (1992)
•• Coursework emphasized <u>research</u> and included:
- Social Science Research
- Statistics for Social Sciences
- Experimental Psychology I & II
- Introd. to Business & Marketing
- Advanced Research Project
- Data Processing
- Senior Evaluation Project

••<u>Activities:</u> Member, Psychology Club; Captain, Hockey Team

RESEARCH PROJECTS (College)

BOSTON UNIVERSITY, Boston, MA
In fulfillment of degree requirements, completed two projects:
- **Questionnaire Survey:**
  Designed and executed a research study to identify the nature of <u>eating disorders in five population groups.</u> Administered a Medical Questionnaire. Scored the responses and input data into an IBM PC. Performed statistical analysis using Multiple Regression technique. Interpreted the findings. Wrote a report.
- **Marketing Research:**
  Participated in a study to assess the <u>feasibility of opening a new store</u> for sporting equipment. Analyzed the population demographics in the surrounding area. Identified the user market. Prepared a video commercial to publicize the store.

**EXPERIENCE
June 1991–
April 1992**   **Research Assistant** (Intern)

MASSACHUSETTS GENERAL HOSPITAL, Boston, MA
—Used hospital Questionnaire to conduct survey of Substance Abusers.
—Compiled and scored the responses; entered data into an IBM PC.
—Analyzed the respondents into demographic groups and by socioeconomic status.
—Tabulated and interpreted the results.

ADDITIONAL EMPLOYMENT
Worked every Summer (1985–1990) to help fund educational objectives.
Presently working as a <u>Catering Organizer</u> at College.

BEVERLY SINGLETON

421 Van Wyck Boulevard • Staten Island, NY 10095 • (718) 555-0000

OBJECTIVE: Entry-level position as ACCOUNT EXECUTIVE/SALES REPRESENTATIVE in one of the following areas:
Advertising Space . Magazine Sales . Media Time . Subscriptions

STRENGTHS:
- Bachelor's degree in Business Management and Marketing; senior project to develop a Business Plan/Marketing Strategy.
- Who's Who in American Universities and Colleges (1992)
- Internship in a corporate Communications Department.
- Research thesis on Commercial Time Sales (60 pages).
- Knowledge of Demographics . Psychographics . Nielsen/Arbitron ratings.
- Excellent communications skills, via telephone and in person.
- Successful interaction with business executives in both work and social situations.
- Able to set and achieve high personal goals; very energetic.

EDUCATION: MARIST COLLEGE, Poughkeepsie, NY
B.A. in Business Management and Marketing (May 1992)
Coursework included:
- Consumer Behavior
- Managerial Marketing
- Senior Project
- Sales Management
- Data Processing
- Statistics

RICHMOND COLLEGE, London, England
Attended Classes (Summer 1991)

INTERNSHIP: **Corporate Communications Assistant**
Sept. 1991– THE INTERNATIONAL HOTEL GROUP, New York, NY
May 1992
—Worked in the corporate headquarters.
—Researched newspaper/magazine articles concerning a labor dispute.
—Telephoned outside parties/agencies/publications for additional information.
—Attended corporate meetings convened to discuss a strike.
—Visited and interacted with area communications representatives.
- Wrote a research paper on Labor-Management issues.

STUDENT
EMPLOYMENT: Cocktail Waitress
Present THE BIG LITTLE HOTEL & BAR, Poughkeepsie, NY

1989–1991 Waitress
VARIOUS RESTAURANTS IN NEW YORK CITY

JOHN LANGSTON

10-G Park Place • Flushing, N.Y. 11355 • (718) 844-0000

OBJECTIVE   Entry-level position in **Mechanical Engineering/Engineering Design**. Offer my A grades, projects, and hands-on laboratory experience.

STRENGTHS
- Bachelor's degree studies in Mechanical Engineering.
- Successful projects in Engineering Design .. CAD/CAM .. HVAC .. and Heat Transfer; obtained excellent grades.
- Programming skills (FORTRAN . Pascal . Ansys . GKS . IBM PC).
- Proposal writing.
- Research and problem-solving skills; able to find alternative solutions.
- Excellent communications and teamwork skills.
- Mature and responsible work attitudes; supervisory/leadership skills.

EDUCATION   NEW YORK INSTITUTE OF TECHNOLOGY, New York, NY
Bachelor of Science in Mechanical Engineering (to graduate 12/93)
Coursework:
- Engineering Design
- Design & Graphics
- CAD/CAM
- Machine Design I & II
- Analysis & Design of Mechanisms
- HVAC
- Advanced Engineering Mathematics

- Fluids + Laboratory
- Thermodynamics + Laboratory
- Heat Transfer + Laboratory
- Solids + Laboratory
- FORTRAN .. Pascal
- ANSYS (Stresses & Strains)
- GKS Software .. IBM PC

STUDENT PROJECTS   Obtained A and B grades for senior courses that involved writing proposals and executing projects. These included:

HVAC: - Prepared an HVAC analysis for a two-family residence (Awarded 95%)

Engineering Design: - Collaborated in designing a Supplemental Home Heating System that employed a greenhouse to heat a single-story structure and cut heating costs. (Awarded 90%)

CAD/CAM: - Analyzed stresses and strains (Rockwell Hardness Tester) (Awarded 90%)

ACTIVITIES
- Member, American Society of Mechanical Engineers
- Senior class representative (Mechanical Engineering) to Engineers' Council

EMPLOYMENT   Helped fund 60 percent of tuition costs by working as follows:

1990–Present   Assistant Office Manager, JONES LAW OFFICE, N.Y.C.

1988–1990   Drug Store Clerk, GOLDEN'S PHARMACY, Bronx, NY

1987–1988   Deli Clerk, EFRAIM'S GOURMET, Flushing, NY

JAMES RODRIGUEZ

52 Mulberry Lane • Newtown, PA 18103 • (215) 480-0000

OBJECTIVE: Entry-level FINANCE in the International Department of a bank or in a multinational corporation where my A grades, marketing, and foreign language skills would be assets.

EDUCATION: STATE UNIVERSITY OF PENNSYLVANIA
B.A. in International Business (June 1992)
THE WHARTON SCHOOL OF BUSINESS (Summer 1992)
International Monetary Economics
•• Completed coursework included:
    Multinational Corporations   International Business
    Money & Banking   Marketing
•• Thesis: Lifting Sanctions Against South Africa (A Grade)
•• Paper: Re-investing in the New South Africa (A Grade)

LEADERSHIP
ACTIVITIES:
- Vice-President, International Business Society
- International Relations Representative to College Senate
- Founding Father, [deleted] Fraternity
- Representative to International Fraternity/Sorority Council

INTERNSHIP: **Marketing Aide to Financial Consultant**
1991–1992
(5 months)   MERRILL LYNCH PIERCE FENNER SMITH, Pittsburgh, PA
    —Assigned to several projects, including the organization of a Seminar, Investment in the '90s.
    —Worked within a budget.
    —Researched the names of likely participants.
    —Located a suitable venue; organized timely invitations.
    —Assisted at Seminar held on three consecutive evenings.
    —Made follow-up calls to attendees.
    • Awarded A grade by Penn State University and Merrill Lynch (for Internship, Special Paper and Presentation).

EMPLOYMENT: Helped fund tuition costs by working as follows:
1989–Present   **Marketing Assistant**
THE FOREIGN INVESTMENT CORP., Pittsburgh, PA
    —Worked summers, vacations and full-time at present.
    —Prepare databases of past, present, and prospective clients.
    —Assist in preparing marketing brochures.

1991   Shift Manager
(Part-time)   YE OLDE DUTCH BAR, Newtown, PA
    —Scheduled personnel; cash receipts; inventory.

LANGUAGES: French, German and Italian (read, write, and speak).

SUZANNE BROWNING

50 Pinewood Street, Scranton, PA 18106 • (215) 876-0000

OBJECTIVE: Entry-level position in BIOTECHNOLOGY or MICROBIOLOGY.
(Hospital .. Veterinary Services .. Food Technology .. Agriculture)

STRENGTHS:
- Certificate as Biotechnology Technician; Major in Genetic Engineering.
- Outstanding student (class rank of 1/30).
- Research project using advanced techniques; obtained A grade.
- Computer skills (IBM PC . Lotus 1-2-3 . Quattro Pro . WordPerfect).
- Research and problem-solving skills.
- Responsible work attitudes; conscientious; am a team person.

EDUCATION: [Deleted] COLLEGE OF TECHNOLOGY, Philadelphia, PA
1990–1992 Work/Study Program
Certificate as Biotechnology Technician (June 1992)
<u>Coursework included:</u>

—Physics & Mathematics	—General Biology
—General Chemistry + Lab	—Microbiology + Lab
—Organic Chemistry + Lab	—Biotechnology + Lab
—Physical Chemistry	—Genetics + Lab
—Immunology + Lab	—Genetic Engineering
—Botany + Lab	—Food Engineering

<u>Thesis:</u> Awarded **95 percent** for research in Genetic Engineering (80 pages):

<u>Comparison of different strains of I.B.D.V. [Infectious Bursal Disease Virus] at the Protein and DNA level.</u>
Project was part of a 7-year research program to investigate a virus that attacks the immune system of ducklings. Compared proteins and DNA. Used state-of-the-art techniques and equipment, including: P.A.G.E. (S.D.S. Polyacrylamide Gel Electrophoresis) .. Western Blotting .. Restriction Enzymes .. Reverse Transcription .. P.C.R. Machine .. Blotting and Hybridization.

1986 SCRANTON HIGH SCHOOL, Scranton, PA—<u>Graduated</u>

STUDENT EMPLOYMENT: Funded tuition costs and living expenses 100% as follows:

1988–1991 <u>Assistant (Intern)</u>
BLUE CROSS ANIMAL HOSPITAL, Philadelphia, PA
—Responsible for feeding small animals (cats and dogs); administered injections; monitored patient progress.

1987–1988 <u>Licensed Practical Nurse</u>
VARIOUS HOME CARE AGENCIES, Philadelphia, PA
—Worked as a Nurse's Aide in hospitals and private homes.

LILLIAN M. JONES

360 Ortega Place • San Francisco, CA 94122 • (415) 235-0000

OBJECTIVE: Entry-level position in an ARTS-related environment where my communications, organizational, and research skills would be assets. Areas of interest include:
Auction House . Art Gallery . Museum . Arts Organization

SUMMARY:
- B.A. (Art History); Arts course in Paris museums/galleries.
- Three internships (Auctioneer/Art Dealer; Art & Antiques and Architectural Digest magazines).
- Knowledge of day-to-day operations of an auction house.
- Research, cataloging, and tagging skills and experience.
- Able to assist in preparation of brochures and mailings.
- Planning and organizing of successful sorority functions.
- Secretarial and typing experience.
- Energetic .. enthusiastic .. excellent "people" skills.

EDUCATION:
1989–1992

TULANE UNIVERSITY, New Orleans, LA
B.A. in Art History (June 1993)

Activities:
- Student Ambassador to Senate
- Student Orientation Coordinator
- Member of Executive Board, [deleted] Sorority
- Senior Organizer, inter-sorority functions

Summer 1990

SUMMER ABROAD STUDY PROGRAM, Paris, France
Six-Week Art Course (Louvre and Rodin Museum)

INTERNSHIPS:
Summer 1992

Intern, COOPER AUCTIONEERS, New Orleans, LA
—Researched markings on bric-a-brac (plates, paintings, guns, vases).
—Worked with Consignor sheets.
—Arranged for photographs of items to be auctioned.
—Assisted in compiling information for auction brochure.
—Tagged furniture; handed out paddles to bidders.
—Took domestic and international bids via telephone.
—Assisted in preparing for auctions, including mailings.

Fall 1991

Intern, ART & ANTIQUES Magazine, New York, NY
—Worked in the Circulation, Promotion, Production, Editorial, and Advertising departments.
—Performed heavy research duties in libraries.

Summer 1989

Intern, ARCHITECTURAL DIGEST Magazine, New York, NY
—Gathered information regarding forthcoming exhibitions.

NAOMI RICHARDS

4107 Victory Parkway, Cincinnati, Ohio 45229 • (513) 234-0000

OBJECTIVE Entry-level position in the MEDIA industry (TV/Video) where my technical skills in Camerawork and Editing would be assets.

STRENGTHS
- B.A. in Media Communications (hands-on courses in Television Production I & II and Media for Education).
- Technical skills as Cameraperson, including two successful projects for college speech and debating classes.
- In- and out-of-class Video projects experience, including Research .. Editing .. Camera Set-up .. Lighting .. Props.
- Strong research skills; able to organize/prioritize.

VIDEO PROJECTS (Out of Class)

DEPARTMENT OF ENGLISH, [deleted] College, Los Angeles
- Class Presentations—Two Experimental Projects (1992)
—Assisted a Professor of English to videotape each student in his Speech class (to assist in correcting speech errors).
—Invited each student to view his/her presentation.
—Repeated the project in a Debating class.

This experimental project has been adopted by Department.

- City-Wide Student Protest on Tuition Hike (1992)
—Videotaped the protest march down to City Hall and back to the sit-ins at [deleted] College.
—Interviewed students and professors.

Video was sent to Governor.

VIDEO PROJECTS (In Class)

MEDIA COMMUNICATIONS DEPARTMENT, [deleted] College, Los Angeles
- Bleeps & Blunders (1991)
—Directed a 10″ video of mistakes made in college settings.

Entered in Annual Film Festival.

- The Rise of Print (1991)
—Participated in educational video on history of printing.
—Involved in two segments (Introduction and Guttenberg).
—Duties: Research . Set Locations . Camera Work . Editing.
—Assisted in postproduction activities.
- Directed, wrote treatments, and performed for a number of 3- to 5-minute Skits (Television Production I).

EMPLOYMENT Secretary to a President (1990–Present)
Receptionist/Clerk (1989–1990)
Customer Service Representative (1988–1989)

EDUCATION UNIVERSITY OF CALIFORNIA, Los Angeles, CA
B.A. in Media Communications and Education (1993)

ROBERT O'HARA

280 San Antonio Place • San Marcus, Texas 78022 • (915) 593-0000

OBJECTIVE Position as **Lawyer's Assistant/Paralegal** where my research, organizational, and supervisory skills would be assets. Bilingual.

EDUCATION SOUTHWEST TEXAS STATE UNIVERSITY
Certificate in Advanced Paralegal Studies (1991) .. 92% average
••An intensive 5-month ABA-approved training program:

- Bankruptcy
- U.C.C.
- Contracts
- Immigration
- WESTLAW/LEXIS/D.P.
- Securities

Diploma—Legal Assistant Training Program (1989)
••Completed a 307-hour General Certificate Program:

• Legal Research	(60 hours)	A grade
• Litigation	(45 hours)	A grade
• Domestic Relations	(22½ hours)	A grade
• Trusts & Estates	(45 hours)	A grade
• Corporations	(45 hours)	A grade
• Real Estate/Contracts	(45 hours)	B grade
• Torts	(45 hours)	A grade

.. Research .. Analysis .. Case Studies .. Role Playing

SOUTHWEST TEXAS STATE UNIVERSITY
B.A. in Political Science (1987) ... B+ average

RELATED SKILLS

- Office management experience; supervision of clerks.
- Able to organize, prioritize, and oversee work.
- Strong research and data collection skills.
- Able to interview and interact well with clients.
- Writing skills (special papers and memoranda).
- Able to exercise sound independent judgment.
- Computer skills (IBM PC . CRT . UNYSIS PC . WordPerfect).
- Light typing (letters . memos . proposals . documents).
- Able to work well under pressure of deadlines.

POSITIONS HELD

1988–Present

Office Manager
COMPUTER SOFTWARE, INC., San Marcus, TX
—Responsible for day-to-day administration of an office.
—Interact extensively with members of the public.
—Interview clients to determine their needs.

1982–1987

Senior Teller/Customer Service Representative
FIRST FEDERAL SAVINGS BANK, San Marcus, TX
—Trained and supervised new hires.

STACEY STERLING

300 West 12th Avenue • Denver, CO 80203 • (303) 828-0000

OBJECTIVE: Entry-level MARKETING position where my experience in a variety of marketing projects and interest in new product development would be of value.

STRENGTHS:
- Degree in Marketing .. Cum Laude .. Scholarship Recipient.
- Completion of student projects in: Market Research . Market Surveys . Direct Mail . Direct Advertising . Sales Management.
- Telemarketing experience selling consumer products.
- Research and data collection skills; strong analytical skills.
- Oral and written communications skills.
- Work well under pressure; hardworking; high energy level.

EDUCATION: DENVER INSTITUTE OF TECHNOLOGY, Denver, CO
B.S. in Marketing (June 1992) .. GPA = 3.6/4.0

Projects:
- Member of 4-person team that played a 12-week computer simulation game concerning the introduction of 3 new softdrink products. Variables included: advertising . inventory . sales force . development of product formulas . sales projections and inventory projections. Held executive board meetings; invested monies; made budgetary allocations; prepared income statements and balance sheets. Wrote an 80-page paper that included an accurate projection of next year's performance. Won the game in competition with five other teams.

- Prepared a marketing research report to advise Sunnyside Club whether or not to build an extension (banquet room). Analyzed the previous year's records, prices being charged, and level of expenditures on the banqueting profit center. Recommended that prices be raised rather than increase volume.

- Direct advertising assignments included analyzing TV commercials, response rates, and target markets.

- Sales Territory Mapping based on number of accounts, volume, and territory.

PETER S. REYNOLDS COLLEGE, Denver, CO
Associate's degree in Data Processing (1990) .. Cum Laude

ACTIVITIES:
- Member, American Marketing Association
- Vice-President, College Marketing Club

EMPLOYMENT: Helped fund tuition costs (60%) by working as follows:

Present   Waitress, B&J RESTAURANT, Denver, CO
Summer 1990   Telemarketing Representative, DETERGENTS, INC., Boulder, CO
1988–1990   Catering Manager, GREAT HOTEL, Denver, CO

DEBORA ANDERSON

80–10 20th Street • Brooklyn, NY 11370 • (718) 800-0101

OBJECTIVE: Position in SOCIAL/HUMAN SERVICES where my strong research skills and teaching/writing ability would be assets.

EDUCATION: QUEENS COLLEGE, City University of New York, NY
B.A. in Psychology (Nov. 1992)
Minor: Substance Abuse (Drug Addiction)
Courses: Sociological and Clinical Aspects of Substance Abuse (offered by Health department at school).

KINGSBOROUGH COMMUNITY COLLEGE, Brooklyn, NY
Associate of Arts degree (1990)
•• Tutored nursing students in Psychology.

**HONORS &
AWARD:**
- Graduated Magna Cum Laude (G.P.A. = 3.7/4.0)
- Golden Key National Honor Society Award (for academic excellence)

FIELD WORK:
• Conducted field work on Substance Abuse at Daytop Village in Jamaica, Queens—a treatment center for adolescents.
• Involved in self-help groups for women.
• Attended meetings of ALANON (12-step groups).
• Obtained Group Counseling experience in all above groups.

**SPECIAL
PAPERS:**
- Wrote research papers with emphasis on Substance Abuse.
- Wrote a paper on amphetamines that was described by Prof. U. No Hoo, C.S.W., as "scholarly." (Prof. Hoo set up one of the first Methadone treatment programs.)

REFERENCES: Professor U. No Hoo, C.S.W., Assistant Professor of Sociology & Assistant Chairman of Department, Queens College.
Professor V. Clever, Assistant Professor of Health & Physical Education (Substance Abuse), Queens College.

**PREVIOUS
EMPLOYMENT:** DREW & JOHNSON, INC., Advertising Agency, NYC
Assistant Vice President (1989)
Credit Manager (1986–1988)
Office Supervisor (1983–1986)

Note: Only in a change-of-career resume is it a good idea to include the names of references in your *new* field. Such people can help you to overcome the skepticism and resistance of employers to those with zig-zag backgrounds. (When relocating to another state, the names of respected *local* residents will similarly help you.)

Part Four

HOW TO
OPEN DOORS TO
DIFFERENT JOBS

12

TARGETING JOBS WITH DIFFERENT RESUMES

Resumes are no longer simply compiled and mass-mailed, but rather are composed, stylized and formulated like a musical score, tailor-made for the reader.
—IRENE COHEN, C.E.O., New York employment agency [42]

WHY WRITING DIFFERENT RESUMES IS IMPORTANT IN THE '90s

In a highly competitive buyer's market, employers have little time for a vague, all-purpose resume that fails to address their specific needs. Instead, they demand to see evidence of focused interest and expect an "I-wrote-this-resume-just-for-you" type of approach. In other words, a *tailored* resume. How to write 2–4 focused resumes that address the needs of each "buyer," is therefore the subject of this chapter.

To remind you, you do have a variety of skills to offer because everyone has transferable skills, some of which are very marketable. As we have seen, your present skills may qualify you to perform up to 70 percent of all office jobs which involve the same basic skills (communicating, interacting with people, solving problems, and so on). That is why the five pages of skills sentences in Chapter 2 are so important. In fact, your best bet is first to learn how to market these. Upgrading your technical skills must therefore rank only as an "extra" be-

cause skills that you acquire in a classroom will usually cover only 10–30 percent of the total content of a job!

A tailored resume—one that offers a specific combination of skills—will maximize your chances of meeting with an employer and persuading him or her that you *can* do the job. As we saw in Chapter 3, your formal "qualifications" *don't* have to be a perfect fit because it is not usually or even necessarily the best *qualified* candidate that gets hired. (Richard Lathrop) (Nowadays, that candidate may be asking for too much!) What usually matters more, is knowing how to *present* your selling points—on paper and in person.

As for deciding whether to apply or not, how often can you tell if you'll be under- or overqualified? Since only 15–20 percent of all help-wanted advertisements are *really* accurate, how can you be sure that you'll be 131 percent or 87 percent or only 34 percent qualified for the vacancy? Only by talking with employers about their problems will you be in a position to discover what they *really* need and see that you do have equivalent experience and valuable skills to offer—many of them anyway. But to unlock that door today, a tailored resume is your best job search tool—even if you are only half-qualified.

If putting together your CAN DO'S on paper is your problem, you may need the help of a competent resume-writing professional. (They do exist!) He or she will analyze your background, identify your transferable skills and show you how to market them as *selling points* rather than as the vague "functions" of the unpopular functional resume.

Now let's see how multiple resumes are constructed.

"PEACHES," "NECTARINES," AND "PLUMS"

To explore all of your options in today's job market you will therefore need to construct two to four different resumes because a combination of your skills and experience that might appeal to one audience will probably be of little interest to another.

In this chapter you will learn to present yourself to one employer as a "peach," to another as a "nectarine," and to a third as a "plum" by presenting your CAN DO's in different ways. (Bakers do the same when they produce white and wheat loaves of bread. The products are different, but 95 percent of the ingredients are the same. Similarly, it won't require much more skill to make resume "magic.")

The first thing you have to do in order to focus your resume is to decide what you wish to "bake." As we have already seen (Chapter 4), focusing starts with writing a clear Job Objective. That, in turn, will guide you in selecting and organizing your data. Such a focused resume is the exact *opposite* of an "all-purpose" resume (without Objective), which will probably fail to address the needs of even a single position.

What this means is that (a) you'll need to prepare a focused resume, not a "general" one, and (b) you'll have to vary it in two to four ways to target various jobs. To be able to write such a focused resume you had to identify and describe your skills (pages 21–22) and learn to write a focused Job Objective (page 43) and Skills Summary (Chapter 5).

Line by line, a focused resume is your most valuable marketing tool in any job market.

But how does one prepare two to four versions of one's resume from the *same* education and lifework experience? The short answer is (a) by writing two to four different Job Objectives and (b) by compiling two to four Summaries of Skills and Experience—each with a different "flavor."

Each Summary will include only those items that back up its own Objective and address the employer's specific needs. (Sample items will be your related skills or abilities, your related education, and your related work experience.) When or where you learned or used those skills is *not* important. The main requirement is that each Objective and its Summary should be geared toward the *type* and *level* of position you are seeking.

Next you will be looking at your Work History and selecting and/or emphasizing only those jobs (or duties) that are *related* to each Objective. Unrelated experience should be downplayed or moved down to a special section: ADDITIONAL (or UNRELATED) EMPLOYMENT. It can even be relegated to a two- to three-line footnote near the bottom or end of the resume. (See example on page 137.)

The same rules apply to focusing your EDUCATION. Emphasize only what will support your Job Objective in the most *direct* way. And express your items in a manner that won't contain any possible "turnoff." For example, if you are applying for a position as Zookeeper, you can safely write: "B.S. in Veterinary Science, (1990)." But to apply for a position as Manager in a quality restaurant, you would be wiser to omit your major(s) and record your education as "B.S., 1990."

These techniques really work. One of my clients was recently appointed Assistant Manager in the first-class restaurant of a deluxe five-star hotel in New York City. He had previously majored in Veterinary Science! Another obtained a position as Customer Service Manager, although his actual degree (from SUNY's McCallister Institute) qualified him to attend to the needs of "customers"—but as a mortician! To summarize, by adding a Skills Summary to your resume and learning how to vary the five to ten items it includes, you can easily construct two to four focused resumes and use them to target various jobs.

THE FOUR FACES OF SYLVIA ROMERO

Sylvia Romero (not her real name) was completing her Master's thesis at a Los Angeles film and TV school. But unlike many of her classmates, she hated the idea of working as a waitress. Upon arriving in the United States from La Paz, Bolivia (where she had graduated with a B.A. in Spanish Literature), Sylvia took a few courses to improve her English, and a short course in word processing.

She then marketed her bilingualism, "people," and communications skills and managed to find part-time positions in the offices of two lawyers. Here she assisted them with their Spanish-speaking clients.

All in all, Sylvia had only a few months of office experience, but this was sufficient for her to prepare *three* focused resumes to target three widely different positions, as well as a fourth in her chosen field (Film and Video). Sylvia now decided to look for employment as

1. Word Processor/Secretary
2. Translator/Interpreter (Spanish/English)

Turn to her first two resumes on pages 182 and 183. In the Experience section, the two versions mention the *same* two law offices that Sylvia had briefly worked in. However, her Related Skills and Summary of Skills and Experience sections (at the top of each resume) emphasize different job-related skills and experience: those she had acquired in these two firms, as well as what she had learned by assisting fellow students. To round off Sylvia's two resumes, in each case, different duties are highlighted to tie in with her Job Objective.

OPTION I.
WORD PROCESSING/SECRETARIAL

Under Related Skills (below), Sylvia markets her word processing and secretarial skills and experience. It emphasizes W/P, typing, and office skills.

Each "bullet" backs up her Objective. (In this resume, she *omits* the word "Spanish" from her degree in Spanish Literature.)

OBJECTIVE: A position as **Word Processor/Secretary**.

RELATED SKILLS:
- Bachelor of Arts degree in Literature.
- Experience as Word Processor/Secretary in law firms.
- Knowledge of general office routines.
- Computer skills (IBM PC . WordPerfect . Tandy W/P).
- Typing skills (60 wpm) .. very accurate.
- Able to input legal documents and correspondence.
- Detail oriented.
- Able to work well under time and accuracy pressures.
- Excellent interpersonal and teamwork skills.
- Bilingual (English/Spanish).

EXPERIENCE:
March 1991–
Dec. 1991

Word Processor/Secretary
LAW OFFICE OF PETER SMYTHE, Esq., Los Angeles, CA
—Used IBM PC and WordPerfect.
—Input a variety of legal documents.
—Performed a full range of secretarial/clerical duties.
—Translated from English into Spanish and vice versa.

June 1990–
Jan. 1991

Junior Secretary/Word Processor
LAW OFFICE OF RONEL FRITZ, Esq., Los Angeles, CA
—Used Tandy word processor.
—Input legal documentation and correspondence.
—Performed general/clerical and secretarial duties.
—Translated documents (English/Spanish).
—Interpreted for Spanish-speaking clients.

EDUCATION:
BROWN SECRETARIAL SCHOOL—<u>WordPerfect</u>   (1990)
STANFORD UNIVERSITY—<u>Advanced English Writing</u>   (1989)
UNIVERSITY OF LA PAZ—B.A. (Literature)   (1985)

OPTION 2. TRANSLATOR/
INTERPRETER

The Summary below focuses on Sylvia's foreign language, "people," and communications skills—both orally and in writing. It includes not only her *formal* experience in two law offices, but her part-time and *informal* experience with students, Spanish-speaking tourists, and visiting business-persons.

JOB OBJECTIVE

A position as **Translator/Interpreter** (English/Spanish; Spanish/English). Able to interpret simultaneously. Bilingual education.

SUMMARY OF SKILLS AND EXPERIENCE

- Fluent in both spoken and written Spanish and English.
- Bachelor's degree in Spanish Literature (La Paz, Bolivia).
- Courses in Advanced English and Writing at Stanford University.
- Experience as Interpreter in law firms with Spanish-speaking clients and for tourists/businesspersons.
- Translation of legal, historical, commercial, and personal documents and correspondence.
- Interpersonal and public relations skills; professional image.

PROFESSIONAL EXPERIENCE

1991   **Translator/Interpreter**
LAW OFFICE OF PETER SMYTHE, Esq., Los Angeles, CA
—Assisted Spanish-speaking clients to communicate with an English-speaking attorney specializing in Immigration Law.
—Interpreted and translated the lawyer's questions, comments, recommendations, and advice—from English into Spanish.
—Interpreted clients' requests and replies—from Spanish.
—Translated legal documents and correspondence from English into Spanish and vice versa.

1990 – 1991   **Translator/Interpreter**
LAW OFFICE OF RONEL FRITZ, Esq., Los Angeles, CA
—Assisted visiting Spanish-speaking businesspersons during legal consultations with English-speaking attorneys.
—Interpreted simultaneously from Spanish/English.
—Translated a wide range of legal documents/correspondence.

FREELANCE TRANSLATING AND INTERPRETING

—Translated academic research material on Latin-American history for Ph.D. candidates.
—Interpreted for Spanish-speaking tourists and businesspersons.

EDUCATION

1985–   UNIVERSITY OF LA PAZ, Bolivia—B.A., Spanish Literature
1989   STANFORD UNIVERSITY, CA—Advanced English & Writing

SYLVIA'S THIRD OPTION:
OFFICE COORDINATOR
(TELEVISION/FILMS/VIDEO)

Sylvia decided to be even more ambitious by applying for a *full-time* position in an office. To achieve this she combined her recent office skills and film/video training. That would qualify her to start looking for a position in the television industry (for which she was training).

Now look at Sylvia's third resume (page 185). Notice how the Strengths section emphasizes

1. Her TV production education and experience
2. Her coordinating skills and experience
3. Her office and computer skills, teamwork skills, and ability to work under time and accuracy pressures

Sylvia divided the Experience section into

1. Office experience
2. Film/Video experience

The emphasis is now on Coordination/Liaison. Notice how she uses her Production Trainee school experience. It *is* "working" experience. Ask any trainee.

In the Education section, Sylvia omits any reference to her graduation in Bolivia. She didn't want her English language skills to be questioned. (They were more than adequate.) Her working experience in La Paz does not necessarily mean that she is Bolivian! Also, she is enrolled in a Master's program, so an undergraduate degree is assumed.

OPTION 3. OFFICE COORDINATOR—TELEVISION

OBJECTIVE: A position as OFFICE COORDINATOR/LIAISON where my coordinating, "people," and office skills would be assets. Technical knowledge of TV Production/Assisting.

STRENGTHS:
- B.A. and studies in TV & Film Production.
- Experience as Office Coordinator/Secretary in two fast-paced offices and as Coordinator/Liaison during production of feature films and TV commercials.
- Thorough knowledge of general office/secretarial duties.
- Organizational, scheduling, and follow-up skills.
- Able to work well under pressure and meet deadlines.
- Interpersonal, communications, and teamwork skills.
- Computer skills (IBM PC . WordPerfect . Tandy W/P).
- Typing (60 wpm) . detail oriented . bilingual.
- Interact well with different people and personalities.

EXPERIENCE:
(Office)
1991

Office Coordinator/Secretary
LAW OFFICE OF PETER SMYTHE, Esq., Los Angeles, CA
—Coordinated and scheduled meetings, interviews, appointments, and consultations in a busy office.
—Acted as liaison between attorneys and many clients.
—Coordinated the work of paralegals and clerks.
—Performed secretarial and word processing duties.
—Heavy follow-up of cases with other agencies.

1990–1991

Secretary/Coordinator/Word Processor
LAW OFFICE OF RONEL FRITZ, Esq., Los Angeles, CA
—Performed a wide range of coordinating, secretarial, and follow-up duties similar to the above.

EXPERIENCE:
(Film/Video)
1989–Present

Film & Television Production Trainee

UNIVERSITY OF SOUTHERN CALIFORNIA, Los Angeles, CA
—Involved in production of B&W film shorts and have written/directed a 20-minute narrative video project.

1986–1988

Production Coordinator/Assistant
S. FILM PRODUCTIONS, La Paz, Bolivia
—Worked on feature films and TV productions.

EDUCATION: BROWN SECRETARIAL SCHOOL—WordPerfect   (1990)
STANFORD UNIVERSITY, CA—Advanced English Writing   (1989)
CALIFORNIA U.—M.F.A. program in Film & Television   (1989–Present)

OPTION 4. ENTRY-LEVEL POSITION IN FILM AND VIDEO

OBJECTIVE   An entry-level position in the FILM & VIDEO industry where my graduate studies in Film and Television, experience as Production Assistant, and strong camera/technical skills would be of value.

SUMMARY OF SKILLS AND EXPERIENCE

- M.F.A. program in Film & Television.
- Experience as Production Assistant at various levels (both in school and in a film production company overseas).
- School experience includes Writing/Directing/Producing/Editing:
  —10″ B&W narrative film (Antonio's Perspective)
  —4″ B&W musical commentary (Spanish Harlem)
  —20″ Color narrative video (Politicians) and 2 × Scripts
- Camera experience (Video & Film), as well as Lighting.
- Quick to grasp the technical aspects of Production.
- Well-developed visual and conceptual sense.
- Able to understand and execute detailed instructions.
- Excellent communications and teamwork skills; bilingual.

EDUCATION AND TRAINING

UNIVERSITY OF SOUTHERN CALIFORNIA, Los Angeles, CA
M.F.A. candidate in Film & Television   (1989–Present)
•• Completed coursework included: Editing (Film & Video) .. Production Techniques .. Hands-on Production .. Camera.
•• Workshop in Directing and Acting (Francois du Plessis).
•• Thesis to be completed in 1992.

LA PAZ UNIVERSITY, Bolivia—B.A.   (1981–1985)

PROFESSIONAL EXPERIENCE

1989–Present   Film & Television Production Trainee
UNIVERSITY OF SOUTHERN CALIFORNIA, Los Angeles, CA
—As a student, worked on numerous film projects.
—Experience includes: Cameraperson (Film and Video) .. Camera Assistant (Film) .. Deck Operator (Video) .. Script Continuity.

1986–1988   Assistant to Producer/Coordinator
S. FILM PRODUCTIONS, La Paz, Bolivia
—Worked on sets of feature films and TV commercials.
—Participated in production from concept through completion.

1984–1985   Photojournalist
INTOMBI (Women's Magazine), La Paz, Bolivia

PROBLEMS OF JOB TITLES AND DATES IN CONSTRUCTING VARIOUS RESUMES

What should you do if you want to target a position but your best or most related work experience was *not* obtained in your present or most recent job? This often happens if you have had to accept a temporary or alternative position or if you've been transferred to another position or department by your present employer. In either case, a prospective employer may not be impressed by what you are doing at present (or by your present job title) because it may seem unrelated to his or her needs.

Awkward job titles (and dates) can be a serious resume-writing problem. To a picky employer you might not look like a good "fit" for a particular position.

Should you try to cover up your problem by using a pure functional resume format that sells your functions (or abilities) rather than your work history? No, in most cases the combination resume format will be more effective because it is more flexible and the end product will look more "normal" to the reader. (In a combination format you are free to use the best or most useful features of other resume formats, including the functional.)

You will be shown how to "fix" awkward dates and job titles in Chapter 13, "Fixing Resume Blemishes or 'Warts.'" In this exercise, you'll see how a few "functional" ideas or concepts can be used to create a combination resume that works (rather than construct an entire functional resume from A to Z).

THE TWO RESUMES OF SANDRA JONES

Sandra Jones (not her real name) was experiencing the problem of awkward titles and dates in trying to construct the two resume versions she needed to apply for positions in *media* and *health care*. Her most recent experience had been in public relations—as an assistant to a Director of Communications (for six months). Prior to that she had worked in a health care practice as a medical secretary and office manager.

How would an advertising or communications executive react to her three years as a medical secretary? He or she might not be impressed! And what would health care people say about her public relations experience?

Sandra's marketing problem was that her previous job title as Medical Secretary would *not* support a job objective geared toward a position in the media; nor would Assistant to Director of Communications impress a typical physician. As regards Sandra's objective to return to the health care field, a further problem was how to present her best and most related experience first. This was during the period 1989–1992—*before* her most recent position in public relations.

CHANGING THE "FLAVOR" OF A RESUME: VARIOUS SOLUTIONS

COMMUNICATIONS AND ADVERTISING

Look at Sandra's Communications resume on page 188. After a suitable Job Objective, she records her education and three job-related projects to interest a media recruiter. Next, Sandra describes in detail her PR work and her duties on a monthly newspaper. This is all job related.

However, instead of writing "Medical Secretary/Office Manager," Sandra labels herself Administrative Assistant/Secretary. This is perfectly acceptable because she did perform such tasks. The titles *don't* define what she really did—they seldom do!) (See also Chapter 13.)

Sandra continues to remove the medical "flavor" from her previous job by deleting "CLINIC" from the trade name of her employer, by substituting "fast-paced office" for "practice with high patient volume," by deleting "Health Insurance" from billings, and by deleting "medical" from the reports she had typed. There is no longer anything "medical" about her Communications resume.

SANDRA JONES

90 Eastern Parkway, Greenwich, CT 06830 ° (203) 346-0000

OBJECTIVE Entry-level position: COMMUNICATIONS/ADVERTISING.

EDUCATION BOSTON UNIVERSITY, Boston, MA
B.A. in Communication Studies   (1986)
Projects: Participated in a Political Survey in Eastern Massachusetts; collected and analyzed data.
Designed an Advertising Campaign for a new furniture store.
Produced B&W film shorts. Wrote scripts.

EXPERIENCE **Assistant to Director of Communications**
1992 RETAIL MERCHANTS' ASSOCIATION, Stamford, CT
Established 20 years to lobby for small retailers.
Public Relations:
—Coordinated public relations activities.
—Wrote press releases using IBM PC.
—Organized press conferences.
—Followed through on correspondence.
• Revamped the office; set up an improved filing system.
Newspaper ("Viewpoints") and Film Review Column
—A 24-page monthly aimed at small businesses.
—Wrote, edited, and proofread copy; data entry.
—Made presentations to sell advertising space.
—Performed a wide range of administrative duties, including Bookkeeping .. Billing .. Collection of Advertising Fees.
• Contributed to a film review column.

1989–1992 **Administrative Assistant/Secretary**
SMITHERS, INC., Hartford, CT
—Responsible for day-to-day management and administration of a fast-paced office.
—Supervised six office staff.
—Scheduled appointments; interacted with clients.
—Processed billings and Accounts Payable.
—Typed detailed reports.
• Streamlined office procedures; updated filing system.

1987–1988 **Rental Sales Agent**
AVIS RENT-A-CAR, Logan Airport, Boston, MA

1986 **Interviewer/Telephone Surveys**
FIRST MARKET RESEARCH COMPANY, Boston, MA
—Telephoned residents to sound out their attitudes about the introduction of budget-priced stores in an upscale mall.
—Conducted a financial survey for American Express.

MEDICAL OFFICE

Now look at Sandra's Medical Office resume (page 190). After her Job Objective, she uses a different strategy. Instead of presenting her communications degree and projects (which are *not* job related in this case), Sandra presents a neat Summary that is "medical office" from A to Z. It includes many of the items a medical recruiter would be interested to read.

Next comes a neat resume-writing strategy that can be used by anyone who needs to *reverse the order* of his or her jobs in order to present a preferred position first. Notice that the dates of her two most recent jobs have now been combined in the lefthand margin as 1989–1992. However, in the righthand margin, two time periods are given instead of the usual dates ("3 Years" instead of 1989–1992 and "6 Months" instead of 1990.) By doing this, Sandra can reverse the order of her two jobs and no one will think of questioning it! (See "Why a Professor of Accounting Had to 'Fix' His Dates," in Chapter 13.)

This time the job description is completely "medical." Sandra has played down her public relations experience in two ways:

1. By changing her job title to Office Manager
2. By shrinking the job description from 14 lines to six

At the foot of her resume comes Sandra's Education section—her nonessential (in this case) B.A. In her Communications resume, this item was presented at the top of the page.

SANDRA JONES

90 Eastern Parkway, Greenwich, CT 06830 ° (203) 346-0000

OBJECTIVE   A position as **Medical Secretary/Office Manager**.

SUMMARY
- Three years' experience as Office Manager/Medical Secretary in a high-volume situation; supervised employees.
- Additional office management experience.
- Knowledge of medical terminology.
- Experience in using CPT and ICD-9 codes.
- Patient Billings . Insurance Claim Forms . Bookkeeping.
- Computer skills (IBM PC).

EXPERIENCE
1989–1992

Office Manager/Medical Secretary   (3 Years)
SMITHERS CLINIC, INC., Hartford, CT
Physical Medicine and Rehabilitation
Staff of 5 Physical Therapists
—Responsible for day-to-day management and administration of a practice with a high patient volume (120+ per day).
—Supervised 6 office staff.
—Scheduled appointments and dealt with patients.
—Processed the billing of Health Insurance Claims.
—Used CPT and ICD-9 codes.
—Typed medical reports.
—Responsible for Accounts Payable and Bookkeeping.
—Maintained inventory of medical supplies.
- Streamlined office procedures; updated the filing system.

Office Manager/Bookkeeper   (6 Months)
RETAIL MERCHANTS' ASSOCIATION, Stamford, CT
—Performed a wide range of administrative duties, including Bookkeeping .. Billing .. Collection of Advertising Fees.
—Data Entry using IBM PC.
- Reorganized the office and set up a new filing system.

1987–1988   **Rental Sales Agent**
AVIS RENT-A-CAR, Logan Airport, Boston, MA
—Used IBM system for scheduling bookings and vehicles.
—Heavy problem-solving and customer relations.

1986   **Interviewer/Telephone Surveys**
FIRST MARKET RESEARCH COMPANY, Boston, MA
—Telephoned residents to sound out their attitudes about the introduction of budget-priced stores in an upscale mall.

EDUCATION   BOSTON UNIVERSITY, Boston, MA
B.A.   (1986)

HOW PETER MORLEY COLLECTED HIS SKILLS AND MARKETED THEM

Peter Morley (not his real name) had trained for a career in Radio. In a series of positions he had learned to gather and prepare news for broadcast—always under pressure of deadlines. (He had also worked as a D.J. and knew a lot about contemporary music and artists.)

A few of these skills were easily transferable to his next job—as News Editor/Announcer in a 900-Number Business Service Company that provided information to the public by way of prerecorded announcements. Here Peter acquired a few more skills—listening to customer inquiries and how to evaluate and handle complaints.

When he was laid off, Peter marketed his radio "voice" and new customer service skills to a telecommunications company. Here he was given more in-house training and learned to cross-sell their products.

With six years in Radio, nearly two as Editor/Announcer and some experience in customer service/sales, Peter prepared *three* focused resumes, each offering a different combination of skills and experience.

A. Peter's first option was radio. His new resume (p. 192) includes *three* crucial selling points in his Objective. (These are expressed in the jargon of the industry.) The Experience section *omits* his current position in customer service because it is unrelated. All station names have been changed for obvious reasons. His eight dates may seem awful, but this is *not* unusual in the radio industry. (See also p. 203)

B. As an alternative to a radio station, Peter liked the idea of a record company—to promote their product to radio stations. (See p. 193) Since he had been a D.J., knew a lot about contemporary music and also had valuable contacts in a major market area, he could offer at least *nine* selling points to those who always need air playtime for new releases. (The main purpose of his "Related Experience" section is to provide evidence of his contacts in AM and FM radio stations and his knowledge of music—*not* to tell them what his duties were. Under Education, courses in Marketing are now included.)

C. Finally, Peter needed a resume to seek a better position in customer service—one with easier working hours/shifts. This resume (p. 194) has an objective with *three* "grabber statements" or hooks. Each selling point in the Summary backs it up.

As regards his Experience, Peter now includes the customer service aspects of his previous position and the fact that he had "coordinated" some of these activities. (Regarding his "adjusted" job title, see p. 202) Notice that his Education section now contains an in-house training program that is job-related.

A.
PETER MORLEY

174 Millbrook Road, Suffern, NY 12054 ° Messages: (914) 357-0000

OBJECTIVE A position in a RADIO station where my metro markets experience would be an asset. Offer my wide knowledge of contemporary music (and artists), including AOR, CHR, HOT AC and Personality News. Have a major market "voice."

EXPERIENCE
8/92–12/92

Evening Air Personality/D.J., WPOP-FM, New Haven, CT
—An oldies station serving the New York metropolitan area that features hits of the 50's, 60's and early 70's.

1/91–7/92

News Editor/Announcer, A.B.C. CALL PROCESSING, Monsey, NY
—Worked for a national 900-number business service.
—Interpreted information from Reuters; developed and broadcasted an up-to-the-minute composite of business, financial and stock information for investors.

9/90–12/90

News Director, WHIP-FM & WHOP-AM, Spring Valley, NY
—Had to juggle many tasks simultaneously.
—Coordinated morning newscasts; made extensive contacts with local political figures; stayed on top of breaking stories.
—Primary coverage area included: Southern Connecticut, Eastchester, Dutchess and Sullivan Counties of NY State.

2/89–8/90

Evening Air Personality, WPOW-AM, Patterson, NY
—Delivered news updates, weather reports and sports bulletins.
—Also coordinated engineering for Pow-Wow, a talk show program fed live via satellite around the U.S. and Canada.

9/87–4/88

Intern, WABC-AM, New York, NY
—Prepared on-air service announcements and community calendar messages. Assisted public affairs hosts with weekly shows and newscasters with research and "wire" machines.

5/87–7/87

Market Researcher, WTIP-FM, New York, NY
—Conducted music surveys/market research in NY metro area.

9/86–1/87

Assistant to Station Manager. WTOP-AM, Suffern, NY
—Worked with station manager. Wrote traffic reports; recorded announcements.

1/86–8/86

D.J., WBRO-FM & WHOB-FM, Bronx, NY & Hoboken, NJ

EDUCATION HUNTER COLLEGE, City University, New York, NY
B.A. in Media Communications & Management   (1989)

TAPES Available upon request.

B.
PETER MORLEY

174 Millbrook Road, Suffern, NY 12054 ° Messages: (914) 357-0000

OBJECTIVE: A position in RECORD PROMOTIONS within the Music Industry. Offer my promotions/marketing experience and valuable contacts in Radio and related environments. Able to meet deadlines. Am a go-getter.

STRENGTHS:
- Broad-based Radio experience (six years in Commercial, Public and College radio as Evening Air Personality, D.J., etc); exposure to major market situations.
- Internships in WTIP (Contemporary Hit Radio) and WABC.
- Knowledge of contemporary Classical Rock artists.
- Experience as D.J. in a Rock Oldies station.
- Wide knowledge of AOR format (Album-oriented Rock).
- Valuable contacts within the Radio industry; access to Music Program Directors and their playlists.
- Conducted music market research surveys; studied demographics to confirm that target audiences were being reached.
- Music experience includes: Song Selection (based on music log); Mixing; and Programming.
- Familiar with <u>Gavin</u> Report, <u>Radio & Records</u>, <u>Mac</u> Report.

**RELATED
EXPERIENCE:** <u>Promotions/Customer Service/Sales</u>
1991–Present FONE-TEL & A.B.C. CALL PROCESSING CO., Monsey, NY
—Promotions and cross-selling of products and services.

1992 <u>On-Air Personality/D.J.</u>,
WPOP-FM RADIO, New Haven, CT

1990 <u>News Director</u>
WHIP-FM & WHOP-AM RADIO, Spring Valley, NY

1988–1990 <u>On-Air Personality/Coordinator</u>
WPOW-AM RADIO, Patterson, NY

1987–1988 <u>Intern/Market Researcher</u>
WABC-AM & WTIP-FM RADIO, New York, NY

1986 <u>D.J.</u>,
WBRO-FM & WHOB-FM, Bronx, NY & Hoboken, NJ

EDUCATION: HUNTER COLLEGE, City University, New York, NY
B.A. in Media Communications/Marketing (1989)

C.
PETER MORLEY

174 Millbrook Road, Suffern, N.Y. 12054 ° Messages: (914) 357-0000

OBJECTIVE: A position in CUSTOMER SERVICE where my success in a major telecommunications company and ability to cross-sell products would be of value. Am very organized and persuasive due to my radio "voice" and experience.

SUMMARY:
- B.A. in Communications; training in proactive customer service/cross-selling.
- Experience as Customer Service Representative (Telecommunications) and as Customer Service Coordinator (900 Telephone Service); also WABC Radio.
- Excellent performance evaluations; award for "Best Call of the Month."
- Proven ability to work well under pressure and handle a heavy volume of calls (100–120 daily); sensitivity to clients and their needs.
- Strong research and problem-solving skills; report-writing.
- Due to my polished delivery (previous experience was in Radio), have credibility and convert many complaining customers into buyers of additional services.
- Able to execute promises to customers under strict time constraints; flexibility in handling "difficult" callers.

EXPERIENCE:
1993–Present

Customer Service Representative
FONE-TEL, INC. (Telecommunications), White Plains, NY
—Handle a high volume of incoming and outgoing customer traffic.
—Inquiries are processed via ACD and CFT systems.
—Give callers pricing and rate information; sell them on additional services.
—Heavy problem-solving and research.
—Follow-up problems and complaints.
—Perform related clerical/administrative work; Data entry.
- Received two consecutive awards for Customer Satisfaction.

1991–1992

Customer Service Coordinator
A.B.C. CALL PROCESSING CO. (900-Number), Monsey, NY
—Prepared and recorded information for business customers.
—Answered questions about the stock market.
—Handled and resolved complaints; wrote reports.
- "Did a first class job . . . was valuable."—Manager

1986–1990

On-Air Personality/D.J./Intern—Various Radio Stations, NY

EDUCATION: FONE-TEL—IN-HOUSE TRAINING PROGRAMS
Proactive Customer Service + Cross-Selling (8 weeks)

HUNTER COLLEGE, City University, New York, NY
B.A. in Media Communications   (1989)

USING WORD PROCESSORS TO CUSTOMIZE YOUR RESUMES

For the past thirty to forty years the way to address the needs of various employers was by writing many cover letters. Thus the instrument of targeting was the cover letter rather than the job resume. The result was a variety of letters that accompanied a single, all-purpose resume.

However, with most employers now ignoring those letters, the strategy has to be *reversed*. You'll now need to vary your resume instead—on average, two to four times. And the detailed cover letter now becomes a brief note to route your targeted resume to the right party.

To maximize your chances of success, you should make every effort to obtain access to a word processor or personal computer. With the help of these tools, it's relatively easy to vary an existing resume or to write a new one, each time making a few minor changes. Only a few words or lines may have to be modified, usually in the Job Objective and Skills Summary. In fact, only a few minutes at the keyboard may be required to alter the *focus* of your resume to match the specific needs of a particular company or hiring authority. The result will be more versions of your resume to offer employers different combinations of your skills and experience.

Creating a tailored resume each time you apply for a job is *essential*. In the highly competitive job market of the '90s, the old idea of the "one resume that must fit all jobs" won't work. That type of resume heavily relied on focused cover letters to offer your skills. Without that letter, you'll need focused resumes to target various jobs.

Word processors and PCs are valuable tools in any job search. If your resume isn't on a floppy disk already, you shouldn't delay this much longer. And check that the printing is of letter quality—not dot matrix, which is hard on the eyes, especially when faxed.

To illustrate the use of a PC, let us see how Jane Roberts (not her real name) compiled her two resumes. In Jane's case, she wanted to send different resumes to the Graphic Arts and Fashion industries—fast-paced environments in which cover letters are seldom read and in which a resume has to interest the reader in seeing your portfolio.

USING A PC TO EMPHASIZE DIFFERENT SKILLS AND EXPERIENCE

Jane was anxious about the downturn in New York's garment industry, where she was working as an assistant designer. She was in danger of being laid off. Her two main options were

1. A design position in the fashion industry
2. A position in Graphic Arts/Art Direction

Jane was fortunate in that she could offer useful experience in each of these two fields. In addition, she held Associate's degrees in both Fashion Illustration and Graphic Design. (Was this luck or foresight? Similarly, many other job seekers have also completed a dual major and might have had work experience in each field.)

Jane's two resumes are presented on pages 196 and 197. The main differences between them are as follows:

1. The Job Objectives are different
2. The two Summaries offer slightly different skills
3. The Job Descriptions emphasize either Fashion Design or Graphics/Art
4. The two portfolios contain different items

Compare the two resumes even if you are not interested in either of these fields. The entire exercise consists of either including or leaving out items that do or do not support one of two specific Job Objectives.

JANE ROBERTS

20 West 8th Street #8, New York, NY 10005 ° (212) 677-6700

OBJECTIVE: A position as FASHION DESIGNER.

STRENGTHS:
- Experience as Assistant Designer, covering all aspects of design.
- Additional experience as Assistant Art Director in a pattern company.
- Strong graphic design and visual sense.
- Excellent drawing skills (freehand illustration) .. Gold Key Award.
- Presentation skills.
- Ability to work well with screen printers.
- Able to produce under pressure of deadlines; teamwork skills.
- Computer skills (Macintosh and Adobe Illustrator).

EXPERIENCE: **Designer/Assistant Designer**
1990–Present   X-Y-Z APPAREL MANUFACTURERS, New York, NY
Young Men's & Boys' Clothing
—Develop designs for seasonal clothing lines for major clients that include: ____ .. ____ and ____.
—Duties include all aspects of garment construction—from concept through completion.
—Design all logos . screen art . presentation boards . sketches . inside labels . hang tags . and specs.
—Use Macintosh PC and Adobe Illustrator.
—Sell to major stores such as ____ and ____.
—Shop the domestic market.

1988–1989   **Assistant Art Director**
BLUEBERRY PATTERN COMPANY, NYC
—Assisted Chief Art Director with catalog .. magazine ads .. promotional pieces.
—Became responsible for executing an entire project—from an initial concept through completion; extensive follow-through.
—Created a variety of promotional materials (posters . brochures . small seasonal books . 3-D point-of-purchase pieces).
—Initially, did layouts and spreads for catalog and magazine.
—Evaluated photography portfolios and fashion illustrations.

1987–1988   **Assistant—Creative Department**
BOSTWICK & DICKENS, Advertising Agency, New York, NY
—Exposure to advertising and creation of magazine ads.

PORTFOLIO: Logos (manual and computer) . Screen Art . Hang Tags . Presentation Boards.

EDUCATION: FASHION INSTITUTE OF TECHNOLOGY, SUNY, New York, NY
Graphic Design and Art Direction—A.A.S.   (1987)
Fashion Illustration—A.A.S.   (1984)

JANE ROBERTS

20 West 8th Street #8, New York, NY 10005 ° (212) 677-6700

OBJECTIVE A position as **Graphic Designer/Assistant Art Director**.

STRENGTHS
- Experience as Assistant to Chief Art Director and thorough knowledge of the art direction process; also fashion designing.
- Strong graphic design and visual sense.
- Excellent drawing skills (freehand illustration) .. Gold Key Award.
- Typography (including designing with type; e.g., logos).
- Photography (including evaluating portfolios and illustrations).
- Knowledge of 4-color printing.
- Able to work well under pressure of deadlines; teamwork skills.
- Portfolio (includes full-time/freelance illustration and graphics).

EXPERIENCE
1990–Present

Designer/Assistant Designer
X-Y-Z APPAREL MANUFACTURERS, New York, NY
—Do all graphic art work for new lines of clothing—from hangtags, labels, and logos to screened artwork; also, design textile prints.
—Use Macintosh PC and Adobe Illustrator.

1988–1989

Assistant Art Director
BLUEBERRY PATTERN COMPANY, New York, NY
—Assisted Chief Art Director with catalog .. magazine ads .. promotional pieces (for in-store use and for outside clients).
—Became responsible for executing an entire project—from an initial concept through completion; extensive follow-through.
—Designed magazine pages; developed own formats where needed.
—Created a variety of promotional materials (posters . brochures . small seasonal books . 3-D P-of-P pieces for in-store use); also, designed logos.
—Initially, did layouts and spreads for catalog and magazine.
—Heavy involvement with photography and type in all projects.
—Evaluated photography portfolios and fashion illustrations.
—Continuous involvement in 4-color printing projects.

1987–1988

Assistant—Creative Department
BOSTWICK & DICKENS, Advertising Agency, New York, NY
—Obtained wide exposure to advertising and creation of magazine ads for clients.

EDUCATION FASHION INSTITUTE OF TECHNOLOGY, SUNY, New York, NY
Graphic Design and Art Direction—A.A.S.   (1987)
.. Coursework included: Concepts and the Art Direction Process from A to Z.
Fashion Illustration—A.A.S.   (1984)

PORTFOLIO Posters . Catalogs . Fashion Books (Children and Adults) . Book Covers . Pamphlets . Brochures . Magazine Pages . Corporate Identity.

13

FIXING RESUME BLEMISHES OR "WARTS": AVOIDING A K.O. IN ROUND ONE

Always tell the truth, and you'll have less to remember.

—MARK TWAIN

And David said to Gad: I am greatly troubled;
let us fall into the hand of the Lord,
for His mercies are many;
but let me not fall into the hand of man.

—II Sam. 24:14

In round 1, job resumes are *not* read from A to Z. They are merely scanned for negatives. Personnel clerks and secretaries who do the initial screening, need to *eliminate* you quickly—in seconds. Anything to reduce their nine-inch piles! Your entire application could therefore be zapped in round 1 (even if your qualifications are a good "fit") because eight out of ten resumes will have serious blemishes. So what can you do to remove any turnoffs? The answers in this chapter are based on what has worked for hundreds of job seekers and on what employers have accepted. (They hired.)

Your main reason for writing a job resume is to impress. Marketing yourself means deciding what to reveal and how to present it to picky employers. This is why you need to downplay or omit all possible turnoffs. A World War II lyric expresses this idea very succinctly:

"ACCENTUATE THE POSITIVE . . . ELIMINATE THE NEGATIVE."

But would it really be okay to omit entire jobs (or any other facts)? The answer is yes, provided you do it in an acceptable manner. In other words, *not* by changing any dates (or other facts) but by learning a few easy techniques. The rule, according to Bernard Haldane, is: "NEVER LIE; BUT DO SELECT YOUR TRUTHS CAREFULLY." (From *What Color Is Your Parachute?*) This chapter will show you what you need not mention, what to downplay or camouflage, and what (and how) to omit.

WHY YOU NEED NOT FEEL GUILTY

There are important things you ought to know about your job resume. First, the word *resume* means "summary," and in any summary, by definition, some information must be left out.

Second, your job resume is a sales device and you are its owner. It is *not* the same as an employer's application form. (The latter is a *legal* document you have to sign and date. In a job resume you can include or leave out anything!)

You have the right to omit whatever you choose to leave out. Always omit any facts about your age, race or national origin, marital status, or sexual orientation—any item that could invite unfair discrimination. (Except for work in the FBI, CIA, or security field, your resume need not disclose all of the facts of your work history.)

The main purpose of your job resume is to make a positive first impression—to impress and sell the reader, *not* to confess your past! All job seekers should therefore leave out entire jobs, dates, and anything else that might not back up a Job Objective or that might create a negative impression. Your aim is to get yourself hired—not hanged!

WHAT YOU CAN SAFELY OMIT

At least 30 percent of your resume might be of little or no interest to a prospective employer. This is why your job descriptions (duties) need to become briefer the further you go back in time. Some jobs, descriptions, and dates should be omitted—especially those that don't support your Job Objective (or that you had fifteen-plus years ago).

In short, you need to clean up your resume, but you can do much more. There are perfectly acceptable ways to omit information (and close the gap that results). As a rule, you should omit

- job titles that don't support your Job Objective
- a short-term position (full- or part-time) if it lasted only a few days or weeks
- the job you chose to leave soon after starting it (because your boss was too abusive, sexually harassed you, misled you, or was going into Chapter 11)
- the job(s) you prefer to forget about (office politics, negative experiences, and so on)
- the job where the boss gives you a bad reference (some employers can be vindictive!)
- dates that make you look like a "job hopper"

(you've made too many moves in too short a time)
- dates that make you seem "too old" (don't give employers a chance to "date" you!)
- dates that imply that your training is outdated (can you use fourth-generation, state-of-the-art software?)

THE FIRST TURNOFFS IN A JOB RESUME

What to omit or change starts at the top of your job resume. Something about your name or address could cost you a job opportunity.

The way you spell your **name** might be so unusual that a personnel clerk might think you didn't bother to check. (For example, if it's Jon instead of John.) Rather "normalize" the spelling (because your resume is a marketing device *not* an application form). Similarly, if your name is too "foreign" (like Voobraniyam Rajah Voobraniyam), simplify it and write, say, "Ray Voobranih" or "Nat Rajah." To "Americanize" it is even better. Why? Because personnel juniors might discriminate against you!

Always give a street **address**—never a P.O. box number. Employers want to know where you live. Is it near or far from their firm? Will you be able to work overtime? How difficult will commuting be in winter? Is it the "right" address, say, for a Park Avenue employer? One of my clients got no responses from Wall Street brokerage houses although his resume was truly well-written. He was a manager, but on line two of his resume he had written: "c/o Basement Apartment . . . ." This did *not* project the image of a successful manager! By changing it, his luck also changed!

You don't need to write the name of a "low class" area before a zip code. And writing "100 Gramercy Park East #15" won't announce to the reader that it's a Salvation Army residence or a "Y." To employers, negative-sounding addresses include most institutions and "welfare" hotels, but not, of course, the Carnegie-Melon Institute, the National Arts Club, or the Plaza Athenée.

If you are relocating to a new city or state, always record a mailing address and telephone number in that town or city. If possible, obtain the permission of a friend or relative to use theirs. If not, contact an answering service in that area or let a prospective employer in that city know (via a cover note) that you will be visiting there soon and will be available for a personal interview from the —th to the —th.

You need to give a *telephone number* where you can be easily reached during office hours. If that is a home number, invest in an answering machine (or service)—provided that a good American voice records a businesslike message. (Relatives or friends won't always take your calls in a professional manner.) It *must* be a day number because personnel clerks or secretaries will seldom contact you after 5:00 P.M. (Thousands of job interviews are lost in this way.) It's usually safe to give a business number. Be cautious only if you're working in any type of "high-risk" environment such as the apparel industry, where a leak could embarrass you or even get you fired.

HOW TO "IMPROVE" YOUR EDUCATION

The education and training section of your resume might be your Achilles' heel. In that case, you will have to "strengthen" or "improve" it.

This is important because the way you present the facts of your education (or lack of it) might cause you to be screened out within seconds if it appears that

- You did not graduate from high school (or obtain a GED)
- You did not attend a college or university or have "too little" education
- You graduated with the "wrong" major or concentration
- You have "too much" education and are therefore "overqualified" (see pp. 206–208)
- Your education or knowledge is out of date (or reveals that you may be "too old")
- Your degree or certificate is "foreign"

To present your facts to the reader, the following three-pronged strategy has already worked for many:

1. Impress the reader with your skills, experience, and achievements (in a Job Objective and/or Summary);
2. Delay the moment of truth by shifting your education section to the foot of page one or page two;
3. "Fix" your education so that you won't be perceived as being either "underqualified" or "overqualified."

The good news is that most resumes with weak educational sections can be improved. You can and should do something about the way your education/training (or lack of it) might be perceived. (See page 57.)

FIVE WAYS TO "STRENGTHEN" YOUR EDUCATION

In the following material are five examples of how to "fix" or "strengthen" the way you present your education and training in a job resume. These will be helpful if you have no college degree, if your degree is not related to the job, or if you have "too little" formal education. They will also show you what might be added to strengthen this section of your resume.

1. If you have no college credits, record all job-related courses:

THE LEARNING ANNEX, New York, NY
IBM PC .. WordPerfect 6.0 (1994)

COMPUTYPE ACADEMY, Denver, CO
Secretarial Certificate (1982)

2. If you dropped out of college:

BROWN COLLEGE, Memphis, TN
Liberal Arts degree studies (1989–90)

A–Z BUSINESS SCHOOL, Dallas, TX
Business Certificate (1987)

.. Included: IBM PC .. Multimate .. Business Mathematics.

3. If you have not yet completed your degree studies:

BARUCH COLLEGE, New York, NY
B.S. degree studies in Computer Science
(1991–Present)
. . . 95 completed credits to date

4. "Boost" your education by adding in-house company training:

SHEARSON LEHMAN HUTTON TRAINING PROGRAM
C.B.T. (Computer-based Training) (1989)

DEAN WITTER REYNOLDS TRAINING COURSES
Lotus 1–2–3 and Multimate (1988)

COLLEGE OF ARTS, SCIENCE & TECHNOLOGY, Kingston, WI
A.A.S. in Business Administration (1987)

5. If you took the "wrong" major—don't mention it! First present all of your job-related courses/workshops:

AMERICAN MANAGEMENT ASSOCIATION COURSES/WORKSHOPS
New Concepts in Marketing (1992)
Marketing for the '90s (1991)
Telemarketing (1990)
Negotiating Skills (1989)

COLUMBIA UNIVERSITY, New York, NY
B.A. (1986) [omit "in Political Science"]

WHY MOST RESUMES ARE SCREENED OUT

With so many job seekers applying for certain positions, a personnel junior or secretary scanning your resume for the first time is only trying to find something negative, especially in the Work History section. What could be potential turnoffs?

The following are the main "red flag" items readers watch for:

1. *Does your present job title or do your most recent titles look like the level and type of position you are seeking now?* Have you any *direct* or *related* work experience? Is there any evidence you will be able to do the job and do it well? The point is that although many (if not most) job titles don't tell anyone what you actually did in that job, busy employers tend to assume that a title similar to the one you are applying for will "prove" you have the experience they're looking for.

a. If you are a secretary seeking advancement to Administrative Assistant, does your job title still read "Secretary?" What the recruiter would like to see is Secretary/*Administrative Assistant*. If you have already performed some duties or tasks of an administrative nature, you would be entitled to add "/Administrative Assistant." (See pages 46 and 203.)

b. If you seek a supervisory or management-level position, have you worked at (or near) that level before? Can you fairly record your present or previous job title as [Actual Job Title]/*Assistant* [Acting] *Supervisor* [Manager]?

You might safely write this if you have substituted for your supervisor (or manager) during his or her absences from work. In such a case, the "work experience" statement in your Summary should contain a phrase such as "five years' experience as —— and ——, including in-charge (supervisory, management-level) responsibilities." (See page 203.) More importantly, the first item under Experience should explain this to readers: "• Substituted during absences of the Office Manager."

The suggested addition of a title similar to the one you are applying for (actual title and additional job title) gives employers what they want to see. Do it. It works!

2. *Are your previous job titles different from what you're applying for?* Look at your job objective and then at your last three job titles. Do they look "right"? If your previous job titles sound too different, you must find (or invent) more acceptable ones

that will look "right." This is always necessary when a military person has to translate his or her job titles into civilian language, when anyone seeks to move from the public to the private sector, and so on. (See page 131.)

3. *Are your dates and periods of employment acceptable?* Are you a "job hopper" who has had too many (or short-term) jobs? Anything potentially negative should be eliminated or downplayed. (See page 204.) You can also *combine* any previous jobs (especially if these were very similar). Here's how to do it:

a. If you worked as a manager (or cashier) in two stores, you might combine the two time periods (and employers) as follows:

1988–1990   Manager (Cashier)
(Combined) B.Z. & M.G. STORES
. . . Performed similar duties in both stores as follows:

b. If you are out of work, it might be wise to continue to write **199– to Present** in your resume to avoid being screened out. But in any cover letter, refer to your resume as "my most recent resume." At the subsequent job interview you should *immediately* reveal that the date in your resume needs to be updated:

"Mr./Ms. Jones, I am no longer with XYZ Company. The word *Present* needs to be taken out."

Note: You should *not* reveal *when* you left or were laid off, unless that date is specifically requested. If the interviewer does not ask, it will be to your advantage.

WHY IT'S OKAY TO "IMPROVE" OR E-X-P-A-N-D SOME JOB TITLES

To a busy recruiter scanning your resume, your job titles are an immediate giveaway. They might easily tell him or her that you are unqualified or overqualified. In other words, those titles could create a negative perception of you as a candidate in less than ten seconds!

Unsuitable job titles that don't "fit" the position

you're applying for are among the main reasons why many resumes don't make it to first base. In the new job market, many of these might give the impression that you are "overqualified" (and will expect too much). That is why this subject is discussed in detail later in this chapter. (See pages 206 to 208.) But job titles may also indicate that you are "underqualified." This is a serious resume problem for all career changers and for those job seekers who are compelled to look for work in different fields or at different levels. It is therefore necessary to adjust one or two of your job titles so that these might better "fit" the positions you apply for. The good news is that you can do this fairly and honestly, by *expanding* your existing titles to cover other functions you have already performed (and could therefore substantiate, if questioned). A few may even have to be reworded.

Thus, if you're applying for say, an administrative position, at least two recent titles should have an administrative flavor; similarly for any other type of position. Big company, military, or public sector titles should therefore be "normalized" and translated into equivalent ones that different employers will be able to understand. The exaggerated titles that tend to be given in smaller firms (titles are cheap) should be "downsized" and the nondescript (and often strange) titles in larger companies may need to be reworded and even "upgraded." Above all, instead of presenting a variety of job titles that might look like a fruit salad, shaping them will create the focused look that employers want to see.

But the very thought of "tampering" with any job title a previous employer gave you, will make some readers feel uneasy because it might seem like being less than truthful. To some folks, that label is as permanent as the "Bar X" branded on steers on a Texas ranch! That, of course, is baloney. No job title is a tattoo any more than a divorced woman's married name needs to be retained forever. A particular employer's job label refers only to what your position is within the hierarchy or pecking order in his or her own company. It defines who you report to and how much you should be paid, but it seldom describes what you really do! To other recruiters, the titles given in, say, large banks, government departments, or major telecommunications companies might seem like so much gobbledygook!

A mere ten years ago a job title would still give you a sense of the level of the position held by an employee. But nowadays, senior accountants in large CPA firms are being referred to as "Associates" and experienced lawyers are labelled "Law Associates." In other areas, junior science graduates are called Research Associates and many of today's Sales and Customer Service Associates are only high school graduates! This shows you how meaningless a job title can be and why, for the job search, it needs to be modified. More than anything, the fact that additional duties and functions have today been combined under the same old job title, is a compelling reason why you should also e-x-p-a-n-d yours in a job resume.

To summarize, no present or past job title of yours can ever give any future employer an accurate idea of what your actual duties really are (or were), nor can it cover all of your skills and abilities. For example, because of the way secretaries have been perceived in the past, the title Secretary in a job resume still sounds like "only a secretary." And yet today's secretaries are doing a lot of administrative work as well and may be in charge of the office, make purchasing decisions, and even be responsible for special projects. Many offer a knowledge of word processing, database management, spreadsheet software, and even desktop publishing and production. This is why it would be more accurate and more advantageous for experienced secretaries to record a "better" job title or two:

Secretary/[Administrative Assistant]

[Administrative Assistant]/Secretary

Secretary/[Assistant/Temporary Manager]

By expanding their job titles (and using a two-page format), such job seekers will be marketing their true worth. Other job seekers can easily do the same. *Adding* the title of the position you are seeking (if justified) to the formal one you already have, will help you communicate more of your abilities and advance your career.

Note: By recording *both* titles you'll be covering yourself if your previous employer is contacted for a reference.

HOW TO "CLEAN UP" YOUR DATES

For many readers this page might be the most useful one in *Winning Resumes*. I'll show you the acceptable way to deal with "awkward" dates: those that show you're unemployed, that draw attention to gaps in your employment history, or that "age" you. These are all negatives that could result in your being screened out in round 1.

Dates often need to be "cleaned up." Why? Because there might be *missing periods* to be accounted for. If you draw attention to these, you'll arouse the reader's suspicions. Doubtful dates will invite interrogatory-style interviews in which you'll have to explain and justify. Nobody needs that. (One pedantic job seeker suffered in every job interview for three years because of his obsession with giving complete dates in days, months, and years.) It is *not* necessary to specify the month you started and the month you left any job. Such details belong in the employer's application form—not in your resume, which is a sales device. Compare the two sets of dates on the next page and you'll see what I mean.

PREVIOUS EXPERIENCE

The Risky Way		The Smart Way
(gives days/months)		
2/10/88– 3/15/91	Job E	1988–Present
7/15/83–10/21/87	Job D	1983–1987
9/11/79– 1/3/83	Job C	1979–1983
6/12/75– 4/9/79	Job B	*
11/16/65– 1/11/75	Job A	

*Details of additional employment will be provided at an interview.

The dates on the *right* help you avoid all of the problems I've indicated. They don't tell the reader that you are out of work now, have been unemployed (four times), or that you might be "too old." (In the latter case, don't forget to omit all graduation dates that would give the game away.) And in case you're wondering, there's *no* gap between, say, 1987 and 1988 because 1987 could have ended on December 31 and 1988 might have started on January 1. (See resumes of Deirdre Lovell on pages 140–42.)

WHY A PROFESSOR OF ACCOUNTING HAD TO "FIX" HIS DATES

It's not only those with less-than-perfect credentials who might need to "fix" their dates. Sometimes job seekers with unblemished career histories can make a single move that later causes them much grief in job interviews. Such people would like to highlight their *previous* work experience by changing the chronological order of two jobs, but the standard work history format only works for those with perfect or linear careers.

Gerald M. was a certified public accountant and adjunct professor of Advanced Accounting. But, for personal reasons, he had resigned from a "Big 6" to join a smaller firm. In subsequent job interviews, this move was perceived negatively—as a "demotion!" His original resume recorded the following:

PROFESSIONAL EXPERIENCE

1990–Present	Audit Manager (Current) SMALL PUBLIC ACCOUNTING FIRM

1984–1989	Audit Manager (Previously) "BIG 6" PUBLIC ACCOUNTING FIRM

"We have to do something about those two jobs," Gerald pleaded. "I'm tired of having to explain, justify, and defend the move I made." The best solution was to use a "functional" technique to *reverse* the order of his move—to make it appear that he'd moved *up*. Here's what he did:

PROFESSIONAL EXPERIENCE

1984–Present "BIG 6" PUBLIC ACCOUNTING FIRM
Audit Manager (6 Years)

SMALL PUBLIC ACCOUNTING FIRM
Audit Manager (3 Years)

Duties and Responsibilities:

During this nine-year period I have been in charge of management, planning, and execution of major audits, including . . .

The actual dates of his two positions have been combined on the left as "1984–Present." On the right, *time periods* are given instead of the usual dates ("6 Years" instead of "1984–1989" and "3 Years" instead of "1990–Present"). More importantly, he has reversed the order of the two firms. Most people reading this resume would have no reason to suspect that the move was actually made *downward*—and wouldn't find out unless they asked. (See also p. 189)

HOW TO LEAVE OUT ONE TO THREE JOBS

If you've had too many jobs (or in very different fields), your resume might be screened out. To prepare a focused and "respectable" resume, remove all *months* from your dates, leaving only the years. In this way—without altering dates—you'll be able to leave out entire jobs and close the gaps between them! Those that remain will be related to your Objective and have longer time periods.

JOB OBJECTIVE: **Clerical/Accounting position.**

	Your Old Resume (original dates and time periods)	Your Improved Presentation (revised dates and time periods)
JOB A (Clerical)	11/89–1/91 (15 mo.)	1989–Present (30+ mo.)
JOB B (Sales)	1/89–8/89 (8 mo.)	**omitted** (unrelated)
JOB C (Accounts)	3/87–10/88 (20 mo.)	1987–1988 (24 mo.)
JOB D (Clerical)	6/86–12/86 (7 mo.)	1986 *one* job (12 mo.)
JOB E (Sales)	2/86–5/86 (4 mo.)	**omitted** (unrelated)
JOB F (Typing)	11/84–12/85 (14 mo.)	1984–1985 (24 mo.) (*one* job—not two!)
JOB G (Sales)	5/84–9/84 (5 mo.)	**omitted** (unrelated)

Jobs A, C, D, and F are all related to clerical/accounting work, and there are now no gaps between them. Similarly, a Sales resume (for jobs B, E, and G) can easily be prepared. (Here, recruiters care less about dates.) Should an interviewer ask, you might reply that you chose to present only your *related* work experience.

There are *no* gaps between any of the four time periods on the right because every calendar year ends on December 31st. The date, "1986," gives the impression it might have been for a full year! Finally, compare the number of months actually worked with the *perceived* time periods on the right. They seem to be longer. It's pure resume "magic."

IF YOU'VE WORKED "TOO LONG" FOR ONE EMPLOYER

Many experienced job seekers have become unemployed or disemployed after working for the same employer fifteen to thirty years. For them to write "1960–Present" in their resumes could be the kiss of death!

Working continuously for one company or firm for a long time might be viewed not only positively but negatively—that your experience has depth but lacks *breadth*. Other doubts might be raised about you. Why were you never confident enough to leave the company? Are you ambitious? Are you a good performer? Have you achieved? Are your skills really transferable? Will you be able to adjust to a new environment?

Even if your experience has been limited to only one company, you've already accumulated a wide range of valuable and transferable skills in various positions within the same department, in different departments, or in different companies within the same group. To present your diversified experience, there are three steps to take to create a perception of both breadth and depth—to persuade readers that your skills and experience are more broadly based than they might appear.

Step one is to write a good Job Objective that mentions your good track record, expertise, and/or accomplishments. Next, draft a Summary of Qualifications (or Summary of Skills and Experience) that mentions the various areas, departments, or companies you've worked in. Again, mention accomplishments—preferably in *different* areas. That creates a perception of breadth. (See page 58.)

Third, handle the Experience section of your resume as follows: If you've been transferred from one position, department, area, or company (or branch) to another within the group, your solution is to *break up* the total time period worked into three to four shorter time periods—each with a different-sounding name, job title, or function. For example, different areas, departments, or company names within the same group, or branches of the same bank. (See pages 153–54.)

Do *not* write "1960–Present" in your resume. That will give the game away. Instead, write: "1991–Present; 1987–1990; 1982–1986. Details of additional experience will be furnished upon request."

"OVERQUALIFIED": A MAJOR DILEMMA

Nowadays, many experienced job seekers are suffering from the overqualification blues. It irks the heck out of them to hear "you're overqualified" so often. Sadly, employers are very reluctant to pay for any experience they don't need, so it's a very difficult problem. What can you do about it?

Before thinking of downsizing your resume, I urge you to be 100-percent certain that your present one isn't letting you down. (It probably is. There's a very high probability it needs to be improved: even if it is laser printed on the best quality paper; even if a few executives have checked it out; and even if some resume "professional" wrote it for you [most of them are hacks and quacks].) As we have noted, 85 percent to 95 percent of all resumes don't do the writers justice and even contain negatives. You might need to consult a very rare bird, a good resume professional. (See Chapter 14.) Can your resume be improved? Is it a good marketing tool? Are there any "red flags" that only a trained eye can spot? Downsizing your credentials is only a last resort.

Many highly experienced job seekers might have to rachet down their expectations. For example, for twelve years, Jeremy B. held a senior executive position in the music industry, where his annual earnings were approximately $150,000. Now he confesses: "I'll be lucky if they hire me for $75,000." And a senior executive in the apparel industry is prepared to do the same work as before—but for $75–100,000 instead of $200,000. (In a recent survey conducted by The Conference Board, a New York business research group, 52 percent of white-collar workers took pay cuts before finding new jobs, even after six months of intensive job hunting. *U.S. News & World Report*, 6/28/93)

Even worse is that many employers don't even want to see those whose credentials might be "too heavy" for a position. With every company trying to cut its payroll, the mere sight of heavyweight credentials might be a turnoff—just as looking "too old" is often a red flag. Your main objective is therefore to get to see an employer who is doing his or her best to keep you out. Only by coming face to face with the hiring authority can you offer the benefits of hiring you: that you can do a great deal for them and that you'll be excellent value for the money.

For this purpose, a properly worded (and toned-down) job resume is crucial. It *cannot* be the same as you would use to find a job at your previous level. You would immediately come across as being overqualified. Unfortunately, it is all too easy to *invite* elimination by the way you present your credentials on paper. The statements you make could intimidate a personnel clerk or secretary—especially those big-looking job titles. Or impressive numbers that attest to the extent of your previous responsibilities. Or dates that reveal more years of experience than they need or are willing to pay for. Or education that might be far in excess of what the job requires.

All such indicators of "too much" or "too heavy" experience will have to be "downsized" to fit the job. But more than that, *what* to omit or play down might be even more important. And not only in your resume but in your Salary History, which would be a dead giveaway. This is why it is often used as a screening device. However, by giving your *base* salary only and omitting all incentive plans, bonuses, commissions and benefits, you won't be showing the total income you received. Then you can play it by ear in deciding what to disclose. (See pages 103–105). But even when your resume does do the trick, your dress, manner, and speech might still be too "senior." (It is therefore imperative that you communicate with personnel officers and secretaries in a very patient, respectful and low-key manner.)

Perhaps the most practical solution would be for

206

you to be given a "neutral" job title such as Projects Supervisor, or Efficiency (or Productivity) Analyst (or Coordinator). In this way you could more easily be accepted as performing a lower-level (line) function. Staff will be told your main assignment is to analyze and streamline all of the functions of that job and how it relates to all other functions in the office. That would label you as a "staff" person who is not competing for any other line position.

Before showing you what to do about toning down your qualifications on paper, let us see how you should deal with the job interview itself. The following are typical questions asked, followed by possible replies.

Q. "Won't this job mean a step *down* for you?"

A. "In my eyes, this would be a step *up*. I'll be contributing again."

Q. "Won't you treat it as a temporary one while you look around?"

A. "I've already done that and this position is the best 'fit.' "

Q. "Won't the responsibilities be less?"

A. "Only in some ways. On the other hand, I'll be working in the industry I know best and in a department I am most familiar with. I'll make it more efficient and cut down on waste to save you money. I'm sure I could handle *two* functions in that department."

Q. "We can't offer you a higher salary. Will you be satisfied?"

A. "Mr. Jones, I'm realistic. Like most job seekers, I've cut my living expenses ('a penny saved is a penny earned') and my wife is also working."

Now, let's downsize your credentials.

Toning Down and "Downsizing" Your Credentials

If your previous job titles are too "big," shrink them as follows:

Previous Title	Revised Title
Owner/Proprietor/Partner	Manager (Operations/Sales)
President/Vice-President	Senior Manager
Regional Manager	Local Area Manager
Director	Manager
Divisional Manager	Manager, ___ Department
Chief Financial Officer	Financial Accountant
Public Relations Manager	Public Relations Coordinator
Administrative Manager	Area/Project Supervisor
Departmental Head	Section Supervisor
Manager/Supervisor	Assistant Manager/Supervisor
Assistant Controller	Full-Charge Bookkeeper
Senior Accountant	Staff Accountant

If previous responsibilities were "big," diminish them as follows:

Previous Responsibility	Revised Responsibility
In charge of $100-million division	In charge of a large department.
Supervised 100 staff	Supervised staff.
Profit and Loss responsibility for	Omit this responsibility.
Prepared/developed a budget of	Assisted in preparing a budget.
Hired and terminated staff	Omit this responsibility.

If your education is too "heavy," omit the following:

Education	Omission
If only a Bachelor's degree is required	Omit Ph.D.; add "further studies"
If a Bachelor's degree is "preferred"	Omit M.B.A., M.A., and M.S.
If they require only high school (GED)	Add: "Further studies in ..."

If your accomplishments are too "big," diminish them as follows:

If you created/initiated/designed	Refined and/or implemented
If numbers achieved are "too big"	Use words that understate, (e.g., "Member of team that achieved ...").

If your dates go too far back, omit all jobs fifteen-plus years ago. ("Furnished upon request.")

14

WHO TO ASK FOR ADVICE: NEW ANSWERS TO 50 FATAL RESUME MISTAKES

The more people you talk with, the more opinions you will get about resumes.... Executives will tell you what type of resumes appeal to them and by the process of following their advice, you run the risk of losing all of the positive appeals in your resume.
—Robert Half, Director, International Placement Organization [14]

Dear Reader:

You (and every other job seeker) will greatly benefit by having someone else go over your job resume—and not only to check your spelling and grammar! You need an objective party to help you deal with more important aspects of your resume—to see if you've created a good *marketing* device—one that sells your skills:

1. Is there a potential red flag item or negative that you might have missed? (They are *not* always obvious.)
2. Are your dates okay the way you've recorded them?
3. Do your job titles back up your Job Objective?
4. Are you highlighting or emphasizing the right facts? Do they support your Job Objective?
5. Are your accomplishments still hidden in the text?
6. Have you omitted all unnecessary detail (or dates or jobs)?
7. Are you exaggerating anything? Have you overlooked something important?

There are many ways in which your resume can be screened out. This is why what to omit (or downplay) is at least as important as what to include. As regards possible turnoffs that could lead to your being screened out in round 1, see Chapter 13, on how to "fix" resume blemishes.

And there are just as many ways in which your resume could fail to market your skills—even if it is laser printed or beautifully typeset on the best rag paper. Many job resumes—perhaps 85 percent or more—fail to do their owner justice. Some can even be suicidal. So why take a chance with yours? Lost job opportunities are a very high price to pay! The question, however, is who to ask for advice.

In my view, the only professional to consult about your resume is an experienced and competent resume writer who does it full-time—no one else. Such a person has to deal with resume-writing problems on a daily basis and find solutions that work for his or her clients. Resume writing is a specialized skill. Answers have to be found regarding the choice of format, suitable length, organization, and, above all, what to emphasize and what to omit. Your own input is essential.

Unfortunately, many out-of-work writers, teachers, personnel officers, secretaries, and typists offer you their services. And every corner print shop promises a quick turnaround. Most of these *can* prepare a basic type of resume for you but *not* a marketing tool. Their products might look pretty, but will be bland and lackluster because they will probably fail to present your best selling points. Nor will they minimize or eliminate all of your resume blemishes. Resume writing is a minefield of hacks and quacks. At best, many are sincere but inept. They'll give you an attractive-looking basic resume that lacks any real sell. In today's highly competitive job market, this won't help you.

Nevertheless, most resume professionals can do better than 90 percent of the people who write their own—even if the only difference is an improved layout, proportional typing, or laser printing. But laser printing alone will *not* create the *marketing* tool you need to help you beat the competition. A printer is a printer, not a marketing specialist!

THE QUALIFICATIONS OF A GOOD RESUME WRITER

First and foremost, very strong *analytical* skills. He or she will need to analyze and discover many additional facts about you, your skills, strengths, and achievements. In short, to determine your poten-

tial worth to an employer. This, in turn, has to be translated into skills that are transferable and marketable. Thus, a background that includes both career counseling and work in a variety of jobs will therefore be useful. The resume specialist must know the workplace and what skills are required of various jobs and at different levels.

In particular, he or she could help you target specific positions by carefully matching up the employer's stated needs with what you are able to offer. Many job seekers don't do this well on paper. What they write is neither clear nor convincing, especially when they lack one or more of those requirements. What could be equivalent to it?

Second, a good resume writer must know a lot about the *art of presentation*, in that the quality of your presentation will always be crucial. It is the skilled way in which your information is selected, organized, and presented that will enhance your perceived value and impress the reader. This requires a knowledge of resume "cosmetics" and "surgery"—but not anything unethical.

Third, he or she must have some knowledge and experience of how the buyer thinks—those who screen as well as those who do the actual hiring. A broad knowledge of which items might be *red flags* is therefore essential, along with an ability to draft your best selling points.

Fourth, a professional writer must have a good understanding of how an effective sales device or marketing tool should be constructed in your particular case. There are no "standard" resumes. People are not clones. Yours has to be custom made.

And last, but not least, the writer should be able to write correct English. Why do I mention this last and not first? Because hundreds of English majors consult with such professionals—even graduates with a GPA of 3.9 from Yale, Dartmouth, or Chicago. Clearly, the help they need isn't for better English but the specific language of resume writing. And how to organize and present their data in the most effective way.

But the best qualification of all is his or her proven ability to develop resumes that have already helped many clients—a lot of them.

THE CREDENTIALS OF OTHER RESUME ADVISORS

Even a trained *career counselor* might not be qualified to assist you with your job resume unless he or she also knows how to discover and present your best selling points to an employer—in the language of hiring. As a rule, such persons talk about skills in an academic manner and are *not* marketing oriented. They often use the language of literature—not that of the workplace.

An *English teacher* might not know enough about analyzing your skills, targeting jobs, or what employers would like to see in a job resume. Unfortunately, teachers think like teachers—not like salespersons. Some will even regard a Skills Summary as redundant! Perfect English, by itself, will *not* turn a basic resume into an effective marketing tool. It needs to have sell. Without the sell, a resume is negative. And what about all of those potential turnoffs that could be fatal even though the spelling, grammar, sentence structure, and punctuation are perfect?

Placement counselors are usually better because they are more in touch with recruiters and are more aware of what skills employers are looking to hire. But, as a rule, they know too little about the writing and marketing process.

What about asking a *Personnel Department* or "employment counselor" to help you write yours? Having been a Personnel Manager myself (in a major company) and having assisted dozens of personnel department people with their own resumes, I can assure you that 99 percent of them won't be qualified to help you write yours. Remember, they are trained to *reject* resumes—not to construct them. Asking them to show you how to sell yourself on paper would be like asking a football receiver to play quarterback! (The fact that you, too, may have screened and discarded 1,000 pieces of junk mail delivered to your door won't qualify you to compose even one of those Direct Mail pieces. Experts wrote them.)

"*Headhunters*" tend to be better—if only because their commission may depend on presenting your best selling points to an employer. Unfortunately, however, executive search people deal only or mainly with those who are known to be 5-star performers. Their business depends on promoting only "most placeable" candidates—not those with anything less than the highest credentials. If you are not one of these, they are unlikely to want to assist you. Even worse, their negative advice may seriously discourage you. (To listen to headhunters you would think that no job seeker over 45 or with less-than-perfect credentials has ever been hired!)

The worst person to consult about your job resume is *Mr. or Ms. Corporate Vice-President*. Some of you will know one or two executives whose opinions you greatly value. You might also admire and envy them for holding down your "dream" job and for the success they've achieved to date. So, do approach them. Would they also be willing to make an enabling phone call or two to arrange meetings with their friends in other companies? Such introductions or leads—"who you know"—could help you discover unadvertised job openings. But please, please, you must understand that sitting in their plush corner offices might have little or nothing to do with their own resumes or resume-writing expertise any more than buying Macdonald's hamburgers got President Clinton elected to the White House. On the contrary, such people know little or nothing about the process of resume construction and certainly can't help you write yours. They do want to help, but all of their talk about receiving and reviewing hundreds of resumes will *not* qualify them to advise you on how to write one. Although they might speak to you with the voice of authority, they are like baseball catchers trying to teach you the mechanics of pitching. Only a pitching coach or another pitcher would be qualified to do that. (And selling yourself also involves a "pitch"—a verbal one.)

The main problem with executives is their extreme subjectivity. They can only tell you what they, themselves, happen to *like*—*not* what will appeal to others or what will really work for you. Such advice can even hurt you. (Please reread Robert Half's words of wisdom in the quotation at the beginning of this chapter. He should know.)

What about asking *friends* to help you write your resume? *Never* do this. Friends could derail your entire career. Why? Because you are not clones, and what might have worked for them might not work for you. However, the same friends can also lead you to the proverbial pot of gold. Their tips and inside information will direct you as to where to forward or hand in your resume. In fact, their leads might be the most valuable contribution to the success of your entire job search campaign.

The more people you ask, the more opinions you'll get. But most of these will probably commence with three little words that usually identify a blatant half-truth: "They say that . . ."

If you're a manager, *never* ask your *secretary* to prepare your resume. A secretarial-type presentation will rarely be suitable for recording the sell and accomplishments of any manager. (One secretary who recently prepared a resume for her brother recorded his main outside interest as ballet because he often accompanied her to New York's Lincoln Center. But in his job objective he was looking for a position as construction engineer!)

CHECKING OUT A PROFESSIONAL RESUME SERVICE

In the past thirty-five years or so an estimated one hundred million job seekers have been assisted by professional writers. However, as with anything else, you do need to check them out carefully. The quality and effectiveness of their resume products can vary from 5 percent to 90 percent! And the individuals who render such services will also vary from rank amateurs to exceptionally competent self-marketing experts who can help you attain your career goals. What should you be looking for?

1. Ask whether they offer a free evaluation of your existing resume or of your needs. As a rule, initial consultations are free.

2. How do they try to sell you? Do they hand out a glossy brochure? Do they quote scare statistics such as "only one in 245 resumes results in a job interview," or "only one in 1,470 resumes results in a job offer"?

Be very wary of such tactics. Good resume writers know that such statistics are meaningless and misleading. An effective sales/marketing tool can hit the target the first time!

(The above figures are widely quoted by resume services and even in some career books. The first of these is taken from a very localized and limited survey published in *Electronic Design 16* more than fifteen years ago. But it is only a silly "average," and in fact, some employers granted an interview for 1 out of every 36 resumes they received! The trouble with such surveys is that all resumes are not equal in quality like, say, aspirins or bananas. Nor do all employers have the same hiring needs at the same time. That is why such findings are meaningless. Remember Disraeli's famous remark: "There are lies, damned lies and statistics." Anyhow, *no* discouraging statistic can ever apply to you as an individual. You can always beat the odds by writing a really good resume.)

3. Who will be assisting you with your resume? He or she might *not* be the same as the party who first greets and sells you on the service.

4. Finally, does the resume writer guarantee you anything? Do they make wild promises? Be very careful!

5. Ask to see two or more sample resumes. Try not to be overly impressed by the superior laser printing and beautiful rag bond paper. Instead, focus on content, as follows:

a. Is there a Job Objective? If so, does it still ask employers to "utilize"? Nowadays, those I-want-I-want objectives of the '80s are out. Instead, I-offer-you-value objectives are in. (See page 45.)

b. Is there a Summary or Qualifications Statement? If so, are individual items *selling points* or are they only a string of corny adjectives (reliable . punctual . dynamic . dedicated)? Are they statements with "sell," or vague? (See page 52.)

If the sample resumes you see include neither a job objective nor a skills summary, that resume writer may be using outdated job search strategies that rely too heavily on a cover letter.

c. Are they still using a "pure" chronological or functional format? Only combination resume formats are marketing tools that present both your skills and experience in the same document. (See pages 7, 9 and 11–12.)

d. Do achievements or accomplishments stand out in the sample resumes? Are they indented and bulleted? Or do they lie buried in a paragraph of gray-looking copy?

e. Do they try to sell you matching envelopes? Why? Is it to impress the mailroom or the wastebasket? (Only senior executives need attractive envelopes—to impress the president's "classy" private secretary. Velvety white (9" × 12") Survivor Stock #R1460 is both eyecatching and appealing. All other job seekers should use brown or white Manila envelopes (9" x 12") so that your resume can arrive looking freshly printed and *unfolded*.)

In short, serious resume writers are skilled craftspersons who help you market your skills in the best possible way. They are not only sincere; they are highly competent and their work will be tailored to your specific needs. But many resume services are simply paper mills!

Check them out carefully. Only one in ten is worth using, and the rates of a highly skilled professional may vary from $75 to $150 for an entry-level resume to $200 to $350 for senior executives. But such an outlay could maximize your chances in the job market and help you find that job in a fraction of the time. In fact, that party can help you rescue your entire career!

SELF-PUTDOWNS THAT ARE DISASTROUS

As we noted in Chapter 2, many of us have been exposed to repeated criticism or negative conditioning in our home and school environments— some more than others. Frequent comments like "How many times do I have to show you?" and "When will you ever learn?" could make anyone doubt his or her own value or self-worth. In addition, your daily achievements might often be ignored, brushed off, or even devalued as being due to "luck" rather than your ability or hard work. That is why, when it comes to job hunting, so many job seekers present themselves as nervous and timid supplicants rather than as confident and

enthusiastic applicants. (Richard Lathrop) But how can you hope to market yourself as you need to do unless you are sure—very sure—of your own ability to do the job? That confidence must shine through everything you write or say to a picky employer, especially nowadays.

Unfortunately, many job seekers aren't aware of how dangerous any form of self-putdown can be— orally or in writing. There are many statements that even the most intelligent and experienced job seekers are guilty of making which might easily mean job suicide. Here are a few:

NEVER WRITE OR SAY (TO AN EMPLOYER):

"I would be interested in *any* position."
                              (Don't you know what?)
"I leave it to you to decide where I would 'fit in' best."   (Mailroom!)
"Although I have no experience . . ."
                              (Why are you applying?)
"Although I don't have the required experience . . ."   (Forget it!)
"I feel that I will be able to learn that . . ."
                              (Are you sure?)
"I think I can do the job."
                              (Sorry, we need to be sure.)
"Should you find my qualifications of interest . . ."
                              (Why did you write?)
"If you'll allow me an opportunity to meet with you."   (No, thanks)
"I hope you'll give me a chance."
                              (Why? We don't owe you!)
"I need an opportunity to prove myself."
                              (Why should we give it?)
"I've never had a chance to . . ."
                              (Don't make excuses!)
"The money isn't important."
                              (You won't care about the work either.)

NEVER OMIT TO WRITE OR FORGET TO MENTION:

How you made a difference for other employers. What you achieved or accomplished that led to an improvement in . . .

213

How performance evaluations praised your efforts.

What your written testimonials say about you.

That you have received/won awards for your performance.

That you were in charge during your boss's absences/illness.

50 RESUME MISTAKES THAT COULD BE FATAL

What can you do to improve your own resumes—with or without professional advice? I am going to help you identify 50 of the fatal mistakes that job seekers commonly make in writing their resumes. The advice is based on my experience in "cleaning up" thousands of self-written resumes and making them work. Many anxious and bewildered job seekers have approached me with a statement like: "What could be turning them off? I've mailed 200 so far but not even one 'Dear John' letter." I was asked to identify the problem(s) and help them correct it (them).

The point is that you can't always blame the job market for the fact that your resume may not be working for you. The reality is that many, many resumes are doomed to fail either due to a structural problem (such as using the wrong format) or because they contain one or two blemishes that *no* employer should be allowed to see. (This is in addition to the fact that these resumes may be unfocused, badly organized, poorly written, or printed on cheap copy paper.)

What should you avoid doing? Unfortunately, this is an area where most people tend to guess. As a rule, they express their own dislikes rather than tell you what would really count against you in the world of hiring. (As we have noted, many corporate vice-presidents are guilty of this.) Although you can never hope to predict 100 percent what might cause a recruiter, personnel clerk, or secretary to eliminate your resume, as a professional resume writer I have had to identify and remove many potential turnoffs or negatives, and the advice given is therefore based on what has worked for successful job seekers. Let's take a closer look at

a few examples of the advice most people might give you.

For example, will a single printing "typo" (typographical error) lead to your elimination? No, it *won't*—unless it's for a job where they expect a high degree of accuracy (legal secretary, proofreader, English teacher, etc.). But no one should have a typo in the first 15–20 lines where it will be more easily noticed. (In my experience, nearly every resume done by a professional printer will contain at least one typo. Please don't allow them to pressure you into accepting a final proof. Check it carefully.) And what about margins that are less than one inch? If the resume is well-written and beautifully presented, half-inch margins *won't* be a turnoff.

But, by themselves, good English, wide margins, and a lack of typos will *not* guarantee that you won't be screened out. There are far more serious no-no's that you need to be aware of.

Choice of Resume Format

NEVER use a standard chronological resume format if your work history is not "perfect," if you are changing careers, if most of your experience is unrelated to your Job Objective, or if you have foreign credentials. Use the flexible one- or two-page combination resume.

NEVER rush to use the functional resume format. That type of resume is *not* a panacea for all your resume-writing problems. Most employers dislike that format because they cannot "match up" the functions you claim to be able to perform with where and when you exercised them.

Use the combination resume illustrated in this book to present your selling points instead of functions.

NEVER rely on a cover letter to sell your skills. It may not be read or could be lost in the shuffle. And cover letters are rarely faxed.

Length of Resume

NEVER select a one-page resume automatically. You may have outgrown it. Will one page do justice to your career and achievements?

NEVER remove the "sell" from your resume in order to get it all down on one page. A beautifully presented two-pager with sell often works better than a crowded one-pager that is not a sales device. Employers are never too busy to read a beautiful two-pager.

Name

NEVER spell out your full legal name if it might be too strange, "foreign," or even "disturbing" to a young personnel clerk or secretary. Thus, change from "Abou Mandour Mohamed Abou Mandour" to "Max Mandor." Always shorten or Americanize such a name. (Your resume is *not* a legal document. Full names need only be given on employers' application forms.)

Telephone Number

NEVER expect personnel clerks to telephone you after 5 p.m. They won't. Thousands of job opportunities are lost in this way! Either give a *day* number or invest in an answering machine or service. (And don't expect your relatives or friends to take your call in a professional manner. They usually won't.)

Address

NEVER give a P.O. Box number; always give a street address. Recruiters must know where you live.

NEVER give an address that seems too far away from your future place of work. Will you always be late in bad weather?

NEVER give an out-of-state address. Must they send you a plane ticket? How will they interview you? Give a local address.

Job Objective

NEVER emphasize what *you* want and *you* expect from employers. Instead, tell them the level and type of position you seek and what job-related skills and experience you can offer.

NEVER ask an employer to "utilize" all of your skills, experience, and education. (You must state what your best skills are. Employers are *not* skills analysts.)

NEVER write two completely different Objectives in the same job resume. Readers may think you don't know your own mind.

NEVER lock yourself into one specific job title. Write an e-x-p-a-n-d-e-d job objective.

Skills Summary

NEVER leave out your Summary. It is your best chance to sell yourself on paper. It increases your perceived worth.

NEVER offer more than 15 years' experience. It may "age" you!

NEVER overdo "value" words like *strong, excellent, exceptional*, or *outstanding*. You may safely use such superlatives only once or twice; overdo it and it backfires. You will lose credibility.

NEVER lie about or exaggerate your own accomplishments.

Employment History

NEVER close off your dates to show you are unemployed. Always write "to Present." Employers prefer those who are working. The only exceptions are if you are relocating or if it's perfectly obvious to recruiters that you've been laid off.

NEVER write "Present" when you are relocating to another State or Country (unless you expect them to pay for your move).

NEVER show that you've had too many jobs in too short a time period. Are you a "job-hopper"? Are you unstable?

NEVER show gaps in your work history. (Would no one hire you?)

NEVER indicate that you failed in your own business. And never write "Owner/Proprietor." (Write "Manager" or "Manager/Partner.")

NEVER reveal that you are or have been moonlighting in two jobs. Most employers like to feel that you'll give all your energy to the job they're hiring you for.

NEVER commence with one or two job titles that are not related to the position you are applying for.

NEVER present unrelated work experience first. Record it last.

NEVER reveal too quickly that you have the "wrong" or unrelated or foreign experience to offer. (Write this 20 lines lower down—after you have already impressed the reader in your Objective/Skills Summary.)

NEVER give big company, military, or bureaucratic job titles that won't make sense to anyone outside those environments. (Always translate them and/or find meaningful equivalents.)

Accomplishments

NEVER omit to say how well you performed in any position. It is the best evidence of your ability to do a good job for any future employer.

NEVER bury your accomplishments in the description of any jobs. If these don't stand out, they may be overlooked.

NEVER omit your "sell." Without it, your resume is negative.

NEVER exaggerate how much you achieved. If you were a member of a team, then say how much you contributed to the team effort. Never claim all the credit for yourself.

NEVER give accomplishments that are not recent (in the last 5 to 7 years or so). (Why have you stopped achieving?)

Education

NEVER start with your Education if it is unrelated or weak.

NEVER state a Major or Concentration if it is un-

related to your Job Objective. (They don't need Biology on Wall Street.)

NEVER give the date you graduated if giving it will indicate that you may be too "old" or that your knowledge is "outdated."

NEVER mention your high school awards 5+ years after graduating. Have you achieved nothing since? Why not?

NEVER state your G.P.A. or college awards after 5+ years.

NEVER give the foreign names of an educational institution. Translate it and Americanize it. In the case of internationally accredited colleges always state "accredited."

NEVER give foreign names of degrees, diplomas, or certificates. Write down the local equivalent so that it can be understood.

NEVER give the foreign grades or percentages— only class rankings.

References

NEVER write "References Upon Request" where employers will be more interested in your portfolio, cassette, demo tape, show reels, clip file, or discography.

NEVER give the names, employers, job titles, and telephone numbers of your references in your resume *except*:
(a) Where you are relocating to another State or Country and these are names of local people who know you.
(b) If you are busy with a career change and the names of professors/adjunct professors or people in your new profession could add weight to your application.

General Turnoffs

NEVER send a handwritten update covering your present job.

NEVER use type styles like script, italic, or Old English. Reading them is very hard on the eyes.

NEVER use a low-quality dot-matrix printout with hard-to-read poorly shaped letters and numbers.

NEVER use tiny 8-point-size type to get it all down on one page.

NEVER print resumes on 20 lb copy paper. Use 24 lb bond.

NEVER fold your resume. Mail it in a 9″ × 12″ Manila envelope.

NEVER try to sell yourself on the phone if you have a foreign accent.

YOU'RE HIRED!

Because today's employers are so picky, your ability to communicate your CAN DO's effectively will be your trump card. With *Winning Resumes* as your guide, you'll know how to sell yourself in the job hunt—on paper and in person. To payroll-conscious employers, your ability to "wear more than one hat" will always make you an attractive hire. Generalists are much sought after these days—versatile employees who can handle more than one function. (In a competitive global economy, fewer employers can afford highly paid but narrowly trained specialists. It's less costly for them to export such jobs to India, the Philippines, Poland, Russia, China—wherever they can get it done at a fraction of the cost and without having to pay additional benefits.) More than anything, are you able to improve operations and/or increase their sales or profits in any area? That will virtually guarantee you a job.

Those job hunters who are willing to be flexible *and* focused, can and will succeed—provided that you lower your salary expectations! In this regard, please don't pay any attention to the latest unemployment statistics from Washington; they don't refer to you as an individual and *won't* affect your chances of finding suitable employment. Hiring goes on regardless—during every hiring freeze and throughout the deepest economic recessions—because people are promoted or get transferred; they also fall sick, get injured, become pregnant, stop working, retire, resign, get fired, or die and need to be replaced. (All this happens daily in the "hidden" job market.) And at any given time, certain businesses or industries or geographical regions (like the Southwest at present) will be doing more recruiting than others. In some fields, like environmental control and recycling in hospitals, thousands of new positions are being created. (*New York Times*, 11/30/93) The TV/radio and print media will keep you posted as to what's "hot" at present.

Keep moving. Keep meeting and talking to people—on the phone, in coffee shops, at meetings of support groups, and anywhere else where other job hunters might tell you where they've already interviewed. The more moving you do, the luckier you'll get! Mail and hand out your resumes. But don't rush to reply to help-wanted ads—the first wave of applications are always screened ruthlessly. Above all, keep job hunting—from 9 A.M. to 5 P.M., five days a week. Expect to get many nos before the final yes but don't give up. As any baseball fan in the Big Apple can tell you: "Ya gotta believe!"

Now let's go out and win. You can. You will!

Bibliography

BOOKS

1. JEFFREY G. ALLEN, J.D., C.P.C. *How to Turn an Interview into a Job.* New York: Fireside Edition, Simon & Schuster, 1983.
2. RICHARD N. BOLLES. *What Color Is Your Parachute?* Berkeley: Ten Speed Press, 1989. (Updated annually.)
3. TOM JACKSON. *Guerrilla Tactics in the Job Market.* New York: Bantam Books, 1981.
4. RICHARD LATHROP. *Who's Hiring Who?* Berkeley: Ten Speed Press, 1989.
5. JOHN LUCHT. *Rites of Passage at $100,000+: The Insider's Guide to Absolutely Everything About Executive Job-Changing.* New York: The Viceroy Press, 1988.
6. PHILIP R. LUND. *Compelling Selling: A Framework for Persuasion.* New York: AMACOM/ Macmillan, 1988.
7. RICHARD A. PAYNE. *How to Get a Better Job Quicker,* 3rd ed. New York: Signet/Penguin, 1988.
8. MARSHA SINETAR, *Do What You Love, the Money Will Follow: Discovering Your Right Livelihood.* New York: Dell Publishing, 1989.

9. TOM WASHINGTON. *Resume Power: Selling Yourself on Paper.* Bellevue: Mt. Vernon Press, 1988.

ARTICLES ON JOB RESUMES

10. KARIN ABARBANEL. *NAFE's Guide to a Winning Resume.* New York: National Association for Female Executives, 1987.
11. TOM R. ARTERBURN. "The Advantages of a Tailored Resume." *National Business Employment Weekly,* Dow Jones and Co., 3/12/93.
12. TAUNEE BESSON. "The Advantages of a Functional Resume." *National Business Employment Weekly,* Dow Jones and Co., 5/31/87.
13. DON ERIKSON. "How to Grab Attention When Answering Recruitment Ads." *National Business Employment Weekly,* Dow Jones and Co., 10/15/93.
14. ROBERT HALF. "How to Write a Resume That Brings Results." *The Practical Accountant,* The Institute for Continuing Professional Development, New York, 1971.
15. WILLIAM E. MONTAG. "The Advantages of a

Combination Resume." *National Business Employment Weekly*, Dow Jones and Co., 10/23/92.

16. DOUGLAS B. RICHARDSON. "The Functional Resume." *National Business Employment Weekly*, Dow Jones and Co., 2/2/92.

17. ———. "Making the Most Out of a Functional Resume Format." *National Business Employment Weekly*, Dow Jones and Co., 2/24/91.

18. ———. "Resume Strategies That Work." *National Business Employment Weekly*, Dow Jones and Co., 4/29/90.

19. DAVID ROTTMAN. "How to Write a Resume Tailored to Company Needs." *National Business Employment Weekly*, Dow Jones and Co., 10/9/92.

20. LEANE RUTHERFORD. "Five Fatal Resume Mistakes." *Business Week's Guide to Careers*, McGraw-Hill, Spring/Summer 1986.

21. LINDA J. SEGALL. "How to Write Resumes That Get Employer Attention." *National Business Employment Weekly*, Dow Jones and Co., 3/26/89.

22. JAY L. STAHL. "Why Your Resume Needs an Objective." *National Business Employment Weekly*, Dow Jones and Co., 3/24/91.

23. TOM WASHINGTON. "Creating a Resume with Qualifications—Add a Summary Statement for Emphasis." *National Business Employment Weekly*, Dow Jones and Co., 6/27/86.

24. ROBERT W. WENDOVER. "How Recruiters Judge Resumes." *National Business Employment Weekly*, Dow Jones and Co., 2/15/87.

ARTICLES ON THE JOB SEARCH

25. WARREN ALVERSON. "Job Hunting Without Perfect Credentials." *National Business Employment Weekly*, Dow Jones and Co., 6/18/89.

26. R. D. ARVEY and J. E. CAMPION. "The Employment Interview: A Summary and Review of Recent Research." *Personnel Psychology 35*, 1982, pp. 281–322.

27. DONALD ASHER. "Writing Cover Letters That Route Your Resume." *National Business Employment Weekly*, Dow Jones and Co., 2/17/91.

28. KATHLEEN LUSK BROOKE, PH.D. "The Rise and Fall (and Rise Again) of the Office Secretary." *Working Woman*, June 1989.

29. PERRI CAPELL. "Why Employers Use P.O. Box Want Ads." *National Business Employment Weekly*, Dow Jones and Co., 7/7/91.

30. IRENE COPELAND. "How I Switched Careers." *Cosmopolitan*, August 1987.

31. ARTHUR P. GOULD. "Tailoring the Job Search to the Job." *New York Times* (Business Section, Forum page), 2/16/92.

32. LAURIE M. GROSSMAN. "As Secretaries Buy More for Their Firms, Marketers Regard Them with Reverence." *Wall Street Journal*, Dow Jones and Co., 3/10/93.

33. JOAN IACONETTI. "Why a Job Description Is a Job Distortion." *Cosmopolitan*, January 1989.

34. TOM JACKSON. "A Fresh Approach to Getting Yourself Hired." *National Business Employment Weekly*, Dow Jones & Co., 1984.

35. ALBERT R. KARR. "Unlike Past Recessions, This One Is Battering White-Collar Workers." *Wall Street Journal*, Dow Jones and Co., 11/29/91.

36. RALPH T. KING, JR. "Job Retraining Linked Closely to Employers Works in Cincinnati." *The Wall Street Journal*, Dow Jones and Co., 3/19/93.

37. ROBERT D. MCFADDEN. "Degrees and Stacks of Resumes Yield Few Jobs for Class of '91." *New York Times*, 4/22/91.

38. BARBARA MENDE. "How to Research a Firm Before a Job Interview." *National Business Employment Weekly*, Dow Jones and Co., 10/9/92.

39. DOUGLAS B. RICHARDSON. "Job-Hunting Tactics for Career Changers." *National Business Employment Weekly*, Dow Jones and Co., 6/30/91.

40. ROBERT W. WENDOVER. "How to Defeat the Overqualification Blues." *National Business Employment Weekly*, Dow Jones and Co., 11/29/91.

41. STANLEY WYNETT. "Cover Letters That Work." *National Business Employment Weekly*, Dow Jones and Co., 11/8/91.

42. ANDREW J. ZANGA. "We Have the Jobs. Where Are the Applicants?" *The Employment Press*, *Employment Network Inc.*, Manhasset, NY, 3/21/93.

Index

A